New Ghosts
Old Ghosts

君不见青海头
古来白骨无人收
新鬼烦冤旧鬼哭

Skeletons lie scattered
Across Qinghai's vastness.
New ghosts cry, "Unjust!"
Old ghosts merely weep.

— Du Fu (712-770)[1]

New Ghosts Old Ghosts

Prisons and Labor Reform Camps in China

James D. Seymour and
Richard Anderson

Foreword by Fan Sidong

An East Gate Book

M.E. Sharpe
Armonk, New York
London, England

An East Gate Book

Library of Congress Cataloging-in-Publication Data

Seymour, James D.
New ghosts, old ghosts : prisons and labor reform camps in China / by James D. Seymour and Richard Anderson.
p.   cm.
"An East Gate book."
Includes bibliographical references.
ISBN 0-7656-0097-8 (cloth : alk. paper)
1. Prisons—China.   2. Forced labor—China.   3. Human rights—China.   I. Anderson, Richard.   II. Title.
HV9817.S48   1997
365′.951—dc21   97-26806
CIP

Printed in the United States of America

BM (c)   10   9   8   7   6   5   4   3   2

Contents

Tables

Charts

Maps

Terminology and Prison Structure
(See chart, page 66)

Laogai organization:

bingtuan	usually refers to the Xinjiang Production and Construction Corps (*Xinjiang shengchan jianshe bingtuan*)
division	*shi*
regiment	*tuan*
detachment	*zhidui*
brigade	*dadui*
squadron	*zhongdui*
group	*dui*
district group	*qudui*
squad	*fendui*
team	*xiaodui*
trio	*sanrenxing*

Other terms, abbreviations, and conventions:

jiuye	former inmates working near a prison[2]
laogai	labor reform[A]
laojiao	labor reeducation
PAP	People's Armed Police
PAFD	People's Armed Forces Departments
PLA	People's Liberation Army
RMB	*renminbi* (currency, also known as *yuan*)

A. As used in this book, the term "laogai" may refer to the phenomenon, to the overall structure, or to a local prison system.

Foreword

It has been very satisfying to work with James Seymour and Richard Anderson on the Xinjiang chapter of this book, and to have the chance to reveal to them my experiences in the laogai (labor reform prison camps) there. Although there may be a point here and there where my perspective differs from the authors', they have certainly been fair-minded, and scrupulous about the facts.

I was a political prisoner in China from 1983 to 1994, having spent most of that time in the Xinjiang laogai. Frankly, it was quite a miserable experience. Prisoners' human rights were severely deprived. Most of us faced the double threats of starvation and overwork. Some of us used to occasionally try to protest. Once, I went on an eight-day hunger strike. Eventually I was able to meet with a laogai official. I reported to him the serious maltreatment to which prisoners were being subjected. The situation, however, did not improve. Another prisoner also wrote to the Minister of Justice, revealing that in one short period over one hundred prisoners had been subjected to brutal corporal punishment. Later, officials sent by the superior departments, accompanied by the prison guards who had actually committed the crimes, came to the prison camp to question prisoners about the incidents. Most prisoners were afraid to say anything at all, and thus the truth remained buried. Almost all inmates thereupon lost hope, and gave up on appealing to authorities. Some prisoners found various other ways to vent their frustration, such as collective violence, killing guards, and escaping from prison, and even committing suicide. Things went from bad to worse, with the disorder and gloom of the bingtuan laogai reaching an all-time low in the late 1980s.

ix

The prisons are managed by cadre police,[A] many of whom have abused their authority and acted tyrannically. Some of them have even instigated prisoner thugs to engage in bloody and violent acts. The violations of the law on the part of the cadre-police were often worse than anything that had been committed by the convicted criminals. As a result, the laogai, far from reforming criminals, has in fact been nourishing criminals. The most ironic joke in northwestern China, and at the same time a fundamental reason contributing to the problem of increasing crime in Chinese society, lies in the fact that most convicts are controlled and "reformed" by other criminals — wearing cadre police uniforms.

Luckily, I survived the ordeal and escaped from China. Now I am determined that the truth be revealed. As long as I am able, it will be my duty to reveal the facts about the Xinjiang laogai.

Likewise, Anderson and Seymour have sincerely devoted themselves to human rights issues in China. I believe that their detailed study and unbiased perspective will help the international public to know the truth. But I especially hope that this constructive book will be taken seriously by the Chinese authorities, and that it will encourage them to take steps to improve its human rights record with respect to China's prisons. Even in China's best prisons, such as those in Shanghai (where I also spent some time), conditions do not meet the past claims of the government outlined in the various white papers on human rights.[B]

External factors really can promote change. As this book shows, the authorities have already had to take note of the concerns and critiques of Westerners toward Chinese human rights shortcomings. For this and other reasons, in recent years the national leadership has shown some concern for these problems, and has issued regulations aimed at alleviating the horrible atmosphere within the laogai. So far, though, these new policies cannot be considered fundamental improvement. The essence of any real change would lie in realizing the principle of the rule by law, which constitutes the only effective protection of human

---

A. This term is explained below, page 77, note C.

B. Cited in endnote 12.

rights in any society. The situation in Xinjiang Laogai is still far from characterizable as rule by law.

The laogai is too complicated an institution to be explained in facile terms, and it would be easy to oversimplify the human rights problems. The authors are always conscious of this. Neither can there be facile solutions. It is my long-term conviction that, by means of thorough examination of China's laogai such as represented in this book, everyone can acquire deeper understanding and have more impact than would be the case if they simply relied on political means and economic leverage. At any rate, putting the truth out there is worth a try. The first step is to elucidate the stark facts. Concealment and distortion by anyone does nothing but harm to the cause of China's socio-political modernization.

Those of us who have experienced the laogai's darkness and disorder, and been victimized by the unfair and inhumane treatment, and indeed anyone who supports the rule of law, and humane and just corrections policies, will be gratified and enlightened by the publication of this book.

Fan Sidong
Hong Kong, May 15, 1997

Preface

"Every country has its secrets.
Our prisons are our secret."[3]

This book describes the prisons of the northwestern part of the People's Republic of China, primarily as they existed between the mid-1980s and mid-1990s. Ideally, it should be possible to describe the system as of a certain point in time. Given the difficulties of researching this subject, however, we are obliged to use sources across such a time span of some years. Our data is as late as 1997, but unless otherwise indicated, information indicated as current refers to around the beginning of 1995. Although we do not examine other parts of the PRC in detail, some of our findings will have implications for the country's prison system as a whole.[4] *(Endnotes begin on page 264.)* We do not address the subject of capital punishment, which has been covered elsewhere.[5] Likewise, what we are concerned with is the prison experience itself; we pay little attention to the procedures which originally resulted in people being incarcerated, on which much has been written.[6]

There are practical problems facing anyone attempting to study China's labor reform system. The first difficulty is the official tendency to obfuscate the issue. Rather than providing reliable statistics and allowing outsiders to directly observe conditions, the authorities bombard us with propaganda which is often unreliable or at best confusing. For example, since the very beginning of the *"laogai"* (a network of labor reform prisons and farms[A]), the practice has been to give more than one name to each prison farm or prison factory, and the names are often changed when camps are reorganized or new political instructions received. This can result in a factory's being known over the years under more than ten names. Maps may show any one of these, or (more likely) none at all. As we were writing this book, a new wave of laogai name changes was in full swing. Apparently the plan is to call every such institution a "prison" (a word generally avoided in the past as being out of step with Maoist concepts), and to streamline overall administrative arrangements. But such "transformations" in China tend to take place much faster on paper than in practice, and we do not attempt in this book to take full account of the current round of changes.

Government reports about the laogai, even when of an "internal" nature, can be deeply flawed. Prison personnel produce documents designed more to please superiors than to reflect reality. Often the job is turned over to one or two educated prisoners, who may be more adept at paperwork than are their guards. Everyone — prisoners, guards, and administrators — participates in a conspiracy to "prettify" the picture, for all stand to benefit if a prison is declared an exemplary unit.[7] This especially complicates our job of evaluating the economic role of the laogai. Some provinces actually keep two sets of output statistics, the real ones and the more fantasy-laden. When Beijing receives what it knows to be exaggerated production statistics, they sometimes seem to slash them in half to arrive at something more realistic.

Although there is much that is hidden about China's prisons, there is much information that can be unearthed through diligent research. There are even some provinces where the essential information is openly available,[8] and we cover one of these in this book. Information

---

A. The common system of incarceration in China is generally known as *laogai,* which literally means "labor reform." Strictly speaking, the Chinese term does not include "labor reeducation," which, as we shall explain later, is slightly different from labor reform. However, in common parlance the term "laogai" can refer to the general regime of imprisonment in China.

on most provinces, however, is not so easily obtained; one must plumb the system for the more reliable of the internal documentation. Most difficult of all are two ethnic-minority regions which present the ultimate challenge to researchers because of the intensity of the secrecy: the Tibet Autonomous Region, research on which we leave to others,[9] and the Xinjiang Autonomous Region, which we do our best in this book to fathom.

The Chinese government's distortion, obfuscation, and secrecy make it difficult to count many of China's penal institutions or to estimate how large each is. One motive for all this seems to be to confuse outsiders. If that is the case, until now they have succeeded beyond their wildest dreams. Perhaps also, to help maintain domestic control they want to make Chinese believe that the laogai is larger than it actually is. Whatever the thinking, it usually results in inflated numbers.

Because only insiders have ready access to the facts, for the outside observer there are two essential methodologies: examining internal documents and interviewing former inmates. These have been our primary research methods, though the two approaches have not been used uniformly throughout the study. Thus, different chapters rely more on one or another type of information. Two chapters (on Gansu and Qinghai provinces) rely primarily on documentation; the Xinjiang chapter relies partly on such documentation but more importantly on interviews — primarily with men who were political prisoners there, and to whom we are greatly indebted. Furthermore, not wanting to re-tread familiar ground by repeating similar stories on Gansu, Qinghai, and Xinjiang, we settled on certain main themes or areas of inquiry for each chapter. In Gansu these are the details of the fairly orthodox justice and prison system in the 1990s. In Qinghai, we explore the laogai's peculiar historical development since the 1950s. In the case of Xinjiang, we look at the region's so-called "bingtuan" (Production and Construction Corps) where we believe prison conditions to be about as bad as any in China. Occasionally, in cases where we go into detail regarding a particular problem in the context of one province, we have not felt the need to discuss the subject in the case of other provinces, even though it might be perfectly relevant. On the other hand, with respect to some issues the provinces make interesting comparisons.

Our research has inevitably led us into the quicksand of Chinese statistics. Our responsibility is to use such information judiciously. Rather than rounding numbers up or down, we have usually indicated the numbers we come up with, which we consider plausible (if implausibly precise). It is the reader's responsibility to remain aware that any statistics from China, and scholars' calculations based thereon, give a false sense of exactitude.

One of the major differences between our findings and most others' has to do with the size of China's prisoner population. Although it is not advisable to give all the details regarding how we reach our conclusions on these matters, we have been quite careful and never take any statistics at face value. When we accept an officially published figure, it is because we have independent confirmation. However, a somewhat more relaxed standard applies when we talk about economics. All units are required to generate all sorts of production and sales statistics for the higher levels. Often the underground and barter economies play such a large role that these statistics are not very meaningful. We use these statistics primarily for comparative purposes.

While many of those who helped us cannot be named, we gratefully acknowledge their help. We are happy to be able to duly recognize the assistance of John Ackerly, Elizabeth Berseth, David Brotherton, John Burns, Louisa Coan, Chen Bieming, June Teufel Dreyer, Fan Shidong (Fan Sidong),[A] Jeanne Marie Gilbert, Jie He, Jean Hong of the Universities Service Center at the Chinese University of Hong Kong, Kangsu Lee, former Xinjiang judge Ablajan Leylemanan, Shih-chung Liu, Yadong Liu, Louis Lu, Xiaobo Lü, Linda McNell, Robin Munro (who originally inspired this project), Andrew Nathan, Carl Riskin, Victor Savichev, Mark Selden, Harold Tanner, Michael Tsin, Wan Yanhai, Tseten Wangchuk, Zemin Zhang, and members of the University Seminar on Modern China at Columbia University. (None

---

A. Fan, on whom we relied heavily for information about Xinjiang, is writing his own book about the laogai (in Chinese). He is also the author of *"Wo dui Wu Hongda shuo baibai"* (My goodbye to Harry Wu), *Qian Shou* (Front-Line Magazine), Hong Kong, June 1996, pp. 78-80. Some of Fan's views appear in the Foreword, and also below on page 125.

of these shares any responsibility for the shortcomings of this book, which is borne by the authors alone.)

But we would be remiss if the acknowledgments stopped there. This book was greatly facilitated (albeit unwittingly) by the three provincial administrations under study. Thus, our greatest debt is to the minions in the labyrinthine bureaucracies who have done so much of our work for us. In the historic tradition of Chinese administration, keeping meticulous records is considered a high priority. In Qinghai, for example, a total of 89 employees busily work in the accounting and archives section of the Laogai Bureau. Not that we found obtaining the `data easy, and we do regret having to flout China's draconian secrecy laws (according to which revealing information about arrests and imprisonment can constitute a serious crime[A]). But we must concede that without such pervasive collection of data by the Chinese, any effort to obtain good information on the history and current situation of the laogai would have been impossible.

The Gansu and Qinghai chapters were the primary responsibility of Richard Anderson. James Seymour was primarily responsible for the remainder of the book. However, all chapters were subject to major input from both researchers, who are equally responsible for the entire book.

JDS and RA
New York, June 15, 1997

A. Shortly before the completion of this book, a dissident named Li Hai was sentenced to nine years in prison for "breaching state secrecy." His supposed crime (according to his mother) had been "attempting to establish the identities, ages, addresses, the crimes committed, penalties served, and sites of detention for people implicated" in the 1989 Tiananmen Square democracy movement (World Tibet Network News, Internet, February 21, 1997). Of course, such extreme treatment is not typical, and was due in this case to the sensitivity of the subject matter.

New Ghosts Old Ghosts

Prologue

Though tourists rarely do so, it is perfectly possible to visit an area on the outskirts of Qinghai's Xining that abounds in prisons and prison enterprises. A convenient (if somewhat ironic) starting point might be the luxurious Qinghai Guest House *(Qinghai Binguan)*. From there, cross the South River (Nan Chuan) and walk east on South Mountain (Nanshan) Road. You will soon enter Nantan (South Beach) District (Nantan Jiedao). After about 300 meters watch for a road turning to the right. At that point, on the left is the compound of the Fourth Team *(Dui)*, Second Qinghai Construction Company, which is no longer part of the laogai but was until 1975. Behind the compound of the Fourth Team is the Xining Detention Center *(Xining Kan Shou Suo)*, the city jail. Walk on, and inside the next compound on the left, notice the Qinghai Hide and Garment Factory *(Qinghai Pimao Beifu Chang)*; this outfit still is a laogai company. Behind the main gate of the factory and inside the same compound is the Provincial Juvenile Delinquents Prison *(Qinghai Sheng Qingshaonian Guanlisuo)*. Just after this gate on the same side of the street is the factory shop, where you can view and even buy what is made at this prison. Ahead on the right is the Xining Printing Works; like the construction company, it is no longer part of the laogai. Opposite that, on the left but not visible from the street, is the Qinghai Detention Center *(Qinghai Kanshousuo)*, which is for criminals detained by provincial-level units.

On the same side one soon sees the Nantan Movie Theater. Built in 1961, this is the former Laogai Employees Club and the meeting hall for political assemblages of Laogai Bureau units. To Maoists it all seemed somewhat self-serving. Fearing a revival of the Laogai Bureau's old élitism and arrogance, in 1972 the army converted the club into a movie house, and other units were now allowed to use it. Opposite the theater on the right side are the housing complex and the primary

1

school for employees of the Qinghai Fifth Construction Company, the latter still a laogai company.

Further down Nanshan Road is the Qinghu Machine Tool Factory *(Qinghu Jichuang Chang)*, another laogai factory. On the right side is the Timber Works of the Fifth Construction Company, and the next compound on the right side is the Qinghai Leather Products Factory, both laogai factories. To the south, behind the Leather Products Factory, is the Qinghai Police School *(Qinghai Sheng Renmin Jingcha Xuexiao)*, which has about 500 students and is the most important such institution in Qinghai.

Walking half a kilometer further on Nanshan Road, one crosses a little creek and then comes upon the huge Qinghai Brick Factory *(Qinghai Zhuanwa Chang)*, a laogai concern founded in 1951 (known as the Xinsheng Brick Factory until 1973). It is with bricks made here that Nantan district's buildings have been built. To the south behind the factory is Nantan Park; from 1959 to 1975 it was called "New Life Park" and belonged to the Laogai Bureau.

After refreshing yourself in the park, you can return to the movie house and turn north on Nanda (Great South) Road. After 300 meters the Transport Team, Fifth Construction Company, will be seen on the right, while opposite is the Eleventh Middle School. This school was founded in 1963 and was first known as the Laogai Bureau Employees' Children's School. Since 1969 it has been run by and for Xining City. In front of the school turn left and then right again, and follow Great South Road to the north. Note another school on the left side, the Nanshan Road Primary School. It was founded in 1956 as Laogai Bureau Nantan Employees' Children's School, and was handed over to Xining in 1976. On the right side of the road is the headquarters of the Fifth Construction Company, a laogai enterprise.

On the left, one can now peer down a lane named "Building Up Agriculture Alley" *(Nong Jian Xiang)*, where the Xining offices of many labor farms of Qinghai are located. The alley ends in front of a big cold-storage warehouse from where mutton and yak meat from laogai farms is distributed to the Xining civilian market. Shortly thereafter, on the right, is a small alley, down the right side of which is the Xining Office of the Provincial Prison.

In order to sell their products and to buy what they need, some labor farms maintain their offices in this area. Xiangride has one at No. 87 Nanda Road, Qinghaihu at No. 88 and Haomen at No. 89.

Note on the right the large Qinghai Red Cross Hospital, so called since the spring of 1989. From its founding in 1957 it had been known as the Laogai Bureau Central Hospital. The name change did not affect the ownership or the type of patients treated there, as patients from laogai organizations (including prisoners) enjoy priority admission.

Continuing north, one sees on the left side the Laogai Bureau Hotel *(Laogai Ju Zhaodaisuo)*. Though officially closed to foreigners, we nonetheless wandered in unimpeded and had a look around.

You have now left Nantan, and have almost finished the tour. After another half kilometer you are in downtown Xining, where you can see the Qinghai Laogai Bureau *(Qinghai Sheng Laogai Ju)* on the left, and a few steps further is the Qinghai Public Security Department *(Qinghai Sheng Gongan Ting)* — just before the city's main intersection, Da Shizi.[A]

A. The tour above describes prisons and prison-related facilities only in the southern part of Xining. There are also prisons in other parts of the city and the suburbs.

Chapter 1

Introduction

> "I feel entitled to say that neither labor camps nor concentration camps exist in China today [1954]. No one talks about them, whispers about them or even assumes that they exist."
>
> *Western journalist, after visiting China*[10]

It has been said that a society can be judged by its prisons. Certainly many have judged China by its practice of incarceration. Thus, even though much has already been written about them,[11] one hardly need justify offering a book about China's "laogai" (labor reform system[A]). It has been described as everything from non-existent (as in the above quotation) to enlightened institutions,[12] to hellish places which subject the inmates to degradation and misery.[13] The system is commonly

---

A. Regarding the term *laogai,* see p. xiv, footnote A.

4

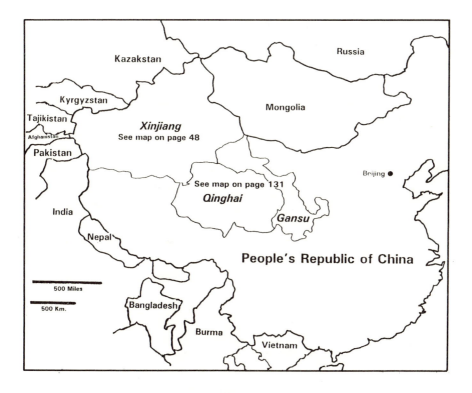

thought (by admirer and critic alike) to have a substantial impact on China in general and on the national economy in particular.[A]

In this book we examine such assertions in the belief that in any human rights endeavor, the starting and ending point must be an objective evaluation of the real situation. The book will feature three case studies, namely the prison systems of China's northwestern province-level units: Gansu, Qinghai, and Xinjiang. The first is predominately Han (ethnic Chinese), the others have large non-Han populations. In the case of each of these provinces, we will discuss the history of the provincial prison system, its size, and the economic impact that it has had at the macro, meso, and micro levels.

One of the more provocative recent studies on punishment in China has been written by Michael R. Dutton. His 1992 book *Policing and Punishment in China* is largely theoretical. "We must avoid ... producing a simple narrative history of regulation and punishment."[14] Thus, Dutton, while far from apologizing for the laogai, believes that it is essentially what spokespersons for the Chinese authorities say it is, though he does put his own gloss on it all. He sees Chinese society in general as one big "factory" in which individuals comprise the raw material. Through work, they are turned into proper socialist citizens. The laogai is part of this system.

> It is in the image of a factory, where education and production are joined as one, where life and labour are organized around the pole of productive collectivity, that *laogai* is set apart from the reformative schemes of the bourgeoisie. But the Chinese did not stop at the factory when deploying technologies of transformation. All the activities of the prisoners are structured into a social web designed to

---

A. According to one widely used text, the labor camps' "inmates undoubtedly ... provide significant economic resources for the state." Frederick C. Teiwes, "The Establishment and Consolidation of the New Regime, 1949-1957," in Roderick MacFarquhar, *The Politics of China, 1949-1989* (New York: Cambridge University Press, 1993), p. 55. Teiwes adds in a note: "Remarkably little firm data are available on the PRC's labor reform system." According to Harry Wu, "The *laogai* camps play an important role in China's national economy." Foreword, in Saunders, p. vii. (For complete citations, see Bibliography.)

maximize transformation and policing. They are locked into relations which establish not only a disciplinary gaze but also a mechanism for transformation. It is the productivist image rather than that of inspection which dominates the Chinese prison.

All this is said to represent a fundamental break with China's past.

> It is in these terms that we can identify a radically different programme to that of disciplinary isolation and individuation. In the Chinese [Communist] programme, isolation gives way to mutuality, the individual to the group. What differentiates this form of collectivity from the classical form . . . is its dynamism.[15]

Dutton's "gulag" includes not only the prisons and labor camps, but the entire system of social regimentation, including neighborhood registration. Parting ways with both Western liberals and Chinese reformers of recent decades, Dutton argues that what he calls the "gulag question" is to be understood as stemming fundamentally from neither lack of proper legal processes nor absence of respect for individual rights, but from China's (and Chinese communism's) utopian bent.

> Some may object to this equating of Gulag and utopia. After all, utopian schemes exist outside socialism. However, nowhere else is there the specific question of the Gulag. Within socialism, "the gulag question" has long since gone beyond the confines of discussion about problems of the prison. We would suggest that this is largely because it is only under socialism that such a well-developed vision of planned and organized social transformation goes beyond the confines of the prison. The collective and disciplinary model used to order and transform the criminal is also of use on the other side of the prison wall, and its transfer could aid in the transition process.[16]

Because China is supposedly evolving toward communism, "the transitional process must always take precedence over individual rights."[17] After we examine the laogai itself we shall consider Dutton's impressions.

Why the Northwest?

How, one may well ask, can we justify concentrating on the prisons of one particular underpopulated[A] corner of China? After all, the country's largest prisons, such as the vast Shayang network of prison farms,[B] are in the east. There are a number of reasons we have chosen to concentrate on the northwest. It would not be feasible to do a thorough analysis of China's prison system as a whole. It is too large a subject, and we simply do not have access to information about every province. On the other hand, due to some fortuitous accidents we have been able to learn about the prisons of these three provinces — which laogai regulations have sometimes treated as a group unto themselves.[18] But should we have limited ourselves to this area simply because that is what we have data on? We think the focus is appropriate.

First of all, the northwest has an international reputation as the land of China's "gulag." Within China as well, "Qinghai Province" is a symbol for what can happen to perceived social misfits. Many a teacher has given independent-minded students the half-joking warning that if they failed to perform (or conform), they might find themselves in Qinghai — a metaphor for the whole laogai system. We believe that it is important to discern to what extent such reputations were, and are, justified.

We will begin with Gansu, partly because it was the first northwestern province the Communists occupied, but more importantly because of the three provincial prison systems, Gansu's is the most similar to the rest of China, and thus offers a good baseline against which the other two provinces can be measured. Because of Gansu's typicality,

---

A. Though vast in area, the official 1992 populations of the provinces (not including the military) were only: Gansu, 23,140,000; Xinjiang, 15,810,000; Qinghai, 4,610,000. Only the population in the Tibet Autonomous Region is smaller than Qinghai.

B. This complex, located in Hubei, is about 36 by 59 kilometers in area (most of which territory is actually not laogai), and has a few tens of thousands of prisoners. It is described in some detail in *FGY*, 1991, no. 5, pp. 6-8, 64-66.

the chapter can be considered a general overview of the Chinese prison system, and we include such data as the percentage of the population sentenced and imprisoned each year, and the role of shorter-term detention centers. Gansu, from Beijing's point of view, is relatively non-sensitive, and therefore there is an abundance of information openly available. As for Xinjiang, there is no doubt that its prison system is unique, widely misunderstood, and of intrinsic interest. Here our focus is slightly different; we deal with the labyrinthine structure of the system and the conditions in the various prisons. We might have expected that the laogai systems in Qinghai and Xinjiang would have developed along the same lines, but for reasons we shall explain, the provincial authorities took quite different tacks, and in the end Xinjiang's and Qinghai's prison systems were like two ships passing in the night — in opposite directions. In the Qinghai chapter we analyze why its laogai has developed over the decades in the remarkable way that it has.

The fact that the three systems developed so differently tells us something about China: that, whatever the center may wish, the result is far from a homogeneous polity. We will also assess the relationship within the prison system in the context of the very different levels of development of the provinces: Xinjiang now being above average (in terms of per capita gross domestic product), Qinghai being about four-fifths the national average, and Gansu weighing in at only half the average.[19] Thus, not even Gansu can be seen as a perfect microcosm of China's prison system. Still, we feel that by becoming familiar with these three systems, one is in a position to understand the larger reality.

There are some subjects which we examine for all three provinces. For example, in each case, we endeavor to ascertain the size of the prison population, and also to evaluate the quality of life in the prisons. But sometimes a single provincial chapter will explore special topics, such as (in the case of Qinghai) the problem of drugs, and the role of the inspectorate. Of course, such subjects are relevant to more than just the one province where we study them, but in such instances we generally limit ourselves to the province where we have the most complete information.

This is a strictly empirical study. We are not particularly concerned with the theory of incarceration, or advancing social science. Certainly we have been determined to avoid ideological considerations and to be guided solely by the facts, allowing them to lead us wherever they would. Sometimes what we found surprised us, and our findings may even be upsetting to some. We seek not to please or offend, but to inform and to set the record straight. Thus, we have searched far and wide for the facts, and used multiple modes of analysis to cross-check our findings. We have used a variety of sources, including interviews with former prisoners, published sources, and secret documents. Regretfully, because the latter are often printed in very small quantities (sometimes as few as five — making it fairly easy to trace leaks), we have sometimes had to refrain from citing our sources. Nonetheless, we trust that readers will appreciate how carefully we have researched this book and how critically we have treated all information that has come our way; and that you will be willing to make the leap of faith on those occasions where a source citation would normally be called for.

That is not to say that the book is guaranteed free of error. This is a subject about which there is much unreliable information, both from official PRC sources and from the regime's more political critics. The latter we largely ignore, preferring to do our own research. The former we deal with as best we can. Often, official disinformation can be spotted because of its internal inconsistencies, but even when this is not the case, we do not take official information at face value and have relied on the various means at our disposal to check it. The problem greater than misinformation is lack of information. Any subject so shrouded in secrecy is difficult to fathom, and it is possible that here and there we have made incorrect inferences from inadequate data. Although we regret any errors of fact or interpretation that we may have made, we are confident that our larger findings will stand the test of time.

Because nearly all inmates of the prisons examined in this book are men, we will use male pronouns. We estimate that nationwide about two percent of prisoners are women. In the 1950s, many prostitutes from cities like Shanghai were sent to the northwest (their situation generally put them in the gray area between prisoner and non-prisoner). Today, women prisoners in Gansu and Qinghai probably approximate the national average in number. However, inasmuch as only men are sent to Xinjiang from the east, the percentage is even smaller there.[20]

This book contains more facts and figures than a work of this sort would normally have. We have various reasons for what may seem as overkill, including the need for absolute clarity in view of the criticism we expect from all sides. When you begin to feel numbed by it all, dear reader, please bear in mind that each newly revealed fact is a blow struck for open inquiry. Each little revelation represents the uncovering of something China's rulers have desperately sought to keep secret, ostensibly from the outside world, but really from the Chinese people. We hope this book will demonstrate the folly of closed government: it cannot be accomplished, and it serves no good purpose.

Incarceration in China is widely viewed as "special," or different from the phenomenon as practiced in other countries. There is no general agreement concerning just what makes it different. Communist writers see the system of labor reform as a uniquely beneficent and constructive process, which results in the rehabilitation of the wayward. Others take a less constructive view. Naturally, views also vary concerning how China came to have its laogai system. Some see it as an outgrowth of traditional Chinese patterns of penology,[A] which were harsh in the extreme, and which often focused on the convict's outlook

---

A. This approach is introduced (with respect to crime generally, and not unduly stressed with respect to the laogai) in Rocca, especially pp. 41-44. See also Dutton (cited in Bibliography), who remarks on p. 4: "Even within those quietly discoursing domains of local-level regulation and policing operating in the present, there still exists the specter of the past. If this were not the case, how could we then account for the maintenance of household registration systems" and other such traditional law-and-order institutions? "Like Su Shaozhi, it is our contention that 'feudal' influence is still very strong in China, although the relation between 'feudal' and socialist forms is both complex and contradictory" (p. 13). For an in-depth critique of Dutton, see Harold Tanner's review essay, "Policing, Punishment, and the Individual: Criminal Justice in China," *Law & Social Inquiry,* Winter 1995, 20:1, pp. 277-303. It is followed by Dutton's response ("One Story, Two Readings," pp. 305-316), and a rejoinder (pp. 317-324), all making for a provocative exchange.

and social relationships as much on past deeds. To evaluate this issue, we need to review a bit of history.

Background

China has had prisons for thousands of years. Forced labor, for both reformative and economic purposes, became common by the seventeenth century. Prior to the twentieth century, however, the prison was only one of a panoply of punishments available to the authorities. Others included various means of torture and humiliation, and banishment.[21] Deliberate humiliation continued as state policy under the Communists for several decades, but recently has been on the decline. Torture is officially outlawed. Prisons, of course, persist, as has something akin to banishment.

Thus, there is historical continuity among the various prison systems, especially in northwest China. This is particularly so in Xinjiang, where the laogai is redolent of the "Military Exile" *(chongjun)* system of the Qing Dynasty (1644-1911). In those days, Chinese offenders were "deported" *(faqian)* to the remotest part of the empire. After the area's conquest in 1757, Xinjiang quickly became the favorite place to send convicts — from the authorities' (but certainly not the convicts') point of view. Most notorious was the Ili area, where prisoners entered a life of virtual slavery in the service of the local Qing military authorities.[A] And it did not all begin in the Qing. Exiling outcasts to the frontiers was an intermittent Chinese practice for two millennia. Given the nature of Confucian culture, such banishment was one of the worst forms of punishment that could be meted out. During the Qin and Han periods (255 BC-AD 221), criminals were often required to perform military service in such remote areas.

During the next thousand years the system was further refined. By Qing times, there were three degrees of banishment; the worst for a

---

A. Deportation (a more severe form of punishment than ordinary "exile," or *chong*) to Xinjiang began in the eighteenth century, and ceased with the Muslim uprisings of the mid-nineteenth century. Bodde and Morris (cited endnote 25), pp. 89-91.

Beijing-area convict was being sent 3000 *li* away, which minimally landed him in the town of Qinzhou (now Tianshui) in the eastern part of Gansu. Being condemned to Xinjiang was the penultimate penalty, second only to execution. As long as the Chinese had firm control over the area, what eventually became Xinjiang was considered a particularly appropriate venue for political offenders, especially for incorruptible officials who had perhaps done their jobs too well. In 1794, no fewer than 445 former officials were living in exile in Xinjiang. Such people were joined by a motley assortment of easterners, including criminals, those punished by virtue of guilt by association, and political and religious dissidents. The lucky ones (which included most former officials) were eventually able to return east. However, the majority remained, and (even if eventually emancipated) would never see their families again.

The first group of non-political prisoners was ordered to Xinjiang in 1758, and over the next decade, thousands more were sent. Some were given as gift slaves to indigenous leaders. Convicts probably comprised about 5 percent of the immigrant population. But one did not have to actually be a convicted criminal to be sent to Xinjiang. There was a category of colonist called "trouble-makers" *(weifei)* who were resettled *(ancha)* in Xinjiang. Examples are twenty-three households of one Hubei clan, who were sent to different parts of the region in the 1760s, and a group of almost a thousand obstreperous silver miners from Yunnan. Such undesirables *(fan)* were considered on probation for a few years before being accepted as ordinary settlers.[22]

Although the Manchus generally restricted Han immigration into frontier areas, northern Xinjiang was something of an exception. By the end of the eighteenth century at least 200,000 Chinese[A] colonists settled there. There was also the military presence, which was quite costly[23] even though most of the garrison soldiers in Xinjiang were local non-Hans. There were some Hans, too; they often populated *bingtun* (agro-military colonies). The *bingtun* perhaps can be thought of

---

A. "Chinese" here includes both Hans (ethnic Chinese) and Hui (Muslims who are otherwise ethnic Chinese).

as the precursor of the latter-day bingtuan, which will occupy much of
our attention when we turn to contemporary Xinjiang. Like the
bingtuan's, the *bingtun* labor force was comprised of both prisoner and
quasi-military labor. At first, the *bingtun* existed largely to provide food
for the army, and non-prisoners working the farms remained for only
three to five years. After 1672, soldiers were urged to settle permanently. Like the various modern provincial bingtuans (which have been
abolished with the notable exception of Xinjiang's), they were still
highly inefficient institutions, unable to produce enough food to supply
the forces' needs. Likewise, mines in which some convicts worked were
only marginally productive.[24] In the mid-nineteenth century, when
Beijing lost firm control of the northwest in the wake of Muslim
uprisings, the northwest ceased to receive offenders on a regular basis
(though some continued to trickle in even in the early twentieth
century).[25]

Over the course of the Qing dynasty, China's traditional system of
punishments gradually broke down. During the first decade of the
twentieth century there was a movement to modernize the prisons. The
model for these changes was Japan's penal system, which itself had
been transformed along European lines.[26] Now the emphasis was upon
surveillance of the individual, rather than punishment of the family.
Michael Dutton writes:

> By the late Qing, a new economy of power was produced through the
> appropriation of Western technologies which shifted the regime of
> punishment away from such sanctions as banishment and torture
> toward incarceration, and away from conceptualizations centring on
> family banishment and torture toward incarceration, and away from
> conceptualizations centring on family-based criminality toward the
> institutional surveillance and policing the individual disciplinary
> subject.[27]

Thus, during the Republican period prisoners were not generally sent
to remote regions, though they were sometimes sent to open up
"wastelands" in China proper. The Kuomintang government did
maintain prisons in the parts of Qinghai that were under their control,
but they did not house prisoners from other provinces there. Only in the

1950s (soon aided by the new northwestern railway) would the tradition be resumed of sending to the northwest prisoners from "inside the last gate of the Great Wall" (*guannei*), as the Chinese have thought of China proper.[28] Not only is there the historical domestic precedent; the Chinese understanding is that sending prisoners to remote areas is a normal practice in countries around the world.[29]

At first, the Communist authorities appear to have thought of the issues of labor and reforming people primarily in the context of politics rather than criminal law. Mao Zedong wrote in 1949:

> As for the members of the reactionary classes and individual reactionaries, so long as they do not rebel, sabotage or create trouble after their political power has been overthrown, land and work will be given to them . . . in order to allow them to live and remold themselves through labor into new people. If they are not willing to work, the people's state will compel them to work. Propaganda and educational work will be done among them . . . and will be done, moreover, with as much care and thoroughness as among the captured army officers in the past. This, too, may be called a "policy of benevolence" if you like, but it is imposed by us on the members of enemy classes and cannot be mentioned in the same breath with the work of self-education which we carry on within the ranks of the people.[30]

This class-struggle rationale continued to be applied long after the prisoner population ceased to be mainly comprised of political offenders, and only in recent years has the philosophy begun to catch up with the reality that the overwhelming majority of inmates are in prison for reasons that have little to do with politics or class background.

By the end of September 1949 the Communists had taken control of the province of Gansu, and also the nearby city of Xining, capital of the largely Tibetan area that the Chinese consider "Qinghai Province."[A] They soon went to work establishing a network of prison camps in the two provinces, and in 1950 Qinghai's earliest laogai enterprises went into production. The next year even saw the establishment of a store

---

A. For Tibetans, it is "Amdo" (though Qinghai also includes part of Kham).

specializing in prison-made goods. From these small beginnings would grow a large laogai network. In the meantime, Xinjiang had come under Chinese Communist control. Then, in May 1951, a top-level national public security meeting was held on the problem of how to handle the country's vast number of prisoners (at the time mostly political outcasts — landlords, Nationalists, and other "reactionaries") to make sure that they would never be able to reestablish the old socio-economic system.[A] It seemed to be a good idea to rid East China of as many political risks as possible, turning them into an asset in northwestern China.[31] As Mao told the conferees:

> The large number of prisoners who are to be sentenced to prison terms constitute a considerable labor force. In order to reform them, to solve the difficulties that the prisons are having, and in order not to let counterrevolutionaries serving prison terms be fed without working for their keep, we must immediately take steps to organize the work of reforming people through labor.[32]

It was now decided to utilize some prisoners imported from the eastern part of the country to try to construct a modern infrastructure for the undeveloped northern and western regions. To support this forced-labor system, the newly arrived prisoners had to build accommodations for the guards and their families, and everyone had to be fed. (Housing for the prisoners themselves would come later.) From the very beginning, throughout the corrections network it was a policy to have prisoners in the countryside grow food for all prisoners and guards. The plan was to make the entire system not only self-sufficient but also profitable, to benefit these poor provinces. The quasi-legal foundation for all this was first laid down in the 1954 "Regulations on Reform Through Labor."[33]

A. According to Harold Tanner, 90 percent of China's labor reform prisoners in the 1950s were counterrevolutionaries. (The term "counterrevolutionary" is not the precise equivalent of "political prisoner" and includes some convicted of ordinary crimes.) "China's 'Gulag' Reconsidered: Labor Reform in the 1980s and 1990s," *China Information,* Winter 1994-1995, p. 43.

In setting up the laogai, the Chinese were much influenced by the Soviet experience and the theorizing of Soviet penologists. Among the earliest theorists was one A. A. Bogdanov, for whom the gulag was supposed to have a whole ethical dimension. Although by the late 1920s Bogdanov had been officially repudiated by the Kremlin, his influence lived on, and his ideas about the morality of forced labor later influenced the Chinese. Thus, although the 1954 laogai regulations were drawn up with the help of latter-day Soviet advice, their moralistic rationale was both redolent of Bogdanov and characteristically Chinese.

It is important to note that the provincial governments in the northwest never made any decision to accept prisoners; the decision had already been made for them. When it marched to the northwest, the People's Liberation Army brought along prisoners. At first, the cities throughout the northwest lacked normal civilian administration; the PLA was in charge of the entire government, including the police and prison administrations. During the early 1950s it was the army that guarded and managed the labor camps, pending the establishment of local civilian administrative organizations. Only then were the prisoners handed over to (one might say: forced upon) the local civilian administrations. So the provincial governments of the northwest inherited, rather than founded, this system.

In the ensuing years, China's authorities would insist publicly that the prison population was very low and that conditions were benign. To bolster such claims, to this day there are sporadic public relations campaigns, and each province is supposed to maintain a potemkin prison to display to foreigners.[A] We are given an upbeat picture of a system with a genuine commitment to humane treatment leading to rehabilitation.[34] But such propaganda efforts are largely ineffective in overcoming the reputation that China's prisons, especially those in the northwest, have gained over the years a reputation as "China's Siberia." Even scholars who are primarily concerned with social science theory readily appropriate the term "gulag" for describing China's

---

A. For information on how foreign visitors are exposed to prisons, see commentary beginning on p. 226, and regulations beginning on p. 247.

prison system.[35] In general, overseas critics claim that there are vast numbers of prisoners there. Some have even said that the country has a forced-labor system as large as the Soviet Union's in Stalin's time, that it has held more than 50 million prisoners since 1949.[36] China supposedly has at least 1,155 prison camps, incarcerating 10 to 20 million offenders (including 700,000 or more purely political prisoners[A]), 2 to 10 million of whom are alleged to be in the northwest.

Before evaluating such claims, we need to look at the evolution of the structure of the prison system.

Structural Overview

Prior to 1983, almost all of China's major penal institutions (prisons, laogai camps, and labor-reeducation camps) were run by the Ministry of Public Security. In that year, Hu Yaobang and Peng Zhen ordered their transfer to the Ministry of Justice, which in most cases has had jurisdiction ever since. While most of the exceptions are not crucial for purposes of this book,[B] one will shortly be occupying much of our attention: the prisons of the Xinjiang Production and Construction Corps, or *bingtuan*.

There are a variety of ways that China punishes people convicted of crimes. Usually, but not always,[C] this involves some form of imprison-

---

A. Harry Wu, quoted in the *Sunday Times* (London), p. 2, November 3, 1996. In his book *Troublemaker* (p. 14), Wu had estimated the number of prisoners as "six to eight million," of whom 10 percent are believed to be political prisoners. (That would be about 700,000 political prisoners.)

B. Such as centers for short-term administrative punishment, the most important prison for political prisoners (Qincheng), and prisons administered by the national railway administration.

C. Aside from fines and immediate probation, what would normally be criminal cases are sometimes handled as civil cases. Pursuant to the practice of "converting criminal cases into civil cases" *(xing zhuang min)*, there is a sort of private settlement between the perpetrator and the victim. Cases of theft, and even mayhem rape, are sometimes handled in this manner, especially in rural areas. (This practice has some parallel in the West. In the United States, if it

ment. The main prison regime is labor reform (*laodong gaizao* or "laogai" for short), which is what we will primarily be concerned with. To place the issue in context, however, the other forms of detention should be mentioned, namely the various forms of administrative detention (*xingzheng juliu*), under which people are held without benefit of any trial at all.

The most severe variety of administrative detention is "reeducation through labor" *(laodong jiaoyang, or laojiao),* intended for those whose behavior is deemed to have fallen "between crime and error." The roots of this system can be traced to the early 1950s (when the institutions went by such names as "new life schools" and "loafers' camps"), but it did not become formalized and widespread until the anti-rightist campaign of 1957-58. In January 1958, the State Council issued a set of regulations concerning rightists in universities. Of the six categories of dissidents, the most errant of the "rightists" were to be subject to labor reeducation. Although there was no formal law on the subject, in August of that year the State Council adopted a brief set of provisions by which petty offenders could be sent to labor reeducation camps.[37] Included in this category were those who did not engage in proper employment, minor counterrevolutionaries, and anti-socialist elements.[38] The system persists to this day. Though there are some notable political prisoners undergoing labor reeducation,[A] their numbers are relatively small. Labor reeducation sentences require little in the way of legal procedures. Until 1979 one could be given *laojiao* sentences of unlimited duration, and conditions were not necessarily better than those endured by regular laogai prisoners. Punishment is

---

proves impossible to convict a defendant criminally, he or she may be given a civil trial. The case of O. J. Simpson is the most famous instance.)

A. Perhaps the best known is Liu Xiaobo, who taught history at Beijing Normal University and was a key figure in the 1989 democracy movement (three-year sentence). Two others, both at the Shuanghe Labor Reeducation Camp in the northeast, are Zhou Guoqiang and Liu Nianchun (brother of exiled leader Liu Qing). The latter two originally received sentences of four and three years, respectively, but in the spring of 1997 these sentences were lengthened (by 288 and 216 days), reportedly because Zhou and Liu refused to write confessions.

now shorter-termed and more clearly defined,[A] and is supposed to be (but usually is not) less onerous than laogai. Altogether, at the beginning of 1995 there were 235 labor reeducation camps around the country, accommodating urban offenders.[B]

The majority[39] of all labor reeducation sentences are imposed directly by the police *(gong an),* but sentences can also be meted out by the courts, and security departments at all levels including those in the larger work units, and the provincial justice departments. It is the latter that actually administer the *laojiao* camps. Because in theory people undergoing reeducation do not lose all civil rights,[C] no trial is necessary; a "mere" administrative determination can result in terms of labor reeducation of up to four years. Because authority to impose these sentences has been so widespread, the authority is often abused, sometimes being invoked as part of a personal vendetta on the part of the sentencer. In 1996 a conference was reportedly held, with representatives from the Ministry of Justice and the National People's Congress, at which participants called for an end to such abuses and for a revamping of the system to end miscarriages of justice,[40] but so far we

---

A. But according to a 1979 ruling, the normal period was "one to three years;" a fourth year could be added "if necessary." "State Council Supplementary Provisions Concerning Reeducation Through Labor," *Chinese Law & Government*, September 1994, p. 63. In past decades, some people are reported to have spent upwards of ten years undergoing labor reeducation. *Detained at Official Pleasure*, p. 10.

B. Very few *rural* miscreants undergo labor reeducation. In 1980 some consideration was given to including more rural offenders. In the end, however, it was decided that only a narrow category of rural people would be eligible for *laojiao* treatment — mainly those who committed crimes in cities, mines, factories, and railroads. *Zhonggong zhongyang wenjian* (Central party document) No. 67, 1980.

C. The regulations are vague on this subject. According to a 1993 decree, *laojiao* prisoners retain the right to vote in elections (*CLG*, September 1994, p. 84), but in practice many such rights are withheld. Before the 1980s there used to be two classes of *laojiao* people, those with and those without political rights.

know these recommendations have not been acted upon. The number of "reeducation" prisoners has fluctuated widely. In 1980 there were about 400,000,[A] but after that an effort was made to keep the population small and manageable, and the number has normally been under 200,000.[B] As we shall discuss in our provincial chapters, however, labor reeducation is less common in the northwest than in China proper.

A more temporary and localized form of administrative detention has been "shelter and investigation" (*shourong shencha*), a practice which dates from 1961. People are not supposed to be "sheltered" for more than three months. However, in the case of political prisoners this time limit is often exceeded, and prisoners have been known to be so held for as long as five years. (Chinese law journals have criticized the illegal application of the "shelter through investigation" detentions.[C])

A. *Zhonggong zhongyang wenjian* (Central party document) No. 67, 1980. This internal document candidly describes how bad conditions in labor reeducation camps were. Maltreatment of inmates was common. Personnel were of poor quality and were underpaid. There were only 11,000 cadres to administer them; 50,000 more were urgently needed. Another 46,000 were needed for laogai institutions. For the entire judicial, procuratorial, and penal system, a million more cadres were required. As a first step, 30,000 were to be recruited for *laojiao,* and 10,000 for *laogai.*

B. In 1992 it was reported that 825,414 had been placed under labor reeducation between 1983 and 1991. That would be an average of 92,000 per year. The 1991 *White Paper on Human Rights* reported only 50,000. If we accept the higher figure, and assume an average stay of two years, that would be 184,000 prisoners at any given time. But because in practice many *laojiao* prisoners serve less than one year, the number is not normally quite this high (though it can fluctuate widely). At the beginning of 1995 it stood at 178,377 (compared with 1,285,948 laogai prisoners in the narrow sense of the term).

In 1996 a Hong Kong magazine published an article (see endnote 40) with what purported to be the details of a Ministry of Public Security report, according to which there were a reported "1,783,300" *laojiao* prisoners. We believe that if any such document exists, it is a forgery.

C. "Even today, when all the affairs in our country are gradually moving along the track of a legal system, the work of shelter and investigation ... is still in a state of there being no law to follow. This situation is not only harmful to

It appears that the number of people "sheltered" over the course of a year is around one million.[A] However, the average duration of such detention is far less than one year (see Gansu chapter), so the number of such prisoners at any given time would be some fraction of a million.

A more benign form of administrative detention is "home surveillance" (*jianshi juzhu*), which sometimes means one's activities are closely followed and circumscribed, or, under special circumstances, may mean house arrest or even (as in the case of political prisoners Wei Jingsheng in 1994-95, and Wang Dan in 1995-96) secret detention for more than a year at a state security "guest house." Such de facto detention is unofficial, and therefore the time spent is usually not deducted from any subsequent prison sentence. However, the numbers of people subjected to home surveillance are too small to affect our overall findings regarding the prisoner population.

By definition, inmates undergoing either of the two *lao* (labor) regimes (which comprise the vast majority of all prisoners) are expected to work.[B] This is not necessarily true of all other categories (though "sheltered" prisoners are often obliged to engage in labor[41]). Of course, prisoners elsewhere in the world, including many incarcerated in various states in the United States,[42] are required to work, but in

---

the struggle against crime, but also harmful to the protection of citizens' personal rights, democratic rights, and other legitimate rights from lawful infringement." Yang Lianfeng and Wei Huaming, "A Preliminary Inquiry Concerning the Incorporation of 'Shelter and Investigation into Criminal Compulsory Measures,'" *Faxue Pinlun*, vol. 5 (1989), translated in *Chinese Law & Government*, September 1994, p. 46.

Actually, lengthy "sheltering" is not always strictly illegal. The "three months" begins only when an individual's identity and address have been confirmed, which in the case of the "floaters" can take a long time.

A. The number of people "sheltered" in 1988 was officially 1.5 million (*Renmin gong'an*, no. 7, p. 18). In 1989 it was 970,000; in 1990, 902,000 (both figures cited by Tao Siju.) All data from *Detained at Official Pleasure*, p. 1.

B. We have no current figure for the portion engaged in labor, but on September 7, 1955, *People's Daily* put the percentage at 83.

China the conditions of work can be extremely harsh. "Reeducation" labor is often even harsher than "reform" labor, inasmuch as the latter is often performed in factories, whereas "reeducation" is usually rural (agricultural work, brick-making, etc.). However, in the northwest, most "reform labor" is also rural, and there is little qualitative distinction between the two categories of labor.

What is a prison? First it should be noted that the word has had various and evolving meanings in the Chinese context. It can refer to any unit where prisoners are kept, most of which are labor reform institutions. In the northwest, a majority of prisoners are in labor reform *farms*. The term "prison" can, of course, be used in a more limited sense to mean a prison (*jianyu)* in the usual English sense of the word — a building or building-complex. In such places in China, inmates do not invariably engage in labor. Political prisoners and certain kinds of ordinary criminals are kept in prisons in the narrow sense. Most of the institutions discussed in this book are not such. Sometimes they do not even have walls surrounding them; the desert may be barrier enough — particularly in the case of camps in Xinjiang's Taklamakan, which has been called "the worst desert on earth."[A]

To count as a "prisoner" for purposes of this book, then, one need not be confined to a building that looks to us like a prison. On the other hand, simply being unable to go home (a situation that has included a lot of people in China) does not make one a prisoner. We do not include people who are in the northwest unenthusiastically, or even against their will, as prisoners. Thus, in our view, those who underwent "rustication" there in the 1960s and 1970s should not be considered to have been prisoners.[43] One might argue that most of China's institutionalized orphans are prisoners, especially considering the often

---

A. Charles Blackmore, *The Worst Desert on Earth: Crossing the Taklamakan* (London: John Murry, 1995).

Even in the American law, "prison" does not necessarily denote a building. According to a 1967 California court decision, "As used in a statute pertaining to escapes, the word may include territory outside a state prison, where an inmate when at work outside is under the surveillance of Prison Guards." *Black's Law Dictionary* (4th ed.), p. 1568.

wretched manner in which they are confined,[44] but we do not include them in this book. Our estimates of prison populations include all persons "sentenced" by any court, the police, or de facto institution to any form of detention, including those in the large units of the Laogai Bureau as well as those in jails or detention centers.[45]

We do not include in our statistical total any former prisoners who have jobs provided for them in the immediate vicinity of their former prison. The phenomenon, called *jiuye,* will be examined in detail in chapter 6, when we will survey what happens to people after their formal release. As we shall see, some "released" prisoners are forced by circumstances to remain associated with their camp but are at least technically free. When a convict is sent to the northwest, his *hukou* (residence permit) back home is normally suspended, often permanently.[46] Upon eventual release, the person has no automatic right to return home. Until the 1980s a majority of released prisoners probably went on *jiuye.* For now, suffice it to reiterate that for purposes of this book we do not count them (much less their families) as prisoners. Though not all observers share this view,[A] the logic of doing otherwise might require us to count as a "prisoner" any citizen in the country who could not establish a domicile at an agreeable location.

In short, our definition of a "prisoner" is a person condemned to any form of confinement for perceived wrongdoing. This is in line with international statistical practice, where persons not fitting this definition are usually not counted as prisoners. In truly ambiguous situations, we err on the side of inclusion rather than exclusion, just as, by the word "sentence," we include informal and extra-legal dispositions when no court is involved.

In China, the terminology used in connection with penal institutions changes with bewildering regularity. Beginning in the first half of the 1980s, some provinces (notably Shandong) began to use the term "prison" more widely than before. This change did not come to the northwest until the mid-1990s, when laogai camps were for the first

---

A. According to the 1994 *Laogai Handbook* (p. 1), people on forced *jiuye* "are deprived of their freedom. They are prisoners by any common sense definition."

time officially called "prisons." Thus, in 1995 the Qinghai Provincial Laogai Bureau was renamed the Qinghai Provincial Prison Administration Bureau *(Qinghai Sheng Jianyu Guanli Ju)*. At the same time, the names of all the province's prisons were either modified or changed completely. All this has generally added one more name to several still-often-spoken old names of each institution. In this publication we will generally use the pre-1995 names, as these are still used locally, and can be compared with the names commonly used in Western publications. Even in China, it will take many more years before the new names have replaced the old ones, if they succeed at all.

There are various motivations behind the latest round of naming. One is to bring Chinese nomenclature in line with international parlance. Another is to rationalize the prison administration by renaming all laogai units as "prisons," and have them under one bureau that bears the same name. A further restated goal is for such agencies to concentrate on prison administration and not on agricultural or industrial production. It is too early to conclude whether this latest move to improve the prison system of China will succeed or is merely cosmetic. So far, one has not noticed any sudden change in either popular parlance or the underlying realities.

Officially, the main purpose of the prison system is always supposed to be neither punishment nor material output, but rather the spiritual transformation of miscreants and their conversion into productive, socially responsible citizens. As one spokesperson explained in 1987:

A labor reform institution makes deliberate choices and institutes controls in order to adapt to the special needs of the reform of prisoners. It deliberately invokes the reformative aspects (which bear on the thought and the consciousness of the laborer), thus greatly strengthening the capacity of this productive labor to reform the human being. The prisoner, obliged to participate in productive labor, is subjected to the restrictions of its various elements (such as work quotas, work evaluation, quality control, the organization and coordination of labor, etc.) causing him *to be constantly aware of his own existence and consciously adapting to this existence* . . . This gradually leads to qualitative change, and hence to the realization of the goal of reform.[47]

Though the system is supposed to be self-supporting and, if possible, profitable, the priority is claimed to be reform, not productivity.[48] Indeed, during the early years at least, the laogai was admittedly unprofitable. As Minister of Public Security Luo Ruiqing commented in 1954, "The income from production of reform through labor . . . has been accumulated, in the form of fixed capital and fluid capital, to an amount approximately equal to the expenses appropriated by the state for reform through labor."[49] That means that for all the funds poured into the laogai, the only material return was in the form of capital construction — mainly infrastructure and the prisons themselves. There were some costs that were borne by tax revenues, and even though the prison labor was unpaid, it might well have been about as economical to hire non-prisoners to do the work as to maintain the cumbersome laogai system, then consisted largely of none-too-robust intellectuals and genteel types.

In later years, when this work force was comprised mostly of people convicted of crimes, attempts would be made to increase productivity, and also to give some meaning to the "reform" aspect of labor reform. However, these efforts were not very successful. Whatever they may have said for outward consumption, in the early 1980s China's new leaders were well aware that the laogai was in desperate condition.[50] Since then, they have been claiming the prisons have become much more enlightened institutions, and more emphasis is now being placed on educational programs designed to prepare inmates for their eventual reentry into society. In 1981 the government announced a national ten-year plan to set up specialized educational programs in the laogai.[51] We shall evaluate the success of these programs and their impact on the northwest laogai.

In China, prisoners normally serve out their full terms, but we will see that there are often exceptions. There is a theoretical right to appeal, even while serving sentence. Although there have been instances of such appeals successfully lodged,[A] the practice is discouraged.

A. An example of one was a prisoner who had been convicted of "hooligan-

Prisoners are told that getting a sentence reversed is only a "dream," and that one would do better to give up on that and start to reform.[52] Still, although there may be almost no hope of gaining a legitimate early release, there are less orthodox ways of doing so.

Indeed, it is important to note that few of the developments in the history of the laogai have taken place within a framework of real law. It is true that in 1954 the State Administration issued a brief set of "Labor Reform Regulations," but no effort to spell out any details was made until 1982, when the government drafted such provisions as "Rules for Prisoners"[A] and the so-called "Detailed Regulations on Prison and Labor Brigade Control and Education Work." But even these were quickly seen as inadequate, and during the relatively enlightened mid-1980s the need was seen for a real prison law. In March 1986 the Ministry of Justice began to draft such legislation. However, only in September 1994 was the "draft" approved by the State Council Standing Committee. Finally, at the end of the following year it was adopted by the National People's Congress after minor changes. (For text, see page 252.)

Before turning to our three provinces, two features of the system common to all should be mentioned. Most of the laogai exists within the "Justice" system, at the top of which is the Ministry of Justice *(Sifa Bu)* in Beijing. Each province has a "Department of Justice" *(Sifa Ting)*. In general, the prisons of each province have been managed by a division of the Department of Justice called the "Laogai Bureau." (However, as we shall see, the laogai in Xinjiang's bingtuan has been an exception.)

Second, the government has established a system that is supposed to

---

ism" (an often-abused legal catch-all). According to *Xinsheng bao* (September 25, 1993, p. 2), the bingtuan cadres agreed that he had been unjustly sentenced, and they assisted him in his appeal, which was successful. After his release, he is said to have made good, and, out of gratitude, sent books back to the prison. (Whatever realities may have underlain the appeal process, it is interesting that this newspaper, read primarily by prisoners, carried this account of a successful appeal.)

A. Dated February 18, 1982, this was a vague set of rules for prisoners to follow, dealing with such matters as study, work, and obedience to cadres.

enable it to check up on China's administrative organs. The Ministry of Supervision has an inspection *(jiancha)* branch in each province, prefecture, and county. In turn they maintain a special sub-branch responsible for checking the prison system. In May 1988, the Ministry of Supervision decided at a conference in Shanghai that the supervision of prisons in China needed improvement. This resulted in more staff being assigned to the task. Permanent offices *(jiancha ke)* were ordered established in prisons and labor camps with more than 3,000 prisoners, and even in smaller institutions holding perpetrators of serious offenses.[53] In the beginning of 1989 the structure of the system was modestly expanded; it now had a total of 59 labor reeducation and labor reform supervision stations *(laogai, laojiao jiancha paichu yuan)*. The 854 persons employed by them were mainly responsible for checking local prisons and the administration of the prison supervision system at the provincial level. In addition, they maintained permanent offices in most prisons and labor camps *(laogai, laojiao zhu chang jiancha zu)*. In early 1989 there were 568 such offices, with a total staff of 1,378 persons.[54] Considering that many of the staffers were busy with routine office work, we estimate that one person from the Ministry of Supervision was in charge of supervising the treatment of 1,000 to 2,000 prisoners. That such a job was impossible for so few to do must have been obvious to the leaders in the Ministry of Supervision from the start, but this was considered an improvement over the earlier situation, when Ministry of Supervision officials had typically visited each prison just once a year.

In the following three chapters, we shall examine how all this functions in practice in the northwest, and the extent to which the labor reform system lives up to the standards that are supposed to prevail.

Chapter 2

Gansu

Of the three provincial Laogai systems we shall examine, secrecy is least a problem for us in the case of Gansu. The government of this province has been comparatively open when it comes to information on its prison and laogai system,[55] including the numbers of criminals sentenced each year. The reason for this transparency is apparent: The prisons are only for the convicts of this province (whose own total population is of modest size); criminals have not been sent there from other provinces since the 1950s. Thus, unlike Xinjiang and Qinghai, the prison system here is small and need be no "state secret." The relative availability of data (both open, and "closed" but available to the persistent researcher) makes possible certain kinds of analysis not possible in the case of our other two provinces. Thus this chapter has a more narrow focus and shorter time span (1993-1995) than will subsequent chapters. Although the information we have used is still not quite complete, it is intensive.

Geographically, Gansu can be thought of as consisting of two parts.

(See map on page 130.) First, there is the eastern part, which is largely agricultural but with industrial centers, making it rather like the rest of China proper. Then, to the northwest, there is the more "central Asian" panhandle, which is largely desert with occasional oases. Some of the major penal institutions are located in the panhandle, particularly around the city of Wuwei. The reason for this location is partly historical: In the mid-1950s a railway and road to Xinjiang were built through northwestern Gansu; some of the laborers were prisoners from Lanzhou (the provincial capital) and from eastern China. After these infrastructure projects were completed, the camps remained in place, and they are there to this day. These include several large laogai camps[56] to which long-term prisoners from eastern Gansu are sent.[57] This is the only area in Gansu that has a concentration[A] of prisoners anything like those we shall see in Qinghai and Xinjiang, and there are additional institutions farther to the northwest. Altogether, from the Wuwei area and the Xinjiang boundary there are seven prison camps.[58] While the prisoners are no longer "outsiders" in the sense that they usually have been, say, in Xinjiang, they still come from long distances (eastern Gansu being up to two days away by train).

Table 1

Long-Term Sentences by Courts in Gansu, 1994		
Sentenced ↓	Persons	Convicts
To Death or Life in Prison	583	4.7%
To terms of 5 to 20 years	4278	34.6%

A. "Concentration" in the sense of a large number of prisoners in the area relative to the number of civilians living in the area.

There are other prisons elsewhere in the province. Lanzhou has two prison factories[59] and two labor reeducation *(laojiao)* institutions. Far to the east, in Tianshui, there is a Provincial Juvenile Offenders Prison.[60] These, along with some other large prisons and prison farms, give Gansu a total of around nineteen prisons. In addition, the province has 130 or so local jails, including county-level detention centers where people who have been sentenced to one year or less are kept.

More difficult than identifying Gansu's penal institutions is gauging their size. Here the available data is somewhat limited, and requires close analysis.

Sentencing Patterns

Some indication of the size of Gansu's prison population can be found in the number of convicted criminals per year. The number of Gansuans reported[61] to have been sentenced for serious crimes during 1994 is shown in Table 1. Except for those executed, virtually all of these convicts were sentenced to prison terms. The total number of persons reported to have been given any sort of punishment (including fines and probation) was 12,369.[A]

Table 2

Persons Sentenced by Courts to Gansu's Prisons, 1994			
Sentenced to 5 years or more, or to death	Sentenced to prison/jail for less than 5 years	Total put in prisons or jails by courts	Total put in laogai and *laojiao* prisons
4,861	5,513	9,974	10,801

A. The remainder unaccounted for (7,508) were sentenced to less than 5 years, fined, probationed, or found innocent.

The conviction rate showed an increase of 22.1 percent over 1993. As elsewhere in China, the crime rate has often been on the increase.[62] To be sure, this is not invariably the case, and during the following year (1995) both Gansu's crime rate and the number of persons newly incarcerated actually declined by some 6 percent.[63] But because we believe the crime rate has since resumed its increase, we consider the 1994 figures to be the more typical, which is why we are examining that year instead of the anomalous 1995.

To gain a broader view of sentencing, we must expand our inquiry to include lesser sentences. Table 2 provides information on this subject. The data suggests that in a typical year, Gansu sentences four thousand or so people to long prison terms (which will have a major, long-term impact on prison populations), and five thousand or so to shorter terms[A] (which will have a lesser impact).[64]

Total Prisoner Population

The above discussion has some relevance to the question of the size of the prison population, but it does not really tell us what it has been. Sentencing statistics tell us how many convicts enter the system in a given year, but they do not tell us how many remained from before, nor how many were released. We do have one earlier comprehensive official statement on this matter: In 1984, a foreign reporter was told by one Gansu official that there were then 20,000 prisoners in laogai institutions in the province.[65] Of course, this official claim, while it may not be completely meaningless, is not to be accepted at face value. At best it has to be taken as the lowest possible number. It appears to exclude all prisoners not detained in laogai institutions, and the last four digits have probably been rounded to zeros.

Otherwise, since 1984 the provincial bureau that is in overall charge of prisoners, the Department of Justice *(Sifa Ting),* has kept rather quiet about the size of the prison population. It has, however, prepared an internal annual document which serves as the basis of an annual "work report" which contains the more important numbers and which is pre-

---

A. Of these, about 1,500 have been sentenced to local jails.

sented to the deputies of the Gansu People's Congress *(Gansu Renmin Daibiao Dahui)*. Parts of this report, excluding the most sensitive numbers, are normally published by the *Gansu Daily* and in the *Gansu Yearbook*. Table 3 contains the figures that were reported to the congress. To briefly return to the subject of sentencing: We now have two sets of figures from different sources for new prisoners in 1994: Tables 1 and 2 with data from the courts, and Table 3 with Laogai Bureau data. The two sets are similar, but for a number of reasons do not fit together precisely. For example, the court statistics count only persons sentenced that year, while the laogai/*laojiao* figures include only persons who actually enter a prison or labor camp that year.[A]

Table 3

Imprisonment in Gansu, 1994			
Persons sent to labor reeduction in 1994	Persons in the laogai on January 1, 1994	Persons in the laogai on January 1, 1995	Persons in laogai and est. number of persons in *laojiao* prisons* on Jan. 1, 1995
2,862	23,409	25,757	28,800

*Although the exact figure for *laojiao* (labor reeducation) prisoners for the beginning of 1995 is unavailable, we have figures on the subject for earlier years, and in the right column of the table adequate provision for *laojiao* has been made.

A. To elaborate further on the discrepancies, the court statistics may include the following persons sentenced but who do not arrive in the prison system during the same year: Persons executed immediately after the sentence; persons released under medical parole after sentencing, but before arriving in a prison; persons sentenced but not yet caught; persons escaping just after sentencing; pregnant women who cannot start their sentence inside a prison until the child is born; persons sentenced during the last weeks of the year who do not arrive at a prison until after December 31.

The number of people put in the laogai in 1994 was 7,939, and the number released was 5,591, so the net laogai increase was 2,348. Although this does not include jails, prisons, and *laojiao,* the long terms involved means that this figure is the one that has the greatest impact on prisoner population. And inasmuch as we have the total of persons receiving any sort of sentence (12,369 — see page 31), we are in a position to take the other populations into consideration. First, let us deduct the ones with commuted sentences (-1,326), which gives us a net total of 11,043 persons imprisoned or executed. The difference between this figure and 10,801 (total sentenced to either form of *lao*) is only 242.[A] Thus, while the statistics for the number of persons receiving real sentences, and the number of persons arriving in prisons, do not jibe precisely, they do coincide fairly closely. This fact, along with other evidence, indicates that the figures in these tables are reasonably accurate.

Now let us return to the question of total prisoner population (as distinct from annual sentences). The total number of 28,800 in Table 3 still excludes certain categories of prisoners. It does not show persons in such places as the local jails; those still must be added to our total figure. Another category of prisoners not reflected in the table are persons arrested and sentenced by the police themselves to brief (one or two weeks) detention *(zhi'an gouliu)*. This includes, for example, persons who are unable or unwilling to pay their fines. We have the province-wide figure of such detentions in 1993; they total 5,861. Although we consider them as prisoners, on an annualized basis they contribute only 100 to 200 persons to our total number of prisoners.

Based on the above information, and also taking into consideration the size of the prison population in smaller institutions, our estimate of the total number of prisoners in Gansu on January 1, 1995, is about 33,000, about 7,000 of whom are in the northwestern panhandle. This is consistent with the sentencing patterns.[B]

A. This number presumably includes those released as innocent, those who only had to pay fines, and those executed.

B. Annually, many convicts are given very short terms. The average must be

The Economy of the Gansu Laogai

There are mathematical relationships between the four variables of the number of criminals sentenced each year, the total number of prisoners, the number of prisons, and the output of prison factories and prison farms. If those figures are put together for a certain area, light is shed on the laogai system as a whole, and figures can be cross-checked by looking at these mathematical relationships. We can compare, for example, the number of prisoners with the output value, or the number of workers in prison factories and prison farms with the number of persons sentenced each year, and then will have a fairly good idea of what the situation is inside the prison system of this area.

In 1994, the prisons and labor reform institutions in Gansu had a gross industrial and agricultural output value of RMB 100.92 million. The Labor Education institutions' output value was 6.92 million Yuan.[66] The sum of these, RMB 107.84 million, is the total 1994 output for all the province's prisons (broadly defined[A]). For the whole province, the gross output value of industry and agriculture that year was RMB 88.2 billion.[67] Comparing the two figures, the share of prison labor in the Gansu economy is only 0.122 percent. As we see in Table 4, the laogai contribution, in both absolute and relative terms, has been steadily declining. The reason is that prison enterprises can no

---

less than two years, so such prisoners would not greatly magnify the size of the prisoner population, which is mainly comprised of long-termers. Only about 4,000 Gansuans are sentenced to prison terms of more than five years. If the average time served were eight years, that would suggest that the total number of long-term prisoners would be 32,000 minus the number who had died in prison. This calculation tends to confirm, but is not the basis of, our conclusion that the province has 33,000 prisoners. The following reviews how we arrived at that figure: 28,800 (taken from table 3: all laogai, *laojiao* and juveniles) + 2,500 [in small (below 500 prisoners) prefecture-level institutions, and in prison on January 1, 1995] + 1,700 (prisoners in county jails on January 1, 1995) = 33,000 total for January 1, 1995.

A. But not including *jiuye*. (Our prisoner figures never include *jiuye* unless we indicate to the contrary.)

longer compete in today's more modern economy.[A]

Now, let us look more closely at the components of this output. Throughout most of China's northwest, the vast majority of the inmates are employed in agriculture. In the case of Gansu, however, the laogai's ratio of factories to farms is similar to the other provinces in China (that is, they are mostly engaged in non-farm work). Still, we need to have a closer look at the Gansu laogai's agricultural sector. Later, we will make comparisons with the other two northwestern provinces. The figures of the Gansu Provincial Laogai Bureau on agriculture and its share of the entire Gansu agriculture will also be analyzed.

Table 4[68]

Agricultural and Industrial Output Value of Gansu Laogai & *Laojiao* Units, 1993-1995, in Million RMB					
Year	Laogai	*Lao-jiao*	Total of prison economy	Total of Gansu economy	Prisons' share of province total
1993	118.50	4.70	122.85	64,600	0.190%
1994	100.92	6.92	107.24	88,200	0.122%
1995	97.20	11.00	108.20	111,400	0.079%

A. Inasmuch as prison enterprises often employ some civilian workers, the percentage of prison-labor-derived output must be an even smaller percentage, because prison labor is not solely responsible for the output value. The precise amount of "civilian prison output" cannot be calculated and is difficult for us to estimate, as prison factories and laogai farms indicate the total output value only. In some of these joint prisoner-civilian enterprises, the prison-labor share of the output is less than half; we do not consider these prison enterprises, but rather civilian enterprises which happen to utilize some prison labor. The amount of prisoner production in thus-defined civilian enterprises is too small to affect our overall findings.

As was also the case in Xinjiang and Qinghai, in the 1950s prisoners were brought out from the eastern provinces to help with agricultural reclamation. Although the base institutions would remain in the same places, between the 1950s and today the management teams and the ways the farms have been managed have changed many times. Further complicating this issue is the fact that prisoners were in effect "rented out" to other projects or units in need of labor. Thus, when an important road was built, prisoners might have had to work for years on this project, being trucked to wherever they were needed. This resulted in new, but often impermanent, camps being built in various areas. After such projects were finished, the remaining prisoners would usually return to their base camps.

As we explained on page 30, the permanent labor camps still exist in the Wuwei area in the western panhandle. Although the prisoners there often used to work on road and railway construction, in between projects they engaged in agricultural reclamation. Until the Cultural Revolution, prisoners actually working on such farms were under the control of the provincial Department of Public Security. At the same time, however, there was cooperation between the laogai and local governments in the area.

The whole setup was changed in 1969 with the founding of the Lanzhou Production and Construction Corps (*Lanzhou shengchan jianshe bingtuan*) or "Lanzhou bingtuan" for short. The headquarters of this bingtuan actually was not in Lanzhou at all, but in Huangyang township, 35 kilometers southeast of Wuwei. It was a largely civilian organization, but with some prison components. By 1970 the Lanzhou bingtuan consisted of six divisions with 57 regiments under its command. Inasmuch as the units were scattered around the four provinces of Shaanxi, Ningxia, Gansu, and Qinghai, and had to be managed under the chaotic conditions of the Cultural Revolution, the Lanzhou bingtuan was an economic disaster, and had to be dissolved to avoid further financial losses.[A] Its final demise came in 1975, when all

---

A. Described in the Qinghai chapter in connection with the Ge'ermu Farm, pp. 144-146.

civilian units in Gansu were transferred to the province's agricultural reclamation bureau. However, those units which had prisoners were now brought back under the Department of Public Security. Nonetheless, these laogai camps continued to cooperate with the local civilian state farms[A] with regard to irrigation and other reclamation projects. Laogai and civilian projects were not clearly separated, and prison labor continued to be integrated with normal labor.

During the 1980s most of the former state farms, as well as industrial enterprises operated by them, were turned over to the newly founded all-civilian Gansu Agricultural Reclamation Company (GARC). This is an amalgamation of companies (mostly state-owned,

Table 5[69]

Percentage of Area Under Cultivation, 1994	
Gansu, total cultivated area	100.00
Gansu Agr'l Reclamation Corp.	0.77
Gansu Provincial Laogai Bureau	0.04

but one is a private stock company), whose mission would be to develop agriculture and food-processing in the area. From now on these farm enterprises would have one characteristic common to Chinese concerns: they were vastly over-staffed. They also have had no interest in using prison labor.[B] Indeed, to make the GARC efficient, the management has had to cut the whole work force of the companies. Whereas in 1985 it had 68,114 employees,[70] by 1994 the number had

---

A. A "state farm" was a farm which had been under State Farms and Land Reclamation rather than in a commune.

B. In Chapter 4 (Qinghai) we will describe in detail why commercial farms in China are no longer interested in employing prisoners.

been reduced to about 45,000.[71] Whereas, as we shall see in the Xinjiang chapter, lack of separation between agricultural reclamation and prison management can result in bad prison conditions (as was usually the case in most areas of China up to the 1980s), by the early 1990s most provinces managed to solve this problem in one way or another. Gansu did so by excluding prisoners from the GARC work force.

Table 6[72]

Value of Agricultural Output in Gansu, 1994		
Unit	RMB, 1990 prices	Percentage
Gansu total	14,166 million	100.000
GARC	161 million	1.136
Laogai Bureau	11 million	0.077

Table 7

Livestock in Gansu, 1994

	Laogai Bureau[74]	Gansu total[73]
Cows and horses owned	300.0	6,079,400
Sheep and goats owned	4,700.0	10,077,220
Pigs slaughtered or sold	3,300.0	5,727,900
Sheep & goats slaughtered/sold	1,500.0	3,448,400
Wool produced (tons)	5.6	16,743

Although the amount of land being administered by the GARC is still large (many times the size of the laogai bureau's holdings), in 1994 it was still less than one percent of Gansu's total farmland. (See Table 5.) But cultivated area is not the only variable affecting productivity; also very important is how well the various farms are managed and how motivated are the farm workers. The difference in the agricultural output value is shown in Table 6. This information will help us compare and evaluate the various laogai bureaus in China's northwest.

Table 8[75]

Agricultural Produce of Gansu Laogai, 1993	
Apples	5,724 tons
Pears	491 tons
Peaches	81 tons
Apricots	3 tons
Meat total (mostly pork)	215 tons
Mutton	13 tons
Beef	1 ton
Chicken	44 tons
Milk	61 tons
Eggs	133 tons
Fish	4 tons

In addition to planting and harvesting grain, vegetables and fruit, the Laogai Bureau owns livestock, which is tended mainly by the inmates of prison farms. Each livestock portion shown in Table 7 is below 0.1 percent of the figure for animal husbandry for the whole province. This is consistent with various other data, such as the laogai's 0.1 percent share of the population. The data suggest that no more than 0.1 percent of those engaged in animal husbandry are prisoners.

Because of the openness of the Gansu laogai in terms of availability of information (at least compared to other provinces), it is possible to study the institution in merciless detail. Everything from the number of tractors and flour mills to the size and qualifications of the work force is known. Although one soon reaches the point of diminishing returns in terms of the value of such data for an understanding of the laogai, occasional details are worthy of note. Whereas from the 1950s to the 1970s the laogai farms mainly produced grain and vegetables, Table 8 illustrates the wide variety of agricultural products now grown, processed and marketed by them. But these two tables also reveal how infinitesimally small is the laogai's share of the provincial total. In 1995 its share of the agricultural and industrial output has been no more than 0.079 percent (well under the laogai population of 0.127 percent). If we take into consideration that a significant share of the so-called "laogai production" is actually produced by civilian workers, the real figure for products made by prisoners must be even lower.

Political and Religious Prisoners

Simultaneous with the Beijing student demonstrations of 1989, Lanzhou was also a hotbed of political dissent. Gansu has been one of China's poorest provinces, and hardly its best-governed. ("It cannot be denied that our own errors have become a pretext for an extremely small number of people to stir up the unrest and disturbances."[76]) Lanzhou University students, in particular, were politically active; by official count, 1,736 of them actually went to Beijing to participate in the Tiananmen demonstrations.[77] Considering the scale of dissident activities in Gansu itself, which apparently had widespread support (even within the military[78]), it is hardly surprising that Gansu has had its share of arrests.[79] All-in-all, though, the crackdown seems to have been somewhat muted. Students who had gone to Beijing were required to write self-criticisms and join "study sessions." Some students (fewer than 20) were expelled from the university. A few factory workers were also punished. All the people known to have actually been arrested, however, were held for only about two months. In short, the official reaction was rather mild by Chinese Communist standards, and the number of political prisoners in Gansu has not been large.

Gansu's best-known political prisoners are those associated with the China Social Democratic Party *(Zhongguo Shehui Minzhu Dang)*. Probably the largest dissident organization the province has seen, it flourished underground in the early 1990s. Based in Lanzhou, it claimed affiliates in many provinces and a membership of more than a hundred members. It was comprised largely of intellectuals who had participated in the democracy movement of 1989. The Social Democrats published a manifesto in 1992 calling on the National People's Congress to institute democratic reforms. They also demanded release of all of China's political prisoners. At least half of the party membership were arrested soon thereafter. The names of ten of these are known; they were all charged as "conterrevolutionaries." Prisoners include Ms. Guo Dansheng, a Lanzhou University instructor.[80]

Although we have no specific current information on the subject of religious prisoners, it would not be surprising if some of Gansu's Muslims, Tibetans[81] and Christians[A] are in prison for political or religious offenses.

Conclusion

On the basis of open and internal sources, we conclude that at the beginning of 1995 there were about 26,000 prisoners (as defined in our introduction) in the eastern part of Gansu, and about 7,000 in the northwestern panhandle, for a total of about 33,000 (±5%).

The rate of imprisonment in Gansu Province is generally between

---

A. The best-known Christian former prisoners are two Catholic bishops, Casimir Wang Milu, and Mathias Lu Zhengsheng, both of Tianshui. Wang was in prison from 1985 to 1993. Lu served two sentences; the date of his most recent release is not known. *DTC*, pp. 239-240.

125 and 130 per 100,000.[82] As we shall see later in this book, this is somewhat below the national average.

Most Gansu prisoners are obliged to work. However, the output from such forced labor plays an insignificant economic role (less than 0.1 percent of provincial output).

Gansu has some political prisoners, but not a large number.

Chapter 3

Xinjiang:

One Region, Two Systems

Xinjiang, like Gansu and other provinces,[A] has a prison system which is ultimately accountable to the Ministry of Justice in Beijing. Its prisoners are generally regular Xinjiang residents. However, Xinjiang is alone among provinces in that it has another large prison system which functions with considerable autonomy. The prisoners in this system, in most cases hardened criminals, have come from various provinces for long terms (the majority having been sentenced to more than ten years[B]). They have often arrived in contingents of 500 to 1,000 from a single province or municipality. Even though members of such a group are soon scattered to different parts of the prison system, they continue to think of themselves as a cohort, and sometimes maintain contact by the grapevine or by chance encounters in work-

---

A. Strictly speaking, Xinjiang is a "region," not a province. However, we will not always observe the fine distinction.

B. It would seem, however, that in practice, time served in the bingtuan laogai is well under ten years. Although we lack bingtuan-wide statistics on this, in one division the release rate was so high that it appears that the average time served was between six and seven years.

places. Because of their backgrounds and the often hopeless situation in which they find themselves, they are considered particularly difficult to supervise.

To understand the setup, we must study one particular institution that is now unique to Xinjiang.

The Bingtuan and Its Laogai

The Autonomous Region has a large development corporation called the Xinjiang Production and Construction Corps (*Xinjiang shengchan jianshe bingtuan*), to which we shall refer as the "bingtuan."[A] This organization had its origins in 1952[B], and officially came into being two years later.[83] The bingtuan came to include a network of labor reform (*laogai*) camps which will occupy much of our attention in this chapter.[84] But it is important not to confuse that network with the bingtuan itself — a large, loose network of organizations somewhat military in structure. During most of the Mao era, most of the north west's various bingtuans were directly under the Lanzhou Military Region; these included those in Gansu, Ningxia, Shaanxi, and Qinghai. The Xinjiang bingtuan was always something of an exception; it has always been under the Xinjiang Military District. Although since the mid-1980s that district has been subordinate to the Lanzhou Military Region, the bingtuan has continued to enjoy considerable autonomy. The reason for this different command arrangement seems to have been

---

A. Xinjiang's having had a bingtuan was not unique, but all of the other provinces' bingtuans appear to have been at least nominally converted to ordinary state farms, or abolished. Hainan's was abolished in 1979. Inner Mongolia's was about half the size of Xinjiang's. (See He Lan and Shi Weimin, *Mo nan qing: Neimengu Shengchan Jianshe bingtuan xiezhen* [Feelings about the southern desert: The Inner Mongolia bingtuan portrayed], Beijing: Falü Chubanshe, 1994.) But even when the bingtuans' prisoner populations were at their maximum, Xinjiang's had the lion's share (83 percent in 1965).

B. In February 1952 Mao Zedong issued an order on bingtuan formation, but it took some time to get things going, and the official start-up date was October 7, 1954 (by order of the Xinjiang Military District).

practical: The Xinjiang bingtuan was too big and too far away to be managed directly by the headquarters of the Lanzhou Military Region.

Actually, the bingtuan was never a purely martial organization (and today is less military than ever). Although some of the original 103,000 members were from the former First Field Army (which had "liberated" the region), its manpower was immediately assigned to projects that were separate from PLA operations. This was partly because many of its members had been peasant-soldiers who had originally belonged to local Kuomintang garrison units. Some of these were prisoners; others had been temporarily absorbed by the People's Liberation Army after the "liberation" of Xinjiang, but were subsequently dismissed pursuant to a 1952 order of the People's Military Commission. Most of these men (as it turned out, the relatively lucky ones[A]) were placed in the bingtuan. What they underwent was a bit less onerous than normal labor reform; they often experienced conditions not dissimilar to those prevailing on Youth League farms.[B] Then, pursuant to the earlier May 1951 central resolution (discussed on page 16), they were joined by 20,865 prisoners (mostly political), bringing the total bingtuan prisoner population to a reported 123,229. That is a conservative figure; our own estimate is 160,000. During the remainder of the mid-1950s many more (perhaps 100,000) *civilian* Hans (ethnic Chinese) from the east entered the bingtuan. By the end of the decade, about 40,000[85] retired People's Liberation Army soldiers also joined the bingtuan's various divisions.

During this early period there was some oversight of the bingtuan by the central authorities in Beijing (the Party and the economic ministries, especially the Department of Agriculture). For example, Wang Zhen, who had once been military commander in the area, continued to pay

---

A. During the Cultural Revolution, former Kuomintang soldiers who were not in the bingtuan were sometimes tortured. An unknown number were killed.

B. Lewis, p. 284. The status of these former Kuomintang soldiers in the bingtuan occupied the "gray area" between prisoner and civilian. (On how the former Kuomintang troops were absorbed into the bingtuan, see Bodard, *Chinas Lächelndes Gesicht*, pp. 141-146.) The others were ostensibly "free."

special attention to Xinjiang after his transfer to Beijing where he served as minister of State Farms and Land Reclamation. But apparently there were problems with this divided leadership, and after a few years the central authorities considerably relaxed their control, with the ironic result that this organ (if little else in the so-called "Autonomous Region" of Xinjiang) would indeed be largely autonomous.[A] The bingtuan evolved into a vast quasi-military, quasi-civilian, quasi-prisoner work force comprised of people who were obliged, for one reason or another, to remain in Xinjiang. In 1973 the organization had 100,000 urban youths, 2,000 of whom were Party members, and 20,000 belonging to the Youth League.[86]

The political tides over the decades have had their effect on the nature of the bingtuan. The Cultural Revolution, especially, was quite hard on the institution, with the youthful settlers often being subjected to what was later officially acknowledged as having been "a white terror" involving "political and corporal oppression."[87] During the latter part of the Cultural Revolution, the institution came under the temporary control of the regular army — which proved quite unable to solve its problems. For all of the bingtuan's political correctness in terms of Maoist sociology, it simply was not efficient in its use of funds and resources. At one point, in 1975, matters got so bad that the bingtuan was formally dissolved and replaced by a "Xinjiang Uyghur Autonomous Region Reclamation Bureau." The divisions were renamed and converted to typical state farms and other state-managed enterprises. Instead of having the bingtuan-style horizontal integration, everything was now vertical. The arrangement was so centralized that enterprises found themselves cut off from traditional suppliers when they were in a different prefecture (zhou). The result was that economic performance actually worsened. In the winter of 1977-1978 the State Council in Beijing held a National Conference on State Farms.

A. The degree of autonomy has varied somewhat over the years. In the early 1990s the State Council decided that the bingtuan would have provincial-level economic powers. Song (see endnote 105), p. 78. Below, we will examine more specifically the autonomy of the bingtuan laogai.

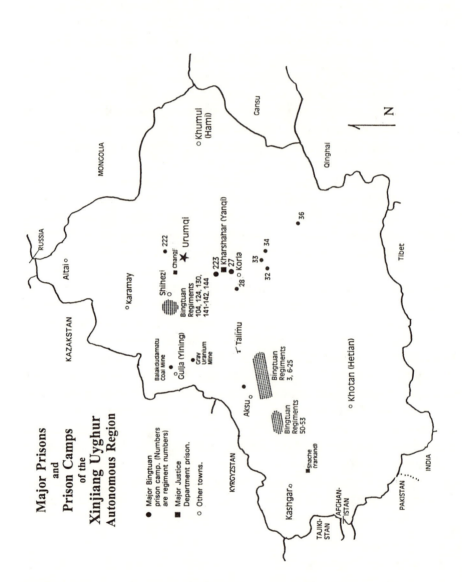

Major Prisons
and
Prison Camps
of the
Xinjiang Uyghur
Autonomous Region

● Major Bingtuan prison camp. (Numbers are regiment numbers)

■ Major Justice Department prison.

○ Other towns.

N

With regard to Xinjiang, the conference decreed that the mess had to be cleaned up, that the former bingtuan enterprises must be made profitable, and that they would have to get along without further subsidies. What ensued apparently was a tortuous process amid much controversy. Finally, at the end of 1981 the central government decided to cut its losses, and revive the bingtuan.

The bingtuan should not be thought of as only a collection of economic enterprises; it has also been seen as a bulwark protecting China's interests in the region, internationally and domestically. The authorities have always been constantly on guard against trouble in this strategically sensitive area, and they have been determined to make sure that the first sign of foreign threat or unpatriotism or religious zeal among the populace could be dealt with quickly. During the coming years, they would have plenty to deal with. Indeed, recently the Party has been appalled by political and cultural trends in Xinjiang. "Our society should not remain indifferent to the present unhealthy tendencies in Xinjiang, which are a manifestation of the people's state of mind. For example, young people wearing T-shirts printed with the American flag and store signs evoking [Islamic] feudal superstition reflect minds that worship things both foreign and ancient, and suffer a 'nationalist inferiority complex.' . . . China's character, sovereignty, and dignity must be safeguarded."[88] We shall return to such issues.

Under the hierarchical arrangements put in place in 1981, the bingtuan would rank fifth among institutions within Xinjiang, just below the regional party committee, the regional government, the PLA's military district, and the People's Armed Police. Since 1981 the head of the bingtuan has been formally selected by the governor of the Autonomous Region, subject to ratification by the State Council in Beijing. The bingtuan soon acquired an alter ego: the Xinjiang Agriculture, Industry, and Trade Group, which in time would preside over a vast array of corporations.[A] The Group (which can be thought

---

A. E.g., Urumqi Co., Aksu Co., Kuerle Co., Hami Co., Supply and Sales Co., Commerce and Trade Co., Goods and Materials Co., Nongken Import-Export Co., Xintian International Economy and Technology Co., various sugar

of as simply another name for the bingtuan) is in some ways a corporate entity[89] and sometimes seems to conduct its own foreign policy. It claims to have concluded cooperative ventures with investors in such countries as the United States, Japan, Germany, Israel, Turkey, Singapore, Italy, Denmark, Thailand, and, most notably, with the World Bank (see commentary, page 228). The bingtuan has a large headquarters in the regional capital of Urumqi, and publishes a daily newspaper, two hefty yearbooks, and much else.[A]

The organization is almost the last in China to be guided by the Marxist-Maoist principle of bridging lifestyles and combining various walks of life. Industrial, agricultural, pastoral, educational, commercial, cultural, and military management are integrated. These aspects of life are all supposed to be brought together at the village or neighborhood level. Such was the rationale of China's communes. The idea was supposed to facilitate leadership, and at the same time improve people's quality of life, enabling people to live integrated rather than compartmentalized lives.[90] Society should be homogenized, with different social strata intermingled. Although during the Cultural Revolution such thinking was applied nationwide, it had actually first been carried out in the Army and even more in such quasi-military institutions as China's various bingtuans. Here, prisoners were added to the social mix, with propaganda depicting them as working in the fields shoulder to shoulder with their guardians. In practice, this would not amount to much more than the same people being responsible for agricultural development and prison management, which meant that neither job was very well done. This problem was once not unique to Xinjiang, but by the early 1990s most other provinces in the northwest and elsewhere

---

refineries, textile mills, power plants, pharmaceutical plants, construction materials factories, metal-working plants, food-processing plants, hotels, an aviation company, and many numbered divisions and agricultural enterprises.

A. One yearbook is narrative, the other (published in Beijing), statistical. The newspaper, *Xinjiang junken bao*, is published by the bingtuan's Party Committee, and appears six days a week. The bingtuan is headquartered on Urumqi's Guangming Road.

had managed to solve the problem by separating the two functions.

Thus, the ideological underpinnings hardly explain much. From the start, the real purpose of the bingtuan was to develop China's "new frontier" *(xin jiang),* though some would insist that what it was really doing was trying to "sinify Eastern Turkestan." The former-Kuomintang bingtuan members proved reasonably loyal to the new regime, and of course eagerly embraced the idea of Han control of the region. (In time, the distinction between former-Kuomintang and former-PLA bingtuan members largely disappeared.) Thus, sinification and agricultural development (both of which had begun earlier in Qinghai, and much earlier in Gansu) continued in earnest in at least northern Xinjiang in the 1950s,[91] with the bingtuan playing a crucial role in this colonization process.[92] It was all part of Liu Shaoqi's grand "border support" plan, the original purposes of which were to ease eastern crowding and sinify the frontier. Both the bingtuan's civilians, and its prisoners (to be discussed shortly), are virtually all Han (ethnic Chinese), whereas a majority of the region's population belongs to the various Muslim nationalities.[A] These are primarily Uyghurs and Kazakhs, although prison camps would also be located in Xinjiang's smaller Mongol and Hui areas. Later, the bingtuan came to be seen as serving a new purpose: a reserve force in case there was domestic unrest.

Over the years the bingtuan came to have less and less of a military cast, with the military aspect largely limited to formal structural arrangements, and by the fact that mid-level cadres (usually demobilized soldiers) maintained a military connection as reserve officers. Except during the late Cultural Revolution, the bingtuan as a whole has *not* (contrary to what has been stated elsewhere) been "run by the People's Liberation Army."[93] Rather, there are four military organizations in Xinjiang, all controlled to one degree or another by the Party. These are the People's Liberation Army (PLA), the People's Armed Police,

---

A. Fourteen percent of the bingtuan's members are non-Han, whereas the Region is 60 percent non-Han. There are certain farms, such as the 64th Regiment of the Fourth Division, which are predominantly minority.

the Xinjiang militia, and the bingtuan militia. The most important of these is indeed the PLA. All of the bingtuan's militia (now numbering 100,000[94]) are trained and supervised by the PLA, which controls its equipment and inventories, and inspects its performance. The Mobilization Department of the PLA oversees militia work. The commander of a military district directs militia operations, while the provincial party secretary serves as political commissar *(zhengwei)* of the district and assists in militia work. The same holds true at the military subdistrict level, although there the authority of the PLA often seems remote.

At the county level and below, militia work is supervised by People's Armed Forces Departments (PAFDs), whose commanders are usually PLA officers appointed by the military district. Although the PAFD is an element in the military chain of command, it has Party representation as well as that of local civilian authorities. Party directives are transmitted to the PAFD through the party's Political Affairs Department at any given level in the administrative hierarchy. The PAFDs serve as local command, administrative, and supply organs for the militia; they are also responsible for militia conscription and veterans' affairs. Being a dual system, either Party or Army may seek to enlarge its sphere of influence at the expense of the other. But an even greater threat to central control is localism, and PAFDs have been known to become quite independent of *any* higher authority.

It is true, as foreign critics charge, that the bingtuan's militia is not independent of PLA control. However, it is not an institution that the PLA cares a great deal about, and anyway the militia only comprises a tiny part of the bingtuan.[A] Actually, the bingtuan's militia has to serve two masters: the bingtuan and the PLA. Thus, some coordination is required, and that is supposed to be provided by a provincial-level Party organ called the People's Armed Forces Committee. The head of the bingtuan (normally a high provincial Party figure) sits on this body. But even more important than these institutional trappings are the

---

A. About 4 percent of bingtuan members belong to the militia. When there is serious trouble in the area, the army usually brings in rapid-reaction "fist" units from Lanzhou rather than relying on the militia.

personal relationships (*guanxi*) of the men involved. Thus it is natural that the bingtuan leaders would try to avoid antagonizing the PLA, and indeed the smoother their relations with the PLA, the better their relations with the provincial government, and with the central government.

In addition to maintaining a militia, there are various other ways that the bingtuan has supported the military. For example, several of its units helped to build the peripheral transportation infrastructure for the missile and nuclear installations in Xinjiang, though apparently they did not generally work on the bases themselves.[95] In the 1950s and 1960s, many of the workers (probably over 60,000) were either prisoners or former prisoners (*jiuye*). Most of these had previously been Kuomintang soldiers, though some were convicted criminals. Of particular note was the Second Division, which by 1960 was involved in construction work at the nuclear test base and missile impact centers. According to one estimate, about two-thirds of the hundred thousand men in this division at this time were prisoners or *jiuye* people.[96] But despite its military trappings, and occasional service to the PLA, the bingtuan was transforming itself into an essentially civilian institution.

In the late 1950s and early 1960s, the former soldiers were joined by many men and women migrants (*mangliu*), and by youths who were influenced by go-west propaganda (and by the absence of local jobs). After that, the bingtuan just kept on growing. Around 1966, large numbers immigrated from such eastern provinces as Shandong, Shanxi, Shaanxi, and nearby Gansu. It is said that by 1967 more than a million youths from eastern cities moved to Xinjiang as part of this "support the border" campaign.[97] Some had left their homes spontaneously, some were government organized. When they arrived in Xinjiang they usually joined the bingtuan. When more land was needed, the bingtuan simply appropriated it, if necessary incorporating some local Uyghurs into the organization at the same time. (For the arriving Hans, conditions often fell far short of what had been promised, and most seem to have felt cheated.) By the 1960s, the bingtuan was farming over 700,000 hectares, or almost a third of the region's arable land, and it also accounted for a third of the economic output.[A] By 1996, the bingtuan had become largely a collection of civilian economic enterprises,[B] with 2.24 million members,[98] or 14 percent of Xinjiang's population. As then-First Regional Party Secretary Saifudin (a Uyghur) once acknowledged, such labor from the east had been a crucial factor in promoting Xinjiang's development.[99]

But at least as important as all this would be the bingtuan's strategic role. In the 1960s, the authorities' main concern was defense against the Soviet Union. But this problem was never unrelated to the local ethnic problem. In 1962 there were serious armed conflicts between Hans and non-Hans, with a reported hundred thousand Uyghurs eventually fleeing across the ill-defined border into Soviet Kazakstan. The bingtuan was expanded to define and defend the frontier. In one case, a whole bingtuan division (the Fifth, from Hami) was moved to Bole, 400 kilometers east of the Soviet city of Alma Ata (now Almaty), to protect the frontier.[C] In all, 58 bingtuan farms (a third of the total) were established along the 2,019-kilometer frontier. Here, labor was integrated with military exercises.

In the 1990s China's official relations with the newly established Republic of Kazakstan warmed. Now, the militia's emphasis is less on border defense, and more on keeping the peace (or China's version

---

A. Figures are elusive. The total value (not including services) in 1966 was reported at RMB 1,200,000. (Donald H. McMillen, "Xinjiang and the Production and Construction Corps: A Han Organization in a Non-Han Region," *Australian Journal of Chinese Affairs*, no. 6, p. 92, note 20.) The "civilian" producers were highly mechanized, whereas the units based on prison labor were not, which is one of the reasons the prison-based economy is so unproductive. In 1984, the value declined 25 percent from 1983. *Renmin ribao,* September 29, 1985.

B. The bingtuan is comprised of thirteen reclamation areas with eleven division-level agricultural organizations — 175 if viewed in terms of regiment-level farms *(tuanchang)*. There are also 55,000 industrial operations (manufacturing, communications, construction, water conservancy projects, etc.).

C. First, the headquarters and 3,000 bingtuan members were moved; children and others followed later.

thereof) at home. Thus, in 1995 the entire militia of the Second Division (Korla) was called up and underwent training to put down ethnic disturbances.[100] That time the authorities seemed satisfied with the bingtuan's performance. Bingtuan deputy commander Hu Zhao-zhang, speaking in 1996, credited the bingtuan with having "carried out the struggle against invasion and penetration and splittist activities quite effectively."[101] (The anachronistic reference to an "invasion" threat must have been spoken out of habit; now the issue was Uyghur separatism.)

Indeed, just as bingtuan leaders once cited the Soviet threat in its pleas for more funding from Beijing, now they often use the separatist threat to argue for the same, playing on the leadership's fears that China might disintegrate the way the Soviet Union did. The bingtuan can exploit an attitude that often comes close to paranoia. China's media sometimes appear to exaggerate the ethnic threat in order to heighten Chinese nationalism. ("International reactionary forces and ethnic separatists at home, in collusion with one another, are bent on subjugating our country. We must not lower our guard. We must mobilize the masses to deal blows at the enemies."[102]) Still, the secessionist danger is real enough, and the bingtuan was never supposed to lose its role as a defender of *Chinese* Turkestan. In 1996, in a televised tirade against religious and ethnic dissidence, the regional party committee claimed: "The bingtuan is a major, reliable force with the assignment of maintaining Xinjiang's stability and building and defending the country's frontiers."[103] Overall, however, the central authorities appeared less than completely confident that the bingtuan could be counted on to fulfill its colonial mission, and called for the "vigorous strengthening" of the bingtuan so that it could be more effective in the struggle against "secession and disruptive activities."[104] Thus, the Party and government at all levels were instructed to foster the bingtuan's further "development and growth."[105]

The Bingtuan's Laogai

The Xinjiang bingtuan has played a noteworthy role in warehousing those perceived as the country's troublemakers. During the Mao era the bingtuan's laogai received mostly *political* prisoners, but since then they have been almost entirely *criminal*. Eastern cities have always been delighted with the willingness of Xinjiang's bingtuan to take prisoners whom, in recent years, no place else would accept. (As we shall see later, now even Qinghai was getting out of this business). It seemed like an inexpensive solution to one of the east's intractable problems. But the flow of prisoners to Xinjiang has been uneven. Indeed, not only did the importing of prisoners sharply decline during the Cultural Revolution, but by 1975 most of those who had arrived in the early 1950s had been released. True, to some extent they had been replaced by prisoners from places like Inner Mongolia and Tibet.[A] But the next real influx of prisoners to Xinjiang did not come until around 1984. This occurred because of the nationwide crackdown on crime that had just taken place.[B] During the ensuing years, prisoners continued to be sent to Xinjiang, but not in quite such large numbers.

For a prisoner to be sent to Xinjiang, he must have been sentenced to a term of at least five years. The sending province draws up a list of whom it wants to ship out, and arranges accordingly with one of the "divisions" *(shi)* in Xinjiang's bingtuan. It would appear that sometimes with high-profile political cases the decision regarding exile is made in Beijing. But such are a small minority, and the decision is almost always made where the offender was apprehended. The procedures often seem to have been somewhat casual. One of our interviewees (Fan Sidong) discovered halfway through his term that no formal order transferring him to Xinjiang had ever been issued. (After Fan complained

---

A. The total number of prisoners sent off to border provinces and Qinghai pursuant to the May 1951 resolution (see p. 16) had been 123,229, of whom 121,938 were released by 1975. In the case of Inner Mongolia, around the time of the Lin Biao incident (1971) Beijing began to fear for the security of the prisoner camps there, and the prisoners were transferred to the northeast and to Xinjiang.

B. According to our informants, the government considered that 80 percent of all criminals were arrested at that time (compared with 10 percent normally, and 30 percent during the somewhat milder crackdown in early 1996). Although these figures seem fanciful, they may provide some insight into official thinking.

about this, proper documentation was eventually issued.)

Most of the labor reform aspect of the Xinjiang prison system is managed by the bingtuan's Labor Reform Work Department,[106] while a smaller but growing share is managed by the Labor Reform Department in Xinjiang's Department of Justice. This dual arrangement was spelled out in 1985, when it was officially reasserted that bingtuan labor reform units were "not under the leadership of the autonomous region's Department of Justice."[A] Before about 1991 even the state supervisory (jiancha) apparatus was hardly active at all in the bingtuan labor camps.[B] In 1994 it was stated that the bingtuan's and province's laogai departments were equal in rank; both were supposed to be under the "leadership of the province." But to the extent that the bingtuan prison administrators are accountable to anyone at all, it would be to the Ministry of Justice in Beijing. Even this is mostly a matter of keeping the ministry informed in a general way about the local situation; there appears to have been no hands-on central leadership.

In addition to the many laogai camps, the bingtuan still maintains[107] its own prison, twenty-four jails (kanshousuo), as well as its own Public Security (Gongan) Bureau, court system,[C] and Justice (Sifa) Depart-

---

A. The Ministry of Justice has jurisdiction only in the case of crimes committed by administrative personnel. However, if a bingtuan court decides on a death sentence, it must request (qing) the Supreme Regional Court to approve (hejun) the sentence before it is carried out. All these arrangements are specified in an instruction jointly issued by the Ministry of Justice, the Supreme People's Court, and the Supreme People's Procuratorate and the Ministry of Public Security, dated September 21, 1985. The instruction appeared in an internal (neibu) publication Zhonghua renmin gongehuo falu guifangxing jiesh jicheng (Collection of standardized explanations on laws of the People's Republic of China), Jilin People's Publishing House, Jilin, 1990.

B. Neither does the Jiancha apparatus appear to have been active in institutions under the Department of Justice. There, however, judicial personnel often served this role. One of our informants, a former judge, paid monthly visits to prison mines, and is our main source of information on this subject, on which see p. 108.

C. There is one bingtuan court for approximately every five regiments. They

ment. These may be subject to some oversight from Xinjiang's similarly designated provincial bureaus. Unless they receive interference, however, the bingtuan's police and courts have generally had full authority to mete out justice (which they did with a vengeance during the Cultural Revolution). People incarcerated within the bingtuan laogai system include not only prisoners sent from the east, but some from Xinjiang itself.[A] We shall show, however, that all of these prisoners combined still have comprised only a very small part of the 2.2-million-member bingtuan.

The bingtuan is divided into prefecture-level divisions. The original plan was to have twelve of these divisions, each with twelve regiments *(tuan)* numbered 1 to 220. In the event, Xinjiang itself would have only ten, which are known as "Agricultural Divisions."[B] Most of the prisoners are in these Agricultural divisions, particularly the First (located in Aksu), Second (Korla), Third (Kashgar), Fourth (Gulja/Yining), Seventh (Kuitun), and Eighth (Shihezi). Now, there are also newer regiments (beginning with the number 221), among them various "detachments" *(zhidui)*, i.e., prison farms. Whether or not a detachment is part of a Division, if it is very large it will be divided into smaller brigades *(dadui)*. These can be contiguous with other prison or non-

---

are accountable to the Division-level court, which may have a staff of 80 or 90.

A. Most bingtuan prisons have a small number of former civilian bingtuan members who have been convicted of crimes. There are also contingents of regular native Xinjiang prisoners, including some who were transferred to the prisons of the First Division after 1985. Yang Zhenhua, p. 416. We believe that the Sixth Division in Wujiaqu also has Xinjiang prisoners.

B. No. 1 (Aksu: 15 regiments in 1988), No. 2 (Korla: 15), No. 3 (Kashgar: 11), No. 4 (Yining: 17), No. 5 (Bole: 10), No. 6 (Changji: 10, plus one in Urumqi), No. 7 (Kuitun: 7), No. 8 (Shihezi: 17), No. 9 (Tacheng: 6), and No. 10 (Altai: 5). There was never a No. 11. Number 12, as we shall see on p. 145, was in Qinghai. In addition, there are also some regiments (e.g., nos. 221, 222, 223) which are under the direct control of the bingtuan. Also in this category is the First Construction Division, with headquarters in Urumqi. This Division has some farms; apparently it produces its own food.

Note that only a small minority of the regiments cited above have prisoners.

prison farms, or they may be isolated. Near the bottom of this structure is the squadron *(zhongdui)*, which typically has 150 men and ten cadres. Here inmates are divided into "teams" *(xiaodui)* of 15 or 20 people who usually occupy one room.[108] The chart on page 66 provides an overall schematic view of what the Xinjiang prison system has looked like, with the bingtuan on the left, and the regular provincial-type laogai structure on the right.

As is typical of public administration in China, within the bingtuan prison system there are two distinct lines of authority. One is managed by professional people concerned with such matters as production. The other is political (policy-oriented), and is concerned with managing incarceration and reform (at the local level, taking direction from the Party). Any differences between the two lines of authority are supposed to be ironed out by consensus. Whether or not this is easily effected, our interviewees agree that prisoners are never exposed to the process or made aware of any "contradictions."

Each laogai unit has one or more specialized administrative bureaus called *laogai ke*. For example, a laogai farm, depending on size, typically will have about three of these *ke*. They specialize in different aspects of laogai management, perhaps focusing on criminals, or counterrevolutionaries, or labor, or reform, or study. Each *ke* has a head *(ke-zhang)*, assistant head, and one or more personnel *(ke yuan)*. The total number of people staffing the organ is usually 7 to 10. The number of prisoners within the purview of a *ke* can vary greatly.

Structure of the Laogai

Table 9 lists the bingtuan units which are known to have had prisons in recent years. Altogether, the number of agricultural prisons (usually, farm complexes) maintained by the bingtuan is thirty-six.[109] If viewed in terms of squadron-level units (single farms), the number is probably 305. Although Chart 1 gives an overall schematic view of the region's prison system, things usually do not follow this "ideal model." In some cases, the actual structure might be much less complex than this, with some levels omitted. For example, there might be no regiment (state

TABLE 9 (See note on page 65)

Bingtuan Units Confirmed as Currently Having Prisons

Division	Regiment (or unit with which prison is affiliated)	County	Estimated number of prisoners	Organizations in charge of prison work	Remarks
First (Aksu)	Reg: Jinyinchuan Prison	Aksu	800		
	3 Reg: Kalakule Prison	Awati	400		
	5 Reg: Shahe Prison	Wensu	800		
	6 Reg: Xinyan Prison	Wensu	400		Location unclear
	7 Reg: Matan Prison	Aksu	600		
	8 Reg: Tamen Prison	Aksu	800		
	9 Reg: Ala'er Prison	Aksu	1,500		Also known as Bingtuan No. 2 Prison.
	10 Reg: Kekekule Prison	Aksu	700		
	11 Reg: Huaqiao Prison	Aksu	500		
	12 Reg: Nankou Prison	Aksu	400		
	13 Reg: Xinfucheng Prison	Aksu	800		

		Also known as:	Ta'nan Laogai Zhidui (Detachment)
14 Reg: Xiahelike Prison	Aksu	900	
15 Reg: Hong-qiao Prison	Aksu	800	
16 Reg: Xinkai-ling Prison	Aksu	700	
Total 14 Prisons		9,900	Ten laogai *zhidui* with 55 *zhongdui* (squadrons)
Second (Korla) 27 Reg: Kainan Prison	Yanqi	700	
28 Reg: Boguqi Prison	Korla	400	
32 Reg: Prison name unknown	Yuli	1,000	
33 Reg: Ku'ermuyi Prison	Yuli	300	
34 Reg: Tie-ganlieke Prison	Yuli	300	
36 Reg: Milan Prison	Ruoqiang	500	
223 Reg: Hamuyuti Prison	Hejing	1,000	
Qiemo Prison	Qiemo	600	Second Division Construction Zhidui
Total 8 Prisons		4,800	

Division	Regiment (or unit with which prison is affiliated)	County	Estimated number of prisoners	Organizations in charge of prison work	Remarks
Third (Kashgar)	Kalabaile Prison		400		Location unclear
	44 Reg: Jindun Prison	Bachu	600		
	49 Reg: Gaimilike Prison	Bachu	600		
	50 Reg: Qigai-maidan Prison	Bachu	1,700		
	51 Reg: Tumutike Prison	Bachu	1,000		
	52 Reg: Qiganquele Prison	Bachu	800		
	53 Reg: Boqia-kesong Prison	Bachu	1,900		
	3rd Div. Con-struction Reg.	Bachu	300		
	Yonganba	Bachu	300		Location unclear
Total	9 Prisons		7,600		

Fourth (Yining)	Uranium mine ("Gray Mine")	Chabucha'er	2,000		
	Balakdudamtu Coal Mine	Near Gulja (Yining) airport	860		Prisoners from both Bingtuan and Sifa Laogai Bureau are kept here
Total	2 Prisons		2,860		
Fifth (Bole)					No prisoners or Laogai unit identified
Sixth (Wujiaqu, Changji)	222 Reg: Fubei Wujing Nong-chang	Fukang	200		
	Gongqingtuan Prison	Changji	500	Laogai No. 1 Zhongdui (in 1996).	
	Sanshihu Prison		500		Location unclear
	Xinhu Prison	Manas	1,000	6th Div. No. 2 Laogai Zhidui	Includes a farm and a water heater factory
	Fangcaohu Prison	Hutubi	2,200		Guarding this camp is the No. 4 Zhongdui
Total	5 Prisons		4,400		

*Prisoners in the Sixth Division are generally guarded by the Fourth Detachment of the Bingtuan People's Armed Police.

Division	Regiment (or unit with which prison is affiliated)	County	Estimated number of prisoners	Organizations in charge of prison work	Remarks
Seventh (Kuitun)	130 Reg.	Wusu	1,000	The Laogai No. 2 Zhidui has its HQ here.	Possibly by 1996 under the same administration as Huang'gou Prison
	Huang'gou Prison		500		Located to the south of 130 Regiment headquarters
	Kuihe Prison		500		Located to the northwest of Kuitun city, probably in Wensu county
	124 Reg: Xia-shuanghe Prison	Wusu	800		Located in the northern part of the area controlled by 124 Regiment
Total	4 Prisons		2,800	The Headquarters of the Laogai Chu (in charge of these prisons) is on Shawan Road, Kuitun City	In the area of the Seventh, the Bingtuan Wujing (PAP) No. 5 Zhidui is responsible for guarding prisons. Their heacquarters is located in Kuitun City

Eighth (Shihezi)	141 Reg: Beiye Prison	500	8th Div. Laogai No. 4 Zhidui	In the area of the 8th the Bingtuan Wujing No. 6 Zhidui is guarding prisons.
	142 Reg: Xin'an Prison	1,500	8th Div. Laogai No. 3 Zhidui	
	144 Reg: Zhong-jiazhuang Prison	1,000	8th Div. Laogai No. 2 Zhidui	
	Xiasangong Prison	500	8th Div. Laogai No. 5 Zhidui	Location unclear
	Shihezi Prison	500		
	104 Reg: Xishan Prison — Southwest of Urumchi	1,000	8th Div. Laogai No. 1 Zhidui	Other name: Bingtuan No. 1 Prison
Total	6 Prisons	5,000		
Ninth (Tacheng)				No prisoners or Laogai unit identified.
Tenth (Altai)			(Had prisoners at least until 1985)	No prisoners or laogai unit identified in the 1990s.
Totals*	48	c. 37.500		Both totals preliminary.

*These are only the bingtuan prisons and prisoners which we have *confirmed*. We estimate that there are an additional 11,000 to 12,000 prisoners, bringing the grand total of prisoners to about 49,000. Prison information is generally for the mid-1990s, but size of prisoner populations refers to c. 1990. In addition to the institutions listed above, the bingtuan operates 24 local jails (kanshousuo), whose prisoners are not included above.

Chart 1
Structure of Pre-1995 Xinjiang Prison System
(Simplified view)

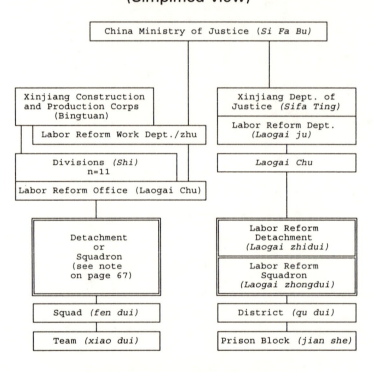

*Double-line box indicates a common
(but not invariable) location of prisons.*

Chart 2

Structure of Pre-1995 Bingtuan (Simplified view)

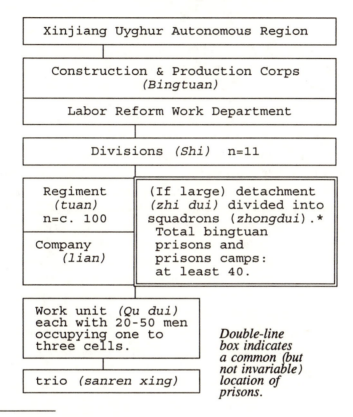

Xinjiang Uyghur Autonomous Region

Construction & Production Corps
(Bingtuan)

Labor Reform Work Department

Divisions *(Shi)* n=11

| Regiment *(tuan)* n=c. 100 | (If large) detachment *(zhi dui)* divided into squadrons *(zhongdui)*.* Total bingtuan prisons and prisons camps: at least 40. |
| Company *(lian)* | |

Work unit *(Qu dui)* each with 20-50 men occupying one to three cells.

trio *(sanren xing)*

Double-line box indicates a common (but not invariable) location of prisons.

*If a detachment (large prison camp) exists, it is divided into squadrons. But in the bingtuan, often the squadrons stand alone rather than being part of a detachment. Apparently a squadron is always accountable to a superior bingtuan level (though sometimes only to a distant regimental headquarters).

farm[A]), with squadrons (of 200 to 300 men) reporting directly to the Division. As for the small units at the bottom, these are work groups; whether and how long they exist depends on the nature of the work being performed at any given place and time. A more detailed view of the bingtuan alone is shown in Chart 2.

On the other hand, the actual arrangement may be more complex, and perhaps downright labyrinthine, with the civilian and laogai "sides" intermingled. Chart 3 on page 69 suggests more realistically (if perhaps bewilderingly) how one of the more complex divisions is organized, in this case showing the Eighth Division in the Shihezi area, just northwest of Urumqi. This is a largely agricultural division, though there is some manufacturing.[B]

The Eighth Division is a large organization, but only between 1 and 2 percent of its people are prisoners. In the mid-1980s there were 4,500 prisoners. Altogether, the Eighth Division has ten or so regiments, the largest of which is No. 142, with a 1995 population of 33,358. Such regiments, however, do not actually administer the prison camps. A regiment is involved primarily because it is the ultimate "owner" of the land farmed by a detachment (prison farm); the land has been entrusted (doubtless with some reluctance on the regiment's part) to the laogai system. Although the regiment has virtually no role in the management of the prison camps, if the camp is a financial success the regiment stands to benefit.[110] But conversely, if a laogai unit gets into trouble financially, the regiment, or the company *(lian)* under it, will be expected to "lend" it provisions.[C]

The Eighth Division is believed to now have twenty-two labor-

---

A. Strictly speaking, these bingtuan farms are "state farms" (*guoying nongchang*), though the term is usually reserved for other state farms which are more centrally administered.

B. Shihezi Prison appears to have an "Agricultural Hydroelectric Equipment Enterprise." *XBN,* p. 319 (under Liu Zhiqiang).

C. This is quite different from the prisons under the Department of Justice, which have no collateral source of emergency help, and must count on the regional (i.e., province-level) authorities.

Chart 3

The Eighth Bingtuan Division (c. 1994)

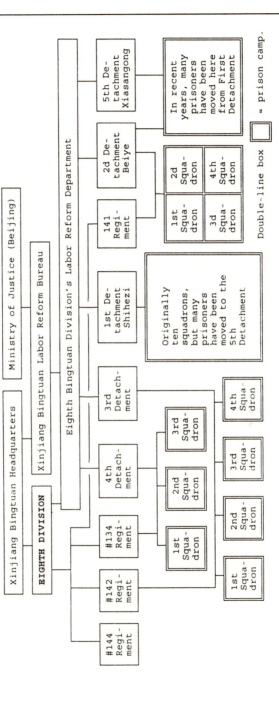

reform squadrons, associated with three regiments. At the end of 1995, the prisoner population was 3,708 (down 18 percent from the mid-1980s). To put this in perspective: altogether, in 1994 the Eighth Division had 18 regiments, 315 industrial enterprises, and a population of 490,854. These prison camps are operated by cadres from the bingtuan laogai detachments 1 through 5. The whole establishment is guarded by men from the Sixth Detachment of the Bingtuan People's Armed Police.

China does not reveal how many prisoners are contained in such institutions, but one can occasionally find such information in internal publications. From such we learn, for example, that the Third Division's Fiftieth Regiment, otherwise known as Qigaimaidan Prison, began taking prisoners from east China in 1983. Over the years, it acquired 4,334 of them, 2,359 of whom remained in 1995. They are divided into seven squadrons *(zhongdui)*. The prison complex has 2,278 cadres *(ganjing)*, of whom 156 are Party members. Twenty-seven have been to college.[111]

Regarding the prisoner populations of whole bingtuan divisions, although data again is not as complete as one might like, we can make some inferences using various tangentially related statistics. Thus, our analysis of the Seventh Division suggests a 1992 prisoner population of 4,338.[A] For 1995, we estimate the number to be 2,514.[B] Such information (which is consistent with our other data) will be useful when we return to the question of the overall size of the Xinjiang laogai.

A. Population derived by means of the following extrapolation: Profit (RMB 4,750,000) divided by profit per prisoner (RMB 1,095). These individual statistics were reported in *Xinsheng bao,* April 18, 1992, p. 1.

B. Population derived by means of the following extrapolation: Number of articles submitted to *Xinsheng bao* (2,489) divided by the average number of submissions (0.99). These individual statistics were reported in *XSB Tongxun,* February 25, 1996, p. 4.

Department of Justice *(Sifa)* Laogai

As noted earlier, there are two prison systems in Xinjiang; in addition to the bingtuan, there is the more orthodox laogai network under the Xinjiang Department of Justice *(Sifa Ting)*.[112] (See Chart 1, p. 66.) The latter's laogai system primarily holds convicts who had been legal or at least de facto residents of Xinjiang. Arrest rates used to be low in Xinjiang compared with China in general. However, in the late 1980s this changed; local arrest rates rose dramatically, and in 1989 Xinjiang sentenced more persons (in relation to the population) than most other provinces. In the 1990s things leveled off a bit, with the region's arrest rate being similar to the national norm. In recent years Xinjiang has continued its upward trend,[113] resulting in a larger prisoner population (even before considering imported prisoners) than one would expect for a province this size. The increasing crime rate is probably related to the vast region's income disparities; Urumqi has become a prosperous city, whereas much of the non-Han population elsewhere is impoverished. Political disaffection among the Uyghurs is also a factor.

After arrest, a native Xinjiang prisoner will usually be sent to the prison in the nearest city. If he is a serious offender whose escape is feared, he will remain there and work in a prison factory. If the case is not so serious but he is still sentenced to a few years or more, he will go to a labor reform farm in his home prefecture. As in the bingtuan, judicial personnel are overwhelmingly Han. However, unlike the bingtuan, most of the people involved in the laogai, both prisoners and minders,[A] are of minority ethnicity — primarily Uyghur and Kazakh. The number of prisoners used to be less than half that in the bingtuan. However, the bingtuan's prisoner population has been declining, while the non-bingtuan prisoner population has been on the increase.

A. According to the 1989 *Zhongguo jiancha nianjian* (p. 211), the entire Xinjiang laogai had 1,896 ethnic minority cadres. They comprised 44.13% of the grand total, which we infer to be 4,296. Inasmuch as the bingtuan prison system is the larger of the two, and the 1,896 minority cadres are concentrated in the Sifa system, Sifa guards must be overwhelmingly non-Han.

TABLE 10

Sifa Laogai Units Confirmed as Having Prisoners in 1990s

Prefecture	Name	County	Estimated no. of prisoners (1990)	Remarks
Urumchi	Xinjiang No. 1 Prison	Urumchi	1,200	
	Xinjiang No. 2 Prison	Urumchi	800	Women Prison
	Xinjiang No. 3 Prison	Urumchi	1,200	
	Juvenile Delinquents Prison	Urumchi	100	
	Zizhiqu Gongan Ting Meikuang (Coal mine)	Urumchi, Lucaogou	200	Coal mine
Total Urumchi	5 prisons		3,500	
Karamay	Wu'erhe Nongchang	Located in the northern-most corner of Karamay.	700	Former name: Xinsheng Nongchang.
Turfan*			100	Prefecture-level jail

*Turfan Prefecture is said to have four laogai camps, but we have been unable to confirm this.

Prefecture	Institution	City	Number	Notes
Hami			200	Unknown; probably prefecture level jail
Changji	Zizhiqu Xiabahu Jianyu (1996)	Changji, Wu-yi West Road	1,200	Old name: Xiabahu Nongchang
Bole			200	Unknown; probably prefecture level jail
Bayingol	Yanqi Jianyu (Laogai Bureau No. 12 Zhidui)	Yanqi	1,100	Other name: Sishili Chengzi Laogai Nongchang. Includes a paper factory.
Aksu	Kuche Laogai Nongchang	Kuche	700	
	Talimu Gongan Nongchang	Shaya	1,000	Other name: Talimu Laogai Nongchang
	Baicheng Xian Meikuang	Baicheng	300	Coal mine
	Kuoruledun Laogai Nongchang	Awati	700	
Kizilsu			200	Unknown; probably prefecture-level jail
Kashgar	Pailou Laogai Nongchang	Shache	3,000	
	Halihuqi Nongchang	Jiashi	800	
	Kelakeqin Laogai Zhidui	Bachu	900	

Prefecture	Name	County	Estimated number of prisoners (1990)	Remarks
Khotan	Kalahan Nongchang	Yutian	1,300	Alternative name: Yutian Laogai Zhidui or Yutian Xian Laogai Nongchang. Headquarters is in Khotan.
Ili	Gongan Nongchang	Xinyuan	1,300	
	Ili Juvenile Delinquents Prison	Gulja (Yining)	100	
	Unknown. Located at 8 Gongyuan St., Alley 4.	Gulja (Yining)	200	Detention station for people caught attempting to leave the country illegally. Operated by the Border Defense Bureau of the Pref. PSB.
Tacheng	Gaxiongbula Nongchang	Wusu	1,300	Old name: Gongan Nongchang
Altai	Gongan Nongchang	Fuhai	500	
Shihezi			100	Unknown; probably prefecture level jail
Grand total	24 prisons confirmed		20,400 prisoners confirmed	Total excludes prisoners in county level jails.

The units overseen by the Justice Department are shown in Table 10. Some institutions deserve special note. Urumqi has one prison for women, another for youths. There is a second prison for juveniles in Gulja (Yining). That town also has a detention house for people caught illegally leaving the country, the only such institution in China of which we are aware. (Central Asians often do not respect international boundaries, which they consider artificial and inconsistent with the ethnic geography.)

Although inmates in this Sifa system are usually regular Xinjiang residents, occasionally a bingtuan member will be sentenced to serve time in a Sifa laogai, and sometimes a Xinjiang citizen, convicted in a Sifa court, will be sentenced to serve his time in the bingtuan prison system. However, such cases are exceptional. Relations between the two systems tend to be poor, and the officials do not like to have to deal with each other. For their part, the prisoners certainly prefer to remain in more familiar institutional territory (bingtuan or non-bingtuan, as the case may be), where they will not be affected by the bad blood between the two systems, and in some cases may even be close to relatives who might be able to use their influence to improve the prisoners' conditions or morale.

Labor Reeducation

As we observed in previous chapters, less serious offenders can be sentenced to "labor reeducation" *(laojiao)* rather than labor reform. Prior to 1979, Xinjiang abounded in labor-reeducation camps, though they were mostly small. Compared to laogai, people doing *laojiao* have a greater likelihood of early release. In one instance in 1978, a whole camp of 20,000 labor-reeducation inmates were declared "rehabilitated" and sent back east — and were immediately replaced by new "students."[114] In recent years, labor reeducation has been less common in the region than before, and since the 1980s labor-reeducation prisoners from other provinces have not been sent here. The main labor reeducation camps known to be functioning today are shown in Table 11. Today, those miscreants who are sentenced to labor-reeducation are people

TABLE 11

Sifa Laojiao units confirmed of having prisoners, 1990s

Prefecture	Name	County	Estimated no. of prisoners	Date if other than 1990	Remarks
Urumchi	Urumchi Laojiao Suo	Urumchi			
Karamay					Unknown
Turfan					Unknown
Hami	Hami Laojiao Suo				
Changji					Unknown
Bole					Unknown
Bayingol	None			Dissolved 1989	Prisoners now in Aksu.
Aksu	Aksu Laojiao Suo				
Kizilsu					Unknown
Kashgar					Unknown
Khotan					Unknown
Ili	Ili Laojiao Suo	Dadamutu,	(near Yining)	1995	Operates a brick factory.
Tacheng	Shawan Laojiao Suo	Shawan		1995	
Altai					Unknown
Shihezi					Unknown
Total (1995)			2,000 estimated		Estimate: 9 camps

who have been living in Xinjiang.[A] Unlike in past years, and in the east still, these institutions are often very small. Even drug addicts are not usually sent for labor reeducation in Xinjiang, as they are in China proper.[B] Thus, labor reeducation in Xinjiang is much less common than it is elsewhere, largely because so many of the prisoners are serious offenders from the east. As we shall see, labor reeducation is also relatively uncommon in Qinghai, but there the reasons are quite different.

Management

Between 1975 and 1983 (when few prisoners were being sent from other provinces), the prisons that the bingtuan did maintain were managed by the bingtuan's small Office of Labor Reform[115] with little or no oversight from the military or anyone else. Then, around 1984 came the big influx of prisoners from eastern China, and soon the bingtuan's laogai was even larger than Xinjiang's regular prison system. Overseeing these networks has required a staff of thousands, which had to be recruited quickly from whatever human material was available for service as prison cadres.[C] Although candidates for this work were

---

A. We interviewed no *laojiao* prisoners, but others stated that conditions in labor reeducation camps were no better than in labor reform camps. According to another report, conditions were once equally brutal but have improved recently in at least one of Xinjiang's labor reeducation camps. Domenach (cited endnote 11), p. 395. In 1995 a German film crew was allowed to film a labor reeducation camp in Yunnan; their assessment was not very favorable.

B. According to our information, those from the Urumqi area go to the Justice Department's Detoxification Clinic (Xiaoduzhan), which is located in the Urumqi Psychiatric Hospital. We do not have information about other parts of Xinjiang.

C. These cadres are called *ganjing* or "cadre police;" most of the personnel inside the prison camps fall into this category. However, there is another type of "police" called *jingyuan,* who occupy the guard room inside the gate and control who enters and leaves the camp.

supposed to have a middle school education and have a "good political background," they have tended actually to be low-income, often illegitimate settlers,[116] who had been scraping a living off the land. As is so often the case in China, these positions subsequently tended to become *de facto* hereditary. (One internal source laments: "Sons simply assume their fathers' positions; there is no other way. Well, at least this solves the young men's career problem."[117])

The cadres comprise an elaborate hierarchy, based on the way the prisons themselves are organized (see page 67). A bingtuan division has a laogai office *(laogai chu)*, which presides over the detachments (usually, prison farms), which in turn have supervisory cadres at the brigade level, and basic-level cadres at the squadron level. The squadron cadres *(zhongdui ganjing)* are the front-line personnel who regularly deal directly with prisoners. This is not considered desirable work; these cadres would rather be working at the brigade level, and the brigade cadres would prefer to be working in the division administrative office. To combat the upward drift and the concomitant tendency for the basic levels to be understaffed, in 1989 it was ordered that cadres at the two lowest levels must comprise at least 60 percent of the division's total cadres, and at least 70 percent of these must be at the squadron level, where there must also be at least one cadre for every 12.5 prisoners.[118]

In the early years the cadres were reasonably competent people, but since the 1950s, misconduct has become pervasive and institutionalized. Efforts to make pay scales contingent on how successful the prisons are (in terms of productivity and reform) appear not to have been very meaningful.[119] Instead, all sorts of dubious means have been devised for cadre enrichment. The immediate superiors are generally aware and tolerant of the corruption. Thus, the cadres could make far more money

---

In this book we use the term "cadre" in the normal loose sense of laogai parlance. The prison personnel generally insist that prisoners recognize them as cadres even if they are not such in the strict sense of "national cadres" *(guojia ganbu)*. See also endnote 367.

working in prisons than they ever had been able to farming.[A] Although the base pay of a low-level prison cadre may be about the same as what a farm hand makes,[B] one's income is multiplied by bonuses and corrupt earnings. Those with seniority receive bonuses of about the same amount as their nominal earnings if there have been no known serious problems in the camp and it is deemed to have been managed well. The highest salaries go to political commissars, who receive a monthly total of about RMB 300 (early 1990s). But they often have unreimbursed expenses, and anyone's pay can arrive months late. Rank-and-file cadres have it the worst. In the past there were occasions when the government even failed to provide them with uniforms; they sometimes wore prisoners' clothes rather than spend their own money.[120] Given such a level of official support, rampant corruption is not surprising. Our sources tell us that the national anti-corruption campaigns of recent years have, at best, only resulted in corrupt dealings being less open and flagrant. Indeed, there is a tendency even to trivialize cadre's crime, designating it as mere "corruption."

In spite of (and in part because of) the corrupt environment, morale has been low.[121] This makes it all the more difficult for the authorities to recruit competent, capable, and responsible corrections personnel. An official report acknowledged the problem, and noted especially the difficulty of finding men suitable for taking over the leadership positions when senior officials retire. "All one can do is select from among the unimpressive."[122] There are two schools which are supposed to turn out more professional cadres for this work (the bingtuan's in Changji, the Justice Department's in Urumqi), but progress has been slow.

A. In 1995 the average per capita annual income for Xinjiang's farmers and herdsmen was only RMB 1,282. *XJRB*, April 21, 1996, p. 1, FBIS, May 17, 1996, p. 75.

B. After two probationary years, a *ganjing*'s base salary (early 1990s) was RMB 100 a month; a farmer might have earned slightly more. By the mid-1990s farmers' incomes were higher, but herdsmen were still making barely RMB 100. *XJRB,* March 29, 1996, p. 2, FBIS, July 18, 1996, p. 79.

An essential feature of the system is the principle of "convicts managing convicts" *(fanren guanli fanren)*. In practice, what this amounts to is a working alliance between the cadres[123] and their convict-allies, to whom hereafter we shall refer as "cell bosses."[A] These are usually serious offenders who assist the cadres in controlling prisoners and punishing the recalcitrant. The cadres themselves are often too callow to be up to dealing with hardened criminals.[124] Although the cell bosses are not directly paid for this work, the perks they do gain are substantial. For example, they enjoyed food having many times the value of that received by the other prisoners.

How does someone become a cell boss? Although there is much competition for these positions, there is no formal selection procedure, and the process appears to be based on something akin to natural selection. There are two main ways to become a cell boss. One is via the bully route — being very aggressive toward the other prisoners and also standing up to the cadres. The toughest man will be recognized as a cell boss. The other approach is to use one's wits and skills, and in that way become ingratiated with the cadres. The latter will quickly appreciate a prisoner who has leadership qualities and is cooperative with them — especially inasmuch as the day-to-day power of the cell boss often exceeds that of the cadres themselves. But this type of cell boss is not as powerful as the first type. According to one of our sources, a squadron's top cell boss usually gets his position by being cruel, and by engaging in bribery (paying the cadre several hundred *renminbi* per month). He then puts together a team of subordinate cell bosses who commit most of the "disciplinary" violence against prisoners. Basically, these lower positions are sold — the going price being a one-time charge of about RMB 1,000. They also must regularly provide little services for the cadres. For example, when the latter take

---

A. *"Laotou yuba,"* literally meaning "prison head prison despot."

This discussion concerns only male cell bosses. Female cell bosses are called *laotie* (literally, "old iron"). On such individuals in Shenyang, see *Fanzui yu gaizao yanjiu,* 1988, no. 5, pp. 44-47. (We do not have information specifically about female cell bosses in the northwest.)

a rest, one would prepare tea, another provide cigarettes, a third provide reading matter or tell stories. They, in turn, are rewarded with soft jobs and de facto recognition of their modest authority, and the likelihood of earning perhaps a year's reduction of sentence. (China's representatives appear to have persuaded the United Nations' Committee Against Torture that the cell bosses do not exist. See p. 236, clause 9.)

Role of People's Armed Police

In the hierarchy of civilian laogai personnel, the field cadres occupy the lowest and least enviable positions. However, even lower in status than these cadres are the members of the People's Armed Police (*wujing*, PAPs), about which a word of background is in order.

Until the early 1980s, China had one main national armed service, namely the People's Liberation Army (PLA). Sometimes prisoners were guarded by these soldiers,[A] but in the case of Xinjiang they were usually guarded by "armed police" who were not part of the People's Liberation Army. The Xinjiang PAPs appear to have been a makeshift operation, dependent on the bingtuan for funds, and not even formally recognized by the authorities in Beijing; reportedly they were not issued arms, which they had to "borrow" wherever they could. This abnormal situation lasted until 1988. In the meantime, between 1982 and 1984 the *national* military police were separated from the PLA; they became the "People's Armed Police," and given responsibility for maintaining internal security.[125] Although they remained a quasi-military organization,[B] until 1995 they would be subordinate to the Ministry of Public

---

A. At other times they were guarded by the bingtuan's own militia (discussed above, pp. 52-55). Before 1980 they were often guarded by the Gong An Bing (security forces under the Ministry of Public Security). There were also armed border guards who were not under direct PLA or MPS command.

B. According to Article 87 of the Details for Implementation of Regulations Governing Correction Work of Prison and Labor Reform, the security

Security[A] (as had occasionally been the case before). In the meantime, the PAP had been considerably beefed up in the wake of the Beijing disaster[126] of 1989, and charged with nipping any future such problems in the bud. Ideology and "political construction" are now supposed to come first.[127] However, it is only uneasily that the central authorities rely on the PAP to protect their power. On at least one occasion, Jiang Zemin addressed a group of PAPs from behind a bullet-proof shield.[128]

Locally, contingents of the People's Armed Police are normally accountable to two superiors: their immediate superiors in the PAP, and the provincial Public Security Bureaus. PAP units which guard prisoners, however, have been under the administrative leadership of the prisons and labor reform units. In the case of the bingtuan, whereas the old People's Armed Police had been administratively separate from the laogai, in 1988 Xinjiang's PAPs lost their autonomy and were brought into the Xinjiang General Unit of the PAP.[129] All of this meant that, in theory, the Xinjiang PAPs were accountable to Beijing. However, the PAP has long been notorious for lack of any Party presence at the lower levels, and this is probably especially true in the northwest. Regularization certainly has not led to any vaunted status for Xinjiang's PAPs, especially the ones who often strike terror into the hearts of the prisoners they guard.

Though it is hardly a daily activity for most PAPs, in Xinjiang the regional People's Armed Police's most conspicuous role has been to repress Uyghur separatism.[130] Sometimes they do this by means of the carrot of anti-poverty campaigns,[131] but more often they use the stick

-----

of prisoners is the responsibility of the Armed Police. The PAP "follows the rules and regulations of the PLA and enjoys the same privileges as those of the PLA."

A. Before this time there had been a small similarly named armed police organization called the *Gong An Bing* (security soldiers) under the Ministry of Public Security. It merged with the PAP. The name was now changed to *Renmin Wuzhuang Jingcha Budui*. The order effecting these changes was Zhongfa 1982, no. 20.

of repression. (In the latter effort, they may on rare occasion actually have enlisted the aid of the prisoners.^A) The first test of the revitalized PAP came during Xinjiang's bloody ethnic disturbances of April 1990 at Baren, in a Kirghiz prefecture north of Kashgar (an area much more central Asian than Chinese in character). At any rate, guarding prisoners was now a relatively minor part of the work of this *Xinjiang* branch of the national PAP. The *bingtuan* PAP, on the other hand, does mainly guard (mostly Han) prisoners. This is an operation that has always been woefully under-financed. These men are paid only RMB 45 per month (plus food and housing), and do not have as much opportunity to enrich themselves off of prisoners as do the cadres. Thus, they tend to be resentful, and relations between the PAPs and the corrections officials are often sour. The prisoners we interviewed were fully aware of the "contradictions" between the bingtuan cadres and the Armed Police, and were under the impression that the whole system was poorly organized. Nonetheless, the PAP continues to grow.[132]

If the Armed Police have bad relations with the corrections officers, their relations with the prisoners can be even worse. Normally, they simply guard the perimeter of the prison camps, and need have little direct contact with the prisoners. Han solidarity notwithstanding, they tend not to relate to the inmates as human beings. They often take out their frustrations on them, coercing them into handing over their possessions, sometimes beating them in the process (though PAPs are responsible for only a tiny fraction of the beatings). On the other hand, the prisoners are sometimes able to exploit the "contradictions" between the PAPs and the corrections officials, perhaps turning the PAPs in for

---

A. United States intelligence sources claim that during the ethnic disturbances in April 1990 the desperate authorities temporarily released prisoners, who were given rifles and told to fight the Uyghurs. However, our interview subjects report that the practice was more effective in the 1950s than in recent decades. Information on the whole subject is sketchy, but we think it unlikely that Xinjiang's prisoners of recent decades (who have mostly been Uyghurs or hardened criminals from the east) would have been asked to deal with ethnic unrest.

theft. Still, the People's Armed Police are not altogether powerless vis-à-vis the corrections officials. Although they normally have no authority over prisoners and are basically kept in reserve for when problems arise, they have ultimate authority for local security in general, and can prevent people, including cadres, from leaving a prison compound. They can even require everyone to leave a work site and return to the compound, a power they sometimes abuse if they do not like the way they are treated.

When a team goes out into the field to work, it is accompanied by at least one cadre. A couple of PAPs may also go, though they are not very effective in preventing escapes. They often perform their job in a perfunctory manner. These soldiers generally loathe their jobs, not least of all because of the low pay. If a prisoner in his charge escapes, the worst punishment a soldier gets may be being sent home, which is probably what he wants anyway.

Escapes

Escaping, then, is not a matter of breaking out of prison; it is almost always a matter of slipping away from a work site.[133] More effective than the Armed Police as lines of defense against escapes are the forbidding Xinjiang environment and the lack of any support system for escapees outside the prison system. Still, escape attempts are frequent (especially by prisoners serving long terms for serious crimes[134]), and some succeed. (Prisoners have been known simply to drive away in official cars![A]) This is especially so in the south, where the forbidding desert, while hard on escapees, also precludes serious manhunts. Region-wide, it is common for up to 4 percent of prisoners to disappear

---

A. On January 10, 1986, a secret notice was issued, the title of which is self-explanatory: "Bulletin from the Ministry of Justice Laogai Bureau Concerning Preventing Escapes by Not Allowing Prisoners to Drive Motor Vehicles." This was widely circulated and based on experience in Guangdong, but the bingtuan laogai offices were specifically mentioned as recipients.

in any given year (though sometimes the rate is only one percent).[A] In one district in southern Xinjiang's First Division there were once supposed to have been 180 prisoners, but 28 of these had escaped. Most of these figures are probably conservative, because district directors tend not to report escapes to their superiors for fear of having their pay docked.

To deal with the problem of escapes, beginning in 1993 many squadrons required prisoners to go shoeless in the camps. Also, a three-man buddy system *(sanren xing)* was instituted. Not unlike in the "three-person supervision groups" *(sanren hujian)* in laogais of other provinces, in Xinjiang this has been enforced at least in the fields, and under a strict version of this regime one must be accompanied by one's two buddies even when leaving a cell to go to the toilet.[135] If a member of such a group causes trouble, the whole threesome can be punished (anything from worse food to physical abuse). On the other hand, if a prisoner reports on another's infractions, he may be rewarded. Such measures seem to have been effective in reducing the very high escape rate to what the authorities considered a tolerable level. In 1991, for example, in the Seventh Division (in Kuitun), satisfaction was expressed that the annual escape rate had been brought down to 3.9 percent.[136] That, however was greater than the national standard (2.5 percent) decreed by the Department of Justice, and much worse than the all-bingtuan figure for the year, which dropped almost in half from the previous year (2.1 percent, down from 4 percent in 1990 and 6 percent in 1988.)[137] We do not know exactly what percentage of escapees are recaptured, but 85 percent is considered

---

A. Police get double pay if they catch an escapee, while guards deemed responsible pay a financial penalty. Escapees are usually caught, with two years being added to the sentence on the first attempt, and more for subsequent attempts. Physical abuse of those caught is also common. See next page.

We were told of one central directive declaring that an escape rate of more than two per thousand was unacceptable.

For more on the subject, see Jin Hao, "My View on the Work of Preventing Escapes" (in Chinese), in *LLLY*, 1989, no. 4, pp. 22-23.

good.[138] Those who are caught can expect a grim fate. In one case, a recaptured escapee was subjected to an organized struggle session *(pi dou)* in which other inmates inflicted beatings, from which he died.[139] Others are sometimes executed in the more orthodox manner, with a bullet to the back of the head.[A] One way of reducing the escape rate in laogai camps is to keep potential escapees in traditional prisons.[B] Nationwide, it appears that prison escapes are on the decline,[140] though we do not know whether this is true in Xinjiang.

Thus, at least until the mid-1990s, the prison camps of Xinjiang were poorly managed. The prisoners suffered, and cadres also had a far from easy time of it. The central authorities have finally become concerned about the situation. Prisoner escapes was one phenomenon that galva nized their attention, but there were others. In 1990 a group of prisoners took over control of their prison camp and killed some officers. It was not the only incident of this sort, but this was a rare instance of the national Ministry of Justice getting involved. The then minister of justice (Zou Yu) went to Xinjiang on an inspection trip. Although he met with some prisoners, the officers selected the more timid for him to interview, and they did not dare speak frankly to him. In the end he appears to have accepted the officers' version of events.

A. Such executions are often carried out under the Xinjiang Department of Justice, even in the case of prisoners who have escaped from the bingtuan laogai. If a former bingtuan prisoner is not executed, he may still end up in a prison under the Department of Justice rather than back in the bingtuan.

B. There are four main such prisons. Prison No. One (in Urumqi) is run by the Autonomous Region. It houses relatively benign offenders, including political cases and women. The bingtuan's laogai apparently has no women. It is not clear what happens when female bingtuan civilians commit crimes, but our guess is that they are put in Xinjiang Prison No. One. As for convicts from the Xinjiang population at large, it would appear that a substantial number are female. According to a 1986 report (see endnote 193), in a batch of 900 local prisoners, 400 were women. Nationwide, about 2% of all prisoners are women. See Kang Shuhua.

Prison Conditions

Certainly the choice of Xinjiang was never made with a view to making life pleasant for prisoners. Even given the best of will and the highest level of corrections skills (neither of which has been in evidence), life would still be harsh under any regime in this land of forbidding deserts separated by even more forbidding mountain ranges. To make things worse, the prison camps have often been placed in remote, widely scattered locations, accessible only by crude means of transportation.

In the earliest days of the Xinjiang *laogai* there were no living quarters at all, and prisoners lived literally in holes in the ground (known as *diwozi* or "earth bird's nests"). But the prisoners were soon put to work building the single-story prison camps that would dot the Xinjiang landscape. The diagram on the next page depicts a typical smaller Xinjiang Laogai Camp.[A] These camps are at least 40 by 60 meters but may be much larger. Each usually has anywhere from a dozen to eighty rooms situated around a courtyard, near the center of which is a well. Each room usually houses a "team" of one or two dozen men. Most of each cell is occupied by a great sleeping platform *(dakang, tongpu)*. (Newer prisons have two-man iron beds.) A small room may house one team *(xiaodui)*, or a large room may house one large team *(dadui)*. The room's small outer windows (30 cm. by 50 cm.) are sealed and barred. There are also a few rooms for the use of cadres while on duty, and a special "guard room" that is used for various purposes, including as the venue for the rare meetings between prisoners and visitors.[B] Food is prepared in the kitchen. It is then sold to prisoners in the adjacent room and usually taken back to the cells to be eaten (though for a while in 1993 Xinjiang bingtuan prisoners were usually required to eat outdoors). Some camps have bathing facilities; most do not.

Such complexes used to be surrounded by three concentric four-

---

A. The diagram is based on information supplied by former bingtuan laogai prisoners. Our understanding is that Xinjiang Department of Justice prisons are not very different.

B. On the terms "cadres" and "guards," see p. 77, note C.

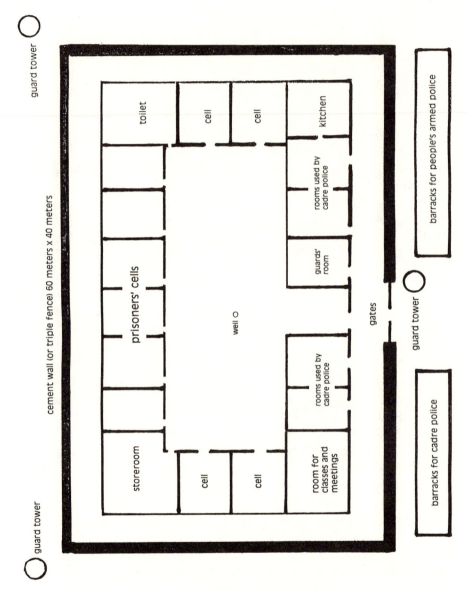

Typical Xinjiang Laogai Camp

meter fences, seven meters apart, but these have mostly been replaced by single cement walls. At any rate, to enter or leave the prison one must go through two or three gates, outside of which are stationed the armed police, and beyond, forbidding desert. The inner gate is guarded by trusted prisoners (who are not otherwise required to work). The latter bear initial responsibility for prison security.

The isolation of the laogai camps, combined with the extremely harsh living and working conditions, give rise to a subculture of resistance. Sometimes this has taken the form of petty sabotage. One former prisoner confided in us that during spring weeding they all used to pick many good cotton seedlings along with the weeds; that way there would be less work to do at harvest time. The corrections officers were not particularly concerned: "They only cared about how much money they themselves could make." Sometimes prisoners would destroy or bury farm implements. A prohibition against "malingering" in the 1990 prison regulations (see page 241 below, §2) was apparently aimed at such practices. Resistance has also been cultural, reflected in poetry, song, art, and sexual behavior.[141]

Sometimes, protest takes the form of self-inflicted wounds (*zishang* or *zican*), a practice often mentioned by our informants. One scholar has likened the phenomenon to hunger-strikes[A] in prisons elsewhere in the world, self-mutilation being "the ultimate degree of resistance to the state."[142] Our sources did not indicate that the phenomenon had any principled component, and tended to describe the practice more in terms of a practical means of escaping from the life of hardship. The literature on Xinjiang tends to confirm this.[B] At the very least, a severe injury would result in hospitalization, with plenty of rest and more

---

A. Hunger strikes rarely occur in Chinese prisons; the known instances involve political prisoners (such as Fan Sidong), not criminals. The rare cases are usually dealt with by forced-feeding, so such protests are not successful.

B. Jia (cited endnote 11), p. 39. Prisoners are described as ingesting round-worms, metal objects, and glass. Occasionally prisoners would simply fake as much, sometimes resulting in an exploratory operation, which itself could result in being excused from work for a half-year.

decent food. If one's injury is serious enough, he may lose his usefulness as a laborer, and the prison administrators may decide to simply release him on medical parole.

The prison administrators are apt to view such behavior in narrow terms, and simply blame obstreperous prisoners themselves for their behavior. Notwithstanding the Ministry of Justice's 1990 "Regulations Concerning the Behavior of Criminals Undergoing Reform" (see page 241), there have been complaints that there is inadequate legal definition of what kind of behavior can be prosecuted. There has been some recognition that the law needs to be clarified in this respect. One local laogai official has advocated that certain acts should be made crimes, including resisting prison control and reform, repeated gambling, stealing public property,[A] self-inflicted injury, refusal to work, and failure to reform after repeated efforts.[143]

There has been little interest on the part of the governmental authorities in providing moral and material support to any genuine corrections effort. Although the bingtuan as a whole appears to have been reasonably successful economically (see page 54, note A), the prison labor system is very unproductive and does not even generate sufficient funds to properly support the bingtuan prison system — even though the system is supposed to be self-financing, relying on revenues generated from the sale of prisoner-produced crops. As we note below, the regional government does receive funding from the eastern province sending out convicts (see page 114); however there never seems to be enough money to do the job right.[B] Although in many respects the economic conditions of the civilian populace (at least in Urumqi) have

---

A. Theft by inmates is a common problem. Petty theft of other inmates' property tends to be ignored, but theft of state property of substantial value (items worth thousands of RMB) is usually punished by severe beatings.

B. One reads, for example, of the great difficulties the laogai had in the 1980s when the new influx of prisoners occurred. For example, between 1983 and 1991 the 32d regiment of the bingtuan's Second Agricultural Division accepted 1,459 prisoners from China proper, and found itself hard pressed to feed, clothe, and house them. Lai Zhengyong, "In Developing the Bingtuan Laogai, Relying on Farms Is a Good Way" (in Chinese), *BLTG*, 1992, no. 5, pp. 34-35.

improved, this is due largely to the newly marketized sector of the economy, and has not resulted in funds flowing into the government's coffers.[144] Governor Tomor Dawamat noted in 1992 that the gap between revenues and expenditures was widening and that the region's financial situation was "grim;"[145] and in 1996 his successor, Abdulahat Abdurixit, still worried about increasing deficits.[146] Thus, even though in theory the prison system exists to resocialize the inmates, prison officials have one priority that consumes all of their attention and energy: to make the system financially self-sustaining.

National law requires that education be provided for prisoners, and in some parts of China it appears that such is the case.[147] The policy, as was stated in the 1992 *White Paper on Criminal Reform,* is that China does not simply punish criminals; there is supposed to be "legal, moral, cultural and technical education."[148] However, there has been virtually no outside funding for the purpose;[A] any expenses have had to be paid for from funds earned by the enterprise. This means that even when there is the will, only the most productive enterprises can afford meaningful education. But in most bingtuan camps it is not seen to be in the interest of the administrators to spend money on educating the prisoners. Not only would so doing cost money, it would reduce production. Thus, any "teachers" are generally the more educated prisoners. Inmates must pay for textbooks, which usually means that two or three must share one book (typically texts used in local junior high schools). Any teaching is limited to the winter, when there is little farm work to be done. Then, in some camps the prisoners have programs for teaching in the three broad subject areas: literacy, technical skills (such as photography, stone carving, electricity), and politics. The latter, unlike the other subjects, has to be taught by political cadres (a category covering about half of the cadres).[B]

A. Ostensibly, RMB 2 per prisoner per month are earmarked for educational proposes, but our sources indicate this is just "for the record," and that the little teaching that is performed is by unpaid prisoners.

B. The term "political cadre" does not appear to mean much, inasmuch as the labor reform units lack political offices, and the Xinjiang prison system has no

However, our informants indicate that politics has not been taught for some years now, and there is independent evidence that the cadres themselves generally have a very low level of political understanding.[A] Indeed, it appears that there is very little education of any sort. One is told that classes are rarely held, with students being encouraged to prepare fake class notes to impress the inspectors.

In short, it is only on rare occasion there is some education in the Xinjiang laogai.[149] Aside from the aforementioned, courses sometimes include even subjects such as geography. It is even claimed that foreign-language study is available, though we know of no such case. In those few camps where education is taken seriously, incentives for succeeding are substantial, and a high grade increases the chances of early release. But our informants report that in most bingtuan camps any schooling is carried out in a perfunctory manner, that prisoners usually see little value in learning what is offered, and that only 2 or 3 percent of prisoners actually advance their educational level.

The Laogai and the Media

There is one activity, however, which some prisoners have found not only educational but mentally stimulating, and that is writing for prison publications. The prison system of each province normally has at least one periodical written and read largely by prisoners, and another for officers. The prison administrators encourage prisoners to write for these publications. Our informants, being disproportionately intellectuals, often were active in this work. One claimed that 80 percent of the articles in the officers' newsletter were actually ghost-written by prisoners. In Xinjiang there is a magazine called *Labor Reform Research*, and a newspaper called *New Life*,[B] the latter considered to

---

political department.

A. In a 1991 study of labor reform camps in China's western provinces, it was found that 98.1 percent of the guards' "ideological training needs improvement." *FGY,* 1991, no. 2, p. 49.

B. *Xinsheng bao.* The same name is used in some other provinces, including Qinghai (which has generally eschewed the term "new life" since the famine of

be one of the country's better such publications. Every subdivision is supposed to supply articles for this paper. Seventy percent of the teams have designated reporters, though only about a tenth of these are active. For them, it is a favorite activity, for on writing days one does not have to engage in labor. Essays, stories, and investigation reports are all welcome, though to be acceptable for publication they must avoid the negative aspects of prison life. If an article is published, the author is paid 4 or 5 *yuan,* and a frequent contributor might even have his sentence reduced by about six months. Thus, for those few prisoners who possess an adequate cultural level, writing for the newspaper provides a rare opportunity to exercise their minds.

While articles for these particular publications must be "constructive" (rather than accurate or muckraking), this has not always been true of the Chinese media in general. Since the 1980s many newspapers (especially those concerned with the law) have carried exposés of the detention and prison systems.[150] Reportage on the laogai is not necessarily limited to the print media. One incident is enlightening: A film troupe was sent to Xinjiang to produce a propaganda movie portraying the wonders of labor reform. To really experience the system first hand, some of the actors arrived in advance and entered one of the camps pretending to be prisoners. To their chagrin, not only were they fed terrible food, they were actually beaten. The film they ended up producing was rather different from what had been intended. It did not get past the censors.

Prisoners often have access to radio. Each squadron normally has one "broadcast room" *(guangbo shi)* for the purpose, but the fare is controlled by the cadres, who sometimes do not want prisoners to hear the regular news. Private radios are not allowed, for fear that foreign broadcasts would be received. Sometimes television is available, with the set having been paid for by the prisoners themselves. As for print

---

the early 1960s). Xinjiang's *Xinsheng bao tongxun,* February 2, 1996, contains considerable data on *Xinsheng bao.* For example, in one year, 1.53 percent of the Eighth Divisions' prisoners contributed articles, whereas only 0.5 percent of the Third Division's did (p. 3).

media, outside newspapers are often provided, even including the semi-classified *Reference News*. The camp may also subscribe to a few magazines. Occasionally a prisoner will have his own magazine subscription, though issues often fail to arrive. By 1996 we received fragmentary information that the situation had improved, and that a squadron might subscribe to over fifty journals and newspapers, including the occasionally provocative *Xinhua wenzhai*.

Rehabilitation

Still, such media-related activities do not go very far in advancing the rehabilitation of offenders, which is supposed to be the main purpose of imprisonment. The Chinese prison experience, it is claimed, resocializes criminals so that they end up as law-abiding, productive members of society. As was stated in the 1992 *White Paper on Criminal Reform,* the goal is "to turn offenders into [people] who abide by the law and support themselves with their own labor."[151] At times, at least a few of China's prisons (those shown to outsiders) have given the appearance of living up to such humane ideals.[152] But outsider access to typical prisons is rare, and as of this writing the International Committee of the Red Cross is still excluded.[A]

To what extent does the prison experience actually result in inmates' rehabilitation? For all the faith the Communists have in the malleability and reformability of man's thinking, the experience of Xinjiang's prisons must be cause for disappointment. Despite the powerful incentives to admit guilt and accept "justice," prisoners often refuse to do either. Instead, as we have noted, there develops a subculture of resistance. According to official internal studies, the effort to reform

---

A. In early 1994, and again in 1997, there were reports that China might permit the Swiss-based International Committee of the Red Cross to inspect China's prisons (*New York Times*, January 23, 1994, and March 2, 1997), but to date there has been no agreement to allow the kind of unfettered access that the ICRC would require. Given the experiences of China's own authorities in ascertaining conditions in the prisons (see above, p. 86), it is unlikely that the Red Cross would have any better results.

prisoners is even less effective in Xinjiang than in other provinces.[153] Whereas in the next chapter we will see how some laogais in Qinghai have a graduated system so that prisoners who make progress get privileges, there is little of the sort in Xinjiang. Thus, there are no meaningful incentives to reform, which is doubtless one reason why the recidivism rate is so high for Xinjiang's former prisoners. These released prisoners have a difficult time finding jobs; except for those who accept *jiuye,* often the best they can do is become street vendors or handymen. Some (especially political offenders) cannot even establish a *hukou* (official residence). Unable to find jobs, many ex-convicts conclude that they have no alternative but to at least skirt the edges of legality (law often having little meaning in China anyway). Furthermore, inasmuch as the more serious and/or incorrigible convicts are sent to Xinjiang,[A] it is not particularly surprising that they would eventually return to a life of crime. But certainly an important factor in recidivism has to do with what these prisoners learned, or failed to learn, from the corrections officers.

As far as the cadres are concerned, it appears that their hearts simply are not in the reform effort. According to an official study, 52.3 percent of those surveyed considered the theory behind labor reform "contradictory and illogical."[154] Another source acknowledged in 1992 that there were too few corrections personnel, and that some were irresponsible, undisciplined, and lacking in probity (*bu lian*).[155] It was said that prisoners had been receiving too much of their "education" from the cell bosses — hardly a good way to learn proper citizenship. (In chapter 5 we shall have more to say about the subject of what happens to people after their release from the laogai.)

A. According to one study, only 39 percent of the prison population of a sample of northeastern prisoners had committed violent crimes. (*FGY*, 1990 no. 5, p. 26.) We do not know what the percentage is in Xinjiang, but it is surely much higher, and very likely double that figure.

The Economics of the Laogai

There are two ways of looking at the economy of the laogai. Much of what happens *within* the system does not fit the usual conception of "economics," but this is nonetheless where we will begin. Later, we will turn to the laogai's economy in the larger social context.

The Economy Within the Laogai

Officially, it is claimed that prisoners' livelihood is well taken care of; that, most importantly, there is sufficient nourishment. In a prison farm near Urumqi, it is claimed, "Each convict is given 25 kilograms of rice or wheat flour and half a kilogram of edible oil each month. Inasmuch as the farms grow their own vegetables and raise their own pigs, inmates have plenty of food."[156] But our information is to the contrary. Indeed, from the perspective of the prisoners, the issue most central to the economy within the laogai is having enough to eat.

In the early to mid-1950s, food was in particularly short supply in Xinjiang and in other northwestern prisons. It was partly for this reason, and partly due to poor medical care, that the death rates were very high. The Ministry of Public Security could do little about the medical care, but in 1956 they did issue an order that "non-working convicts" (probably all ill) should receive more food; northwestern patients were to have a larger food allowance than prisoners elsewhere.[A] This was apparently at the behest of Liu Shaoqi, whose efforts unfortunately came to nothing as a result of the Great Leap Forward. Later, there were similar rulings (1985, 1989). They appear to have generally had at least some short-term effect.

But little impact was felt in the bingtuan's underfunded laogai, where

---

A. "Aside from Qinghai, Gansu, and Xinjiang (where sick prisoners shall receive RMB 0.2 worth of food per day, and very ill ones RMB 0.3), the sick prisoners' food allowance shall be RMB 1.5; RMB 2 for the very sick." There was also a long list of "miscellany" (such as medicine, sanitary items, and cooking utensils) for which the (annual?) allowance was not to exceed RMB 3 in the northwest, RMB 2 elsewhere. Article 50 of the "PRC Laogai Regulations" (1956).

there has generally not been enough food. It has been a problem even for the cadres. After the ravages of inflation even the RMB 150 a month that a corrections officer receives would not be enough to pay for his family's food. Indeed, the amount that an officer was allotted for food *declined* between the mid-1980s and the mid-1990s. Increasingly, food (sometimes amounting to as much as 90 percent of what guards ate) has simply been stolen from provisions intended for prisoners, or obtained by other corrupt means. One of our informants explained that if, for example, a pig was slaughtered, the cadres would receive the lean meat, while the fat would go to prisoners and dogs. The prisoners' staples are steamed bread (made from wheat or cornmeal), but often a dog is given a larger quantity than the men. Even if the prisoners capture a wild animal, they may have to turn it over to the authorities for their consumption. One former prisoner told us a story of how prisoners on work detail caught a wild cat. The flesh was eaten by guards, the skin by cell bosses. The prisoners got nothing.

Aside from food, cadres also often steal agricultural and industrial equipment. If the prisoners are local people (or if the prisoner and a cadre have families in the same town), the prisoner's family may be pressured to make a "donation to the labor reform program," perhaps in the form of livestock. One former prisoner told us of a cadre having visited the prisoner's relatives back east, hinting to them that if they would give him gifts, the prisoner's condition would improve.

In theory, prisoners survive on food paid for out of an allowance given them by the prison.[A] Since 1988, prisoners have received such allowances for food and necessities. The men are supposed to receive between RMB 20 and 100 per month, but we are told that the actual range is 5 to 70 (paid in scrip). With RMB 1 buying only 10 buns, and a real dish of food costing about RMB 4, that money does not last very long. The result of all this is that the prisoners often go hungry unless

---

A. In this book we have elected not to describe the remuneration of prisoners. It is a matter of great complexity, and, in the final analysis, not of fundamental importance. Suffice it to say that prisoners are given the means of survival, and sometimes slightly more if they are big producers and otherwise please the cadres.

they can obtain food from non-prison sources. A common way to make up the deficit is for relatives to send food, such as flour, which will be eaten or, if there is a surplus, sold. Food is better than money, which can only be used to buy scrip — though sometimes prisoners manage to hide some civilian currency and eventually spend it illicitly. If a prisoner cannot receive any outside help, his best bet is to earn scrip or food by performing odd jobs (such as washing clothes) for the cadres and the more affluent prisoners. Other ways are to get paid by rich prisoners for doing the hardest laogai work that they do not want to perform, or to assist someone in a fight.

Cooking is done by a few prisoners selected for the job. In the prison the on-duty cadres used to eat in the same canteen with the inmates, but there was a problem of the cadres taking too much of the better food. In an attempt to prevent such abuses, in recent years in most prisons cadres have been fed in separate canteens, but this has had the opposite of the intended effect, with the best food going to their canteens.

In the mid-1990s Xinjiang's prison camps present a more mixed picture regarding food. In some places the situation has vastly improved. Elsewhere, prisoners receive only 600 to 700 grams a day. Such a low-calorie diet is not unknown even among civilians, but for prisoners engaged in heavy physical labor it is still less than adequate.

Clothing is a problem for most prisoners. They are issued a sheepskin hat once on arrival and a uniform every year or two, but, given the tough work, the uniform does not last. Prisoners can wear their own clothes, but they must bear the prisoner's number in red paint, and also the character *qiu,* or "prisoner." (A central directive banning the latter practice has been ignored in Xinjiang.) In summertime, the main protection against the elements is a straw hat. The soft shoes issued quickly wear out, and prisoners must use their own funds to buy new ones. Gloves, essential for much of the work done, must also be purchased or improvised. Prisoners often make their own gloves by sewing together bits of whatever material is available. In addition to clothing, inmates who can afford them can buy cigarettes, milk powder, eating utensils, and toiletries at the prison store (which is usually opened every second Sunday). Prices are marked up 40 percent to 100 percent, with the profit believed to go to the administrators. This clearly perceived exploitation is altogether alienating. (One former prisoner remarked: "We were even madder about that than about the torture. . . . ")

Health problems — both physical and mental[A]— are endemic. The regional government does provide some, but insufficient, funds for medical care. Every detachment-level camp is supposed to have a complete medical clinic, and indeed in some camps the care is reasonably good, with antibiotics and other medications available. Such a clinic is staffed by a (male) nurse. However, at the lower (squadron) level, any clinic is apt to be a mere tiny room (5 to 20 square meters) staffed by a prisoner whose main function is to report serious problems to the prison administration. Medical conditions which outside the prisons system would be deemed to require treatment are often not considered serious enough to bother with. An example is the chronic diarrhea from which almost all newcomers suffer for months; prisoners thus afflicted not only receive little medical care but are expected to work despite their condition. That has not always been the case. We were told that prior to 1987, on any given day about one percent of prisoners would be excused from work on account of illness, resulting in considerable work loss. Regarding the latter problem, the national authorities have seemed mainly concerned about the phenomenon of healthy malingerers claiming to be sick. Thus, a central directive ordered a clamp-down on this, and since the beginning in 1987 it has been much more difficult to be excused from work. Only a fever of over 39° (102°F) normally excuses a person. An informant who spent a decade in Xinjiang prisons claimed to have known of ten sick prisoners who died of neglect. Injuries (especially common among construction workers) often go unattended.

Although the health situation has still been a problem in recent years, it is not as bad as it had been in the 1950s and 1960s. Now, at least

---

A. Psychiatric disorders among inmates are quite common. Only rarely, and in the most serious cases, are the mentally ill sent to the hospitals. What with the rigors of prison life, their condition often deteriorates. (There have been a few cases of normal prisoners faking mental illness to avoid work.)

when the cadres are persuaded that they have a mortally ill prisoner on their hands, they often make some effort to get the person to a hospital (rarely existing nearby), as they don't want to be held responsible for too many in-camp deaths.

Actually, medical parole has always been at least a theoretical possibility for the seriously ill. A person's eligibility for medical parole is supposed to be determined according to whether various criteria are met, such as inability to perform physical activities. Since 1983, when the explosion in prison population began, medical parole is also one of the most widely abused features of the system. In one sample, about 5 percent of the prisoners were granted "medical parole," but only a tiny fraction of those (perhaps one percent of parolees) were actually sick. The beneficiaries of almost all "medical paroles" have been reasonably healthy prisoners (both criminal and political). Personal connections *(guanxi)* are all important, and a prisoner who has a good *guanxi* network is in a good position to buy his way out — if he has the money. One has to pay off the local cadres, the district administrator, and the doctors. Altogether, this might cost RMB 5,000. After returning to civilian life, such parolees are subject to petty blackmail by cadres, and reimprisonment if they do not "cooperate."

By national standards, RMB 5,000 for buying one's release is probably mid-range. In the more affluent areas of China it can cost RMB 10,000 or even up to RMB 100,000. At the other extreme, in 1992 it was reported that in some provinces a mere RMB 4 or 5 (per commuted year) could buy medical parole. This latter situation finally resulted in an investigation by Beijing. The local corrections officers' explanation was that inasmuch as the center provided little financial support for labor reform and the prison capacity was inadequate, it was necessary to raise funds and reduce crowding. The practice of selling paroles served both needs, but many prisoners could not afford more than a few *renminbi*. Inasmuch as the cadres have little concern for the larger social purposes of incarceration, such thinking is perfectly rational. Indeed, sometimes the fiction of "medical" parole is dropped. In the early 1990s, in particular, local labor reform administrators enjoyed great power to do whatever they wanted to do without considering the law. In one place, all prisoners were let go for RMB 500 per commuted year. Efforts by the central government to curb the practice do not appear to have been very effective, perhaps because they are primarily directed against prisoners, not corrupt administrators.

Whereas fake the "medical parole" phenomenon used to be a response to overcrowding in the prisons (with the attendant difficulties the officers have had in maintaining order), soon the corrections officers found that they had other incentives: easing their administrative burden, and self-enrichment. In Xinjiang, the latter seems to be the most important factor. One former prisoner recounted to us an incident when a cadre had told prisoners that, with the important exception of outright escape attempts, the prisoners were free to use any means available to regain their freedom. Everyone present understood that he was announcing his openness to receiving bribes.

These are simply the most blatant types of bribery. Lesser forms are legion. For example, in a labor reeducation camp a trusted prisoner might be allowed a visit to the nearest town; he only need present such a cadre with something like a bottle of liquor.[157] Such "gift" giving is commonplace, though there seems to have been an effort to curb the practice. One source cites with pride the fact that in one year gifts valued at RMB 53,000 were rejected;[158] another source indicates that in one division alone the annual value of rejected bribes had been RMB 20,047.[159] Such claims should be greeted with even more than the usual dose of skepticism. At any rate, there is no word regarding the value of gifts that were *accepted;* our interview sources indicate that, more often than not, that is what happens.

Proper procedures are often eclipsed by the relationship a prisoner has built with cadres by such means. For example, if a prisoner is an exceptional worker, he is supposed to be considered for early release. We are told that the top 5 percent (production-wise) have a 50 percent chance of being granted commutation. However, measuring productivity inevitably involves subjective judgment on the part of cadres, which means that ultimately it is still *guanxi* that is important.

In addition to material gain, the corrections officers are the beneficiaries of many personal services provided by the prisoners. On the job, prisoners carry food and beverages for the cadres, and such seasonal comforts as umbrellas in summer and quilts in winter. But lowly worksite cadres receive much less impressive service perks than do their seniors, who enjoy things like prisoner assistance in home construction. Typically, a group of five to ten prisoners will work on the construction of an officer's house. The workers are usually near the end of their terms, reducing the likelihood of escape. They are paid no money for such work. Prisoners also assist the cadres by making furniture, working in private gardens, and (from the more educated prisoners) providing secretarial and tutorial help. Sometimes the results of such services are disastrous; in one case a private prisoner employee murdered the cadre for whom he was working.[160]

One phenomenon has a faint echo of Qing times:[A] An educated prisoner is sometimes given responsibility for writing a corrections officer's monthly report (including his comments on various inmates), applications for party membership, even recording the cadre's own "thoughts." Other convicts, especially older ones, may do housework (laundry, etc.), helping officers bathe, giving them massages, making clothes for them, and helping out in a sideline business like a store. Faithful performance of such personal services may gain one early release. But the work is otherwise unpaid, and the price of enjoying such soft work is sometimes accompanied by considerable verbal abuse from the officers.

Then again, sometimes not. One former prisoner, when asked whether such domestic service was not a form of slavery, said that this analogy did not hold, because the officers tended to use the most educated (or at least skilled) men for such work. Thus there was usually an element of respect on the part of the cadres toward these particular prisoners, especially in view of the fact that some of them might one day be rehabilitated and would be in a position to reward or punish former benefactors and tormenters. Thus, there can result a subtle upgrading of the status of some prisoners to the cultural and social level

---

A. Exiled officials used to act as clerks, and sometimes even drafted documents. But since these political offenders were unreliable, sensitive documents were written in Manchu, which few Chinese could read. The most highly educated exiles also played a role in the local education and examination processes. Waley-Cohen, pp. 143-144.

of the cadres. But in the northwest this phenomenon has not been as particularly common. In other parts of the country, prisoners often fraternize with cadres and ingratiate themselves into the prison administration to the point where the distinction between cadres and elite prisoners becomes blurred.[161]

At any rate, corruption and other misconduct is certainly rampant among corrections officers in the northwest, and probably everywhere. One of our bingtuan informants insisted that 5 percent of the latter were simply hooligans *(liumang)* and another 20 percent were not above committing petty crimes. The majority ploddingly do their job, neither participating in nor being upset by the criminal behavior of their colleagues. A quarter of them take a dim view of such conduct, but only one in 20 of them actively oppose the misconduct by, say, reporting it to superiors, inspectors, or the media.

The Laogai and the Economy at Large

At any given time, a local prison work force has been engaged in one of three kinds of production: agriculture, public works, or manufacturing. Most prisoners in Xinjiang are engaged in farming. Grain (mostly wheat) used to be the primary crop, but in recent years cotton has surpassed grain.[A] Xinjiang prison-labor cotton is traditionally renowned for its quality. It has long been the major crop in the Aksu and Yarkand areas, where there are many prison camps.[162] The cotton is sold, and so is some of the food, but much of the latter is retained for use in the laogai, by both the prisoners and administration. There are

---

A. Cotton can be grown in both northern and southern Xinjiang. In general, cotton has been replacing grain as the bingtuan's main crop. In 1994, the bingtuan laogai produced 21,101 tons of cotton (up from 9,000 in 1991), and 27,827 tons of grain (down from 38,000 tons in 1991). However, in the mid-1990s it was decided that because of the need for grain, the northern farmlands could not all be given over to cotton growing, and that cotton should be primarily emphasized in the south, where "the largest cotton-producing area in the country" would exist. Wang Lequan, address to CPPCC, March 27, 1996, *Xinjiang ribao*, March 28, 1996, pp. 1-3, FBIS, April 23, 1996, p. 82.

also various quasi-agricultural activities, such as reed gathering.[163]

As we have noted, by the mid-1980s most of the prefecture-level enterprises had been restored to the bingtuan. (Some small ones, such as those in Hami and Khotan, did remain under the prefectures.) From now on, neither the Beijing nor Xinjiang governments would be much involved, and the bingtuan's economy would operate with considerable autonomy. But it must have been obvious to all that more fundamental reforms were required if the laogai economy was ever to get out of the doldrums. Thus, pursuant to the national trend, an incentive system was introduced with prisoners to be paid according to the quantity and quality of their work. The normal monthly minimum would be RMB 70, and the theoretical maximum was RMB 120.[164] How effective were these measures, and how important has the Xinjiang's laogai been economically since then?

Table 12

The Bingtuan's Laogai Production
as a Share of the Bingtuan Economy, 1994[165]

	Bingtuan Laogai	Bingtuan Totals	Laogai Share
Cotton	21,101 tons	332,900 tons	6.3%
Grain	27,827 tons	1,107,000 tons	2.5%
All goods	RMB 244 million	RMB 9,260 million	2.4%

Industrial output officially accounts for only 3 to 5 percent of the Xinjiang laogai's total, depending upon how "industrial" is defined, so for all practical purposes we are talking about the agricultural sector. At the end of 1994 there were about 172 bingtuan laogai farms, with 25,280 hectares under cultivation. That was 2.6 percent of the bingtuan's total farmland.[166] Half of the bingtuan laogai's farmland was devoted to cotton; 37 percent to grain.[167] A few parts of the system are quite profitable,[168] but on the whole the results have been lackluster. In 1991, the bingtuan's laogai produced a reported 9 thousand tons of cotton,[169] whereas the bingtuan as a whole produced 234 thousand tons.[170] As for grain, in the same year the bingtuan's laogai produced a reported 38 thousand tons,[171] compared with 1,376 thousand tons for the entire bingtuan.[172] Thus, the laogai's 1991 share of these two main bingtuan crops was small — 3.8 and 2.8 percent, respectively. In 1994, the laogai's share of the bingtuan's production was even lower, despite an outstanding performance in the cotton sector.

Although we do not have region-wide laogai figures, it is safe to assume that most of Xinjiang's laogai output is from the bingtuan's laogai, and Table 13 should be read in this light. Furthermore, the share of the *whole* bingtuan (civilian and laogai) of Xinjiang's economy declined from 30.69 percent in 1965 to 13.42 percent in 1993. By 1995, the bingtuan reportedly accounted for one-fifth[173] to one-fourth[174] of the region's total. And by now the bingtuan had fewer prisoners, so the bingtuan *laogai's* contribution to the Xinjiang economy must have been declining even more.

Table 13

The Bingtuan's Laogai Production
as Share of Xinjiang's, 1994

	Bingtuan Laogai	**Xinjiang Total**	**Share**
Cotton	21,101 tons	882,100 tons	2.39%
Grain	27,827 tons	6,428,900 tons	0.43%
All goods	RMB 244 million	RMB 67,368 million	0.33%

As for the output of the whole Xinjiang laogai (bingtuan and Justice Department), we believe that it must be well under one percent of the regional's total. Even the Xinjiang laogai's modest output figures have often masked an even poorer record concerning profitability. Although we do not have complete figures, we do know about one bingtuan division, the Seventh, in Kuitun. This division started taking prisoners in 1984, and over the next four years its laogai produced a cumulative output of RMB 9,740,000, but it actually *lost* RMB 2,780,000 during that period. After a "readjustment" (whose nature and extent one can only guess), things started to improve, and the annual output in 1991-92 was RMB 10,925,000. The per capita output rose five-fold compared with 1988. The annual profit averaged RMB 1,375,000 (RMB 547 per capita).[175] These numbers are not particularly remarkable, especially considering that in 1991 the weather was unusually good. That year, the value of the division's laogai output was claimed to be RMB 22.78 million, or RMB 3,317 per capita.[176] In recent years some laogais have done much better. In 1995 the relatively small laogai in the Second Division (Korla) produced a reported RMB 28.6 million's worth (which we estimate to be about RMB 6,500 per capita), and showed a profit of over two million *yuan*.[177]

But, like most Chinese prison farms, Xinjiang's have usually failed to make a real profit.[A] One source estimates that local civilian farms are 30 percent more productive than prison farms. The corrections officers' private farms are the most productive of all, for they enjoy the benefit not only of free prison labor, but also of purloined chemical fertilizer. The officers may even bring their pigs to the prison camp for feeding until they are big enough to be sold for slaughter. With such abuse of the system, it is small wonder that the actual bingtuan prison enterprises are unprofitable.

In view of the low per-capita productivity, it is perhaps surprising how long the working day is. From April to November, prisoners toil up to fifteen hours a day, seven days a week. Work starts at 5:00 a.m., and continues until dark, with three hours out for meals and sometimes a short meeting or class. Except in the winter, prisoners usually engage in crop growing, but sometimes they are involved in land-reclamation, irrigation projects, and other public works.[178] In Xinjiang, the Chinese authorities place high priority on conserving what little water is

---

A. On this concept, see p. 210, footnote A.

available[179] (often without regard to the downstream ecological consequences). These are often winter projects, and then the working hours are much shorter than in summertime (9:00 to 4:00, with a two-hour break), but the work is arduous, and the temperatures sometimes reach -30° (-12° F.). Much of the often-dangerous work involves building earthen dams,[180] sometimes hauling hard fill by handcart or even in sacks hung around the neck.

We noted earlier that during the 1960s prisoners were used in the construction of nuclear test sites. The most important of these was at Lob Nor, administered from the town of Malan to the northwest,[A] but today no prisoners are allowed there. It appears that since then bingtuan members (civilians and prisoners) are no longer involved in nuclear capital construction work (which has been performed by a special unit known as the Henanese Engineering Corps). For their part, prisoners play new roles in nuclear development. Among those bingtuan units responsible for supplying the personnel at the test site is the Thirty-fourth, in which is located Tieganlieke Prison. It may be that food produced by the prisoners there helps feed the workers.

A much more substantial involvement of prison labor in the nuclear arms business has to do with the mining of uranium near Gulja (Yining).[181] A word of background. The first investigation of the uranium potential of this area was undertaken between 1955 and 1964 (conducted by the 519th Exploration Team of the Second Ministry of Machine Building). The latest report known to us was produced by the 216th Exploration Team of the Ministry of Atomic Industry, prepared between 1990 and 1992. These various studies established that uranium deposits extend across southern Ili Prefecture (and presumably into

---

A. Until recently, the major science and technology center of Malan was omitted from published maps. This town is in the southeastern corner of Heshuo County, in the general vicinity of the bingtuan's Thirty-second Regiment. The area is officially known as the Malan Village Police Administrative Area *(Malan cun gongan guanli qu)*. In military terms, it is Unit 89800 *(89800 Budui)* of the Second Artillery Corps. The population (4,650 in the early 1990s) is almost entirely Han. The reason that there are only three Uyghurs is undoubtedly that Uyghur loyalty to China is so dubious.

Kazakstan). The Ministry of Atomic Industry (which mines other minerals besides uranium) seems to be the largest industrial employer in Ili, and has political clout to match.

Southwest of Gulja on the lands of the bingtuan's Seventy-second Regiment is the huge 731 mining complex, within which is a highly secret laogai operation known as the Gray *(Huise)* Uranium Mine.[A] This institution is the grimmest laogai unit that our research turned up.

Chart 5

Organization of the Uranium Industry in the Ili Area

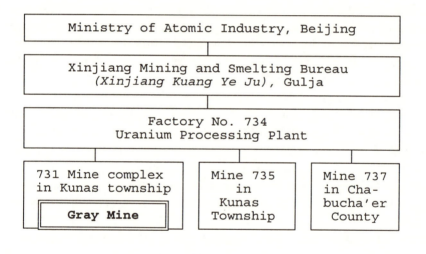

A. To the extent that it is known at all, it goes by various names. The name Gray (Huise) apparently derives from the Chinese term for Uranium Oxide. Locally it is called "Chee-san-ee." The term Chee-san-ee (in Mandarin, Qisanyi, meaning 731) is based on the military designation used by the Ministry of Atomic Industry for this secret installation. The local Uyghurs call it Chee-san-ee as though that were simply a non-numerical geographical name. The Seventy-second Regiment is not involved in the administration of the mine.

Today, two thousand prisoners labor under inhuman conditions (out of four thousand workers in the entire complex). Perhaps due in part to the radioactive nature of the ore, life expectancy is not long, with the death rate probably running between 10 percent and 20 percent per year. There are sixty prison cadres, all packing guns (unusual for the laogai). The place is filthy. Prisoners sleep on barracks floors. The structure of this and related operations is shown in Chart 5.

Xinjiang has at least two other uranium mines which do not employ prisoners. It appears that uranium from all the mines is processed at Factory No. 734. Inasmuch as a great many people have been arrested in Xinjiang since the spring of 1996, there is speculation (so far as we know, unfounded) that the authorities intend these mines to be worked by prisoners as well. Using prisoners in uranium mines does have certain advantages. In the first place, few on the outside know or particularly care whether the men live or die. And it is much easier to keep a prison-labor operation secret than when thousands of civilian laborers were trooping in and out every day.

Aside from uranium, other high-risk forms of mining exist. There are various laogai coal mines, including one at Bulakdudamtu,[182] just outside Gulja. It has 860 prison laborers, mostly (but not exclusively) from the bingtuan. Another, the Buya Open Cast Coal mine, is reported to be near Khotan. Like the uranium miners, they are also often in wretched health, with readily apparent skin problems. Some become ill from black lung disease, but many do not live long enough to develop that malady, as safety conditions are atrocious.[183] Flimsy wooden posts hold up the ceilings, and cave-ins are common. We also suspect that prisoners are used in asbestos mining, particularly in mines of the bingtuan's Thirty-sixth Regiment, which operates Malan Prison. Asbestos mining is a treacherous business, and the processing (which is done nearby) is just as dangerous.

In contrast to places like mines, there are units of the laogai where the work is relatively desirable, namely that in the factories. Though hardly luxurious, living conditions for industrial prisoners are superior to that of their agrarian counterparts, and certainly to those of the miners'. There are typically only four or five prisoners (no more than eight) occupying a cell of at least 20 square meters, with 2 to 5 square meters per prisoner.[A] Although the organization of industrial prisons is somewhat similar to the setup in agriculture, the prisoners receive far better treatment than do those engaged in agricultural work. These institutions might, for example, be responsible for the manufacture of building supplies and simple appliances. Aside from infrastructure works, prisons near Urumqi specialize in the production of such goods as water-heating equipment, processed foods, textiles, leather goods, machine tools, and (scattered around the region) brick kilns. But a great deal of the so-called "industrial" work is of the most menial sort, such as rock crushing (by hand) to make gravel. Although very few prison enterprises develop or utilize useful skills, there are a few handicraft outfits that produce goods like carpets (as in the case of the First Detachment of the bingtuan's Eighth Division). Sometimes prisons have stores attached to them for local distribution of prison-made merchandise.[184]

Despite China's claims to the contrary, prison products are sometimes exported.[185] Indeed, before it became a sensitive international issue, provincial yearbooks used to boast about such exports. Then an order (issued on October 10, 1991 by the ministries of Justice and of Foreign Economic Relations and Trade) forbade the export of prison-made goods, and it appears to have at least made a dent in such trade. Because Xinjiang is so far from the coast, the region's prison products had not been commonly exported overseas. However, with the laogai producing about 6 percent of the region's cotton, and Xinjiang annually exporting hundreds of millions of dollars worth of cotton yarn and cloth,[186] the latter may well contain a small amount of laogai fiber.

Certainly the temptation to export cheap prison-made products of all sorts to the former Soviet Union has been too much to forgo. An interesting case involves a bingtuan company located almost on the Kazak-

---

A. This would appear to be far less than the national standard, though that standard appears to deal with cell size alone, and not with how many people occupy the cell. See below, "Regulations Guiding the Management of the Reform Environment in Prisons," p. 250, Article 16.

stan border.[187] A group of laogai cadres, after bribing various Ili officials, established an illegal distillery using prison labor, and began exporting vodka of dubious quality to Kazakstan. At least 48,000 cases were sold to buyers in Almaty. But an international incident resulted when two people died after consuming the vile drink. The Chinese authorities investigated, and ordered the distillery closed. However, it has since resumed operations, now exporting its brew to hapless consumers in Kyrgyzstan. In the final analysis, however, it must be said that almost all of the northwest laogai's output is consumed locally.

The bingtuan prison system is sometimes able to raise money through commercial enterprises not necessarily directly related to prison work. For example, near Shihezi, the Eighth Agricultural Division runs a restaurant at the Baihua Bazaar. This is said to be one way that the district raises funds to finance the laogai. Not incidentally, most of the employees have connections *(guanxi)* with the prison administrators. Occasionally, a trusted prisoner may be assigned to the establishment.[A] Naturally, such work would be preferable to the normal agricultural labor. Still, even in a situation where prisoners and civilians work side by side, the prisoners do not have an easy time of it. They must put in endless hours doing the less pleasant work, of course for no extra pay or perks. One civilian employee was heard to remark: "I wouldn't do that work for any amount of money. Why can't the convicts at least be fed decent food?" (The value of civilian employees' food is more than twice that of prisoners' food.)

A. One may doubt whether commercial operations are really profitable. Although Xinjiang's *private* commercial enterprises (including wholesale) are sometimes lucrative, those in the public sector sometimes have not adapted well to the market economy, and lose money. They have had a tendency to try to undercut the private sector by engaging in price wars (first a "wool war" and "cooking oil war," and in 1996 a "sugar war"). See Wang Changhai, "Leading Role for State Commercial Enterprises," *Xinjiang ribao,* March 19, 1996, p. 5, FBIS, May 24, 1996, pp. 83-84; and an interview with Aisihaiti Kelimubai (retransliterated Uyghur name), *Xinjiang ribao*, March 16, 1996, p. 2, FBIS, May 24, 1996, p. 85.

Normally, prisoners work in groups, which will have a quota to be achieved. There are even prizes for the squadron which produces the greatest quantity. (No consideration is given to quality.) The work burden is exacerbated by the fact that there are always a few prisoners who are exempted from work — because, for example, they work privately for, or have otherwise ingratiated themselves with, the cadres, or because of illness. At any given time, from 10 to 20 percent of the group will be exempted from the regular work. Whatever the type of work involved, the more men exempted from work, the greater the burden on the other members, there being no adjustment in the group's quota. If a prisoner is highly productive (which means he must be in good physical condition), he may enjoy a shortened sentence.[A]

Although we have found that prison enterprise has little impact on China's over all economy, locally the picture is somewhat different. Much of the money the administrative personnel make has some stimulative effect. To start with, prisons are built with funding from the central government. Local construction teams work on a "cost-plus" basis; i.e. the price is determined after it is built. But even in a place like Shihezi, agriculture (including that of the bingtuan's vast Eighth Division) makes up only about 10 percent of the city's agricultural and industrial output.

Just as in Gansu, there is considerable integration of inmate and civilian work forces. Sometimes local laborers are hired to do some of the agricultural and public-works projects. Conversely, the prison farm also provides local labor to communities, earning cash which it tries (not always successfully) to retain for its own use. Some squadrons have both prisoners and non-prisoners; they may even work together. At the end of the day the prisoners return to their prison camp, while

---

A. Although cadres seem to have considerable discretion to shorten sentences, they do not have authority to lengthen them. This is in line with the policy of having regularized sentences. However, some guards object to this, and argue that it should be possible to lengthen sentences in the case of obstreperous inmates. E.g., Min Zheng, " 'Xing fa' yin zeng she 'jia xing' tiao kuan" (The criminal law should add provision for "enhanced sentences"), *LLLY*, 1989, no. 3, p. 9.

the others return to their homes. Normally the civilians work shorter hours, but at harvest time they put in twelve hours, almost the same as prisoners. In the case of industrial prisons, part (typically a fifth) of the work force also is civilian. These people are often relatives of corrections officers; naturally, they require employment, and these enterprises are logical places to arrange it. These people are well paid, often holding administrative or support positions (such as accounting).

In Xinjiang, as elsewhere in the northwest, there is often no clear separation between the prison and civilian economies, and there is usually at least some actual integration between the two. In principle, we do not see this as morally reprehensible.[188] Given the Communists' view that prisoners should "pay their own way," there is no logical reason why the prison economy has to be autarkic, and indeed that would be even more inefficient. This is something to be borne in mind as China becomes increasingly integrated into the world economy. A small amount of prison produce is bound to enter international commerce. Likewise, foreign investment in China cannot be totally insulated from the laogai economy. By 1996, Xinjiang had enjoyed US$1.5 billion worth of foreign investment. There is also about $1.5 billion in trade with 66 countries.[189] Thus, an institution like the World Bank, which has invested heavily in Xinjiang, is "vulnerable" (if that is the word) to charges that some of its funds finance forced-labor enterprises. (See commentary, page 228.)

The economic data we have for the Xinjiang laogai is not as comprehensive or accurate as what we presented on Gansu, and will offer for Qinghai. However, we have found no reason to believe that the Xinjiang bingtuan's economic experience has been any better than were the miserable performances of the bingtuans in the other provinces. The main problem is that when prison administration and enterprise administration are combined, it is quite likely that neither job will be done well, and the result of the system's quest for profit will be misery for the prisoners.

Size and Nature of the Prisoner Population

Xinjiang's prisoners have been a varied lot, and how many of them there are has long been quite a mystery.

How Many Prisoners?

It will be recalled that in 1955 the number of Xinjiang prisoners probably reached a total of about 160,000.[190] After peaking a few years after the anti-rightist campaign, it began to trend downward. The official 1965 figure for the number of prisoners in the bingtuan alone was 120,000,[191] with releases having been replaced by 20,000 new prisoners from the east between 1963 and 1966. The total sent prior to 1975 was something under 200,000.[A] Over the years, the prisoner population continued to decline. By the early 1980s, hardly any of the earlier detainees remained, and the bingtuan's prisoner population was now comprised of fewer than a thousand mostly young, errant members of the bingtuan itself.[192]

Then, in 1983, the nationwide crackdown on crime was launched. The immediate effect of this was that the already overcrowded prisons in China proper became saddled with a huge influx of new convicts — this at a time when Xinjiang's prisons were relatively underpopulated. Party secretary-general Hu Yaobang decided to rationalize the situation by sending the long-term convicts from the east to the northwest. The leaders of the Xinjiang bingtuan were especially agreeable. It was decided that Beijing would pay Xinjiang a one-time payment of five hundred million *yuan,* in addition to the usual ten thousand *yuan* per prisoner from each sending province. (The poorer sending provinces need not pay so much, for Beijing provides subsidies.) In return for this money, the bingtuan assumed responsibility for transporting prisoners from the east, and then for incarcerating them in Xinjiang.

Different provinces have had different practices. Some, such as Sichuan and the major cities, have a long tradition of sending prisoners

---

A. According to an internal source, the number between 1955 and 1975 was *shi ji wan,* which translates as 1_0,000, with the second digit unspecified.

to the northwest, and now simply continued the practice. Others, such as Yunnan, had no such tradition, and saw little reason to begin now. Some provinces, such as Zhejiang, had little experience in shipping off prisoners, but now found their own facilities taxed; it was cheaper to send new prisoners to Xinjiang than to build new facilities.

Thus, the decline in Xinjiang's prisoner population was reversed. The New China News Agency reported that between 1973 and 1986, 37,000 male prisoners were sent to Xinjiang camps from fifteen eastern provinces and municipalities; we believe the actual number is at least double that.[193] At any rate, the number of inmates in Xinjiang did double between the early 1980s and early 1990s.[194] Again, the new arrivals were mostly young men;[A] some were juveniles. These convicts were seen as highly obstreperous. According to the director of one prison farm, "In cities, they were wild like untamed horses, and had no aims in life. Unless they are ruled by strict discipline and lead a structured and routinized life, they will not change their bad habits."[195] While this is certainly true of many, some were doubtless innocent. Guilty or not, there was strong objection to the transfers from the prisoners, their relatives, and friends.[196]

For a couple of years after 1983, the national crime rate dropped dramatically.[197] This meant that the problem of prison overflow diminished, resulting in fewer prisoners being sent to Xinjiang from the east (though apparently some political prisoners started arriving from Tibet[B]). We calculate that by the early 1990s there were something under 100,000 prisoners in Xinjiang — a figure still considerably lower than other estimates.

The transfer of so many prisoners from China proper has become a

---

A. In one laogai camp in 1986, 3,562 (81 percent of the prisoners) were under 30 years old.

B. According to a former Tibetan prisoner who escaped to Nepal: "One day [in mid-1995, apparently in southern Tibet] two long buses were filled with prisoners, about 50-60 people in each, together with four soldiers in each bus. I heard clearly that one was going to Xinjiang and the other one to China." Tibet Information Network, *TIN Background Briefing Paper No. 26*, 1995, p. 69.

sensitive political issue among the mostly-non-Han people of Xinjiang, resentful as they are over their land being viewed as a bleak, barbaric place, and thus an appropriate dumping ground for China's unwanted. On the other hand, some of the sending provinces were themselves becoming disenchanted with the arrangement because the convicts tended to turn up in their old neighborhoods sooner than expected.[A] The problem has been early releases. Although we have difficulty evaluating the extent of this phenomenon (the former prisoners we interviewed did not consider it very common), there have been complaints from the sending provinces of the convicts' premature return. Whereas prisoners sent to the northwest have generally been given long sentences, Xinjiang only receives a single lump sum per prisoner, paid at the time the prisoner is sent. Thus, Xinjiang has no incentive to actually keep them in prison for the full term, and indeed, money is saved if they are released early. Thus, the sending provinces, which had assumed it had seen the last of the men, have sometimes been faced with the specter of their showing up on local streets again after a few years.

From some relevant data in the prisoner newspaper *Xinsheng bao* we calculate (as a raw figure) the number of bingtuan prisoners in 1995 to have been 34,025,[198] but this we consider to be somewhat lower than the real figure. We estimate that as of March 1997 the number of prisoners in the region's bingtuan is about 49,000.[199] The number under the Department of Justice is more difficult to estimate because it is on the increase, but we believe it to be at least 35,000. Thus, the total of all prisoners in Xinjiang is roughly 85,000.[200]

Social Composition of the Prisoner Population

Prisoners come from widely varied social backgrounds. Although those in the prisons under the Department of Justice are mostly Xinjiang residents, even they can be from many disparate ethnic and socio-

---

A. For example, in the mid-1980s Guangxi sent many prisoners to the bingtuan's Second Division (Korla), but Nanning appears to have become dissatisfied with the arrangement, and by 1990 the flow appeared to cease.

economic groups. They are more apt to be in prison for political-related activities than is the case with bingtuan prisoners. The latter have almost always been convicted of serious non-political crimes. Bingtuan prisoners come from all over China, including Xinjiang itself. Detachments vary greatly, but here is an example of one bingtuan detachment in the Aksu area, as described in an article in an internal bingtuan publication. The detachment's 254 prisoners had these origins:

> 122 from Beijing
> 3 from Shanghai
> 5 from Henan Province
> 56 from Jiangxi province
> 68 from Xinjiang.

But perhaps an even more important social divider than provincial is the urban/rural distinction. One hundred and nine of the prisoners were urbanites in the strict sense *(dingju)*. Urban and rural prisoners tend not to get along very well. Reflecting attitudes of society at large, there is much discrimination against rural inmates, who are called by such pejorative names as *tulao mao* (roughly, "straws hats") and, in the case of native Xinjiang prisoners, *dagua* (melon tappers). It is these rural folk who are obliged to do the dirtiest work, such as cleaning up the camps and removing the human waste. Although the cadres participate in the exploitation of rural prisoners, they also do not appreciate the arrogance of the city slickers. Often of rural background themselves, they sometimes find urban prisoners difficult to deal with. People from the cities are considered pushy and like to show off their superiority. (One can only imagine the attitude of Beijingers, speaking what they consider the quintessential version of the Chinese language, when they are supposed to be heeding northwesterners of dubious educational background!)

The complaints go on and on. According to the same article, "City folk are more cunning and deceptive. . . . Simple persuasion doesn't work. . . . They have a way of tricking the guards into trusting them." City people are more apt to stand up to authority, can be very confrontational, and do not comply with regulations or take orders. In their relations with other prisoners, they engage in demagoguery, incite unrest, and persuade other inmates to follow them and form gangs. They are seen as tough; even treating them roughly does no good. (The article complained that such inmates do not care about normal penalties, and cannot even be persuaded by the use of *xingju*, a term which can include such things as shackles and also instruments of torture.) Of the twelve people identified as gang leaders, all hailed from cities. Of the fifteen serious incidents of insubordination during the period studied, thirteen of them had involved urbanites. At the same time, city people were seen as fun-loving and accustomed to a soft life. To a much greater extent than rural people, they eschewed the labor that is the laogai's *raison d'être*. They are less apt to reform themselves (61 percent of the urbanites in this detachment had been recidivist), and are even reluctant to admit guilt. City people are more likely than rural people to feign illness, self-inflict injury, or try to escape. The sole concern of such people is seen as getting back to the cities.[201]

Regarding imprisoned juveniles, international human rights standards require that they be separated from adults and be brought as speedily as possible for adjudication. Most provinces, including Qinghai and Gansu, separate juvenile from adult prisoners. This is also true of Xinjiang generally, but not in the case of the bingtuan, where offenders in their mid-teens are incarcerated with adults. The number of juveniles in bingtuan prisons appears not to be large, for, unlike adults, they are not sent to these prisons if they only committed comparatively minor crimes. Younger prisoners are treated by cadres and other prisoners somewhat better than are other prisoners. They are given lighter work, especially if the parents send gifts for the cadres. Not surprisingly, the hardened criminals tend to be a bad influence on the young.

Political and Religious Offenders

Whereas the number of *political* prisoners in the bingtuan is quite low, there are still some former political prisoners in the bingtuan's *jiuye* regime (see chapter 5), and there are many political prisoners currently in the Xinjiang regional system *(Sifa)*.

Xinjiang seethes with political dissent. The atheistic Communists have always been hostile to the Islamic faith of the locals. Furthermore, in the 1950s, the Uyghurs and Kazakhs were often forced off their ancestral pasture lands, their traditional land rights not being recognized. All "vacant" land had once been viewed as having belonged to the emperor; now it belonged to the state *(guojia)*, to be settled in most cases by Hans.[A] Bingtuan people (first civilians, then prisoners) were rushed in to fill the perceived vacuum. On their eventual release, the prisoners usually remained in Xinjiang, often unreconstructed. Other issues giving rise to dissension are coercive sterilization of women, racial discrimination in the workplace, and nuclear testing (which poisons the land and causes health problems).

The Chinese complain that some areas have become "fortified villages of national splittism and illegal religious activities."[202] These two are seen as closely linked. "Religious freedom does not mean that religion is free to do what it wants," *Xinjiang Daily* warns. "We must fight those who do not respect others who do not believe [in Islam] and force them to become believers. . . . We must distinguish between lawful religious activities and those which are against the law, and between authentic believers and those who are plotting separatism."[203]

Until recently, a serious political offender in China was often deemed "counterrevolutionary."[B] In 1992 the percentage of counterrevolution-

---

A. Of the total bingtuan population (officially 2,223,957), 90 percent is Han. The only Division with a non-Han majority is the Third (Kashgar), in which Uyghurs make up the majority. The smaller Heguan Chu (not part of a division) is also majority Uyghur. *XBN,* 1995, 280.

B. This is a vague concept (officially dropped in 1997) that enabled the authorities to deal arbitrarily with dissidents. For an analysis, see *CJCC,* pp. 77-81. In 1993 it was announced that the concept of "counterrevolutionary crime" would be replaced by "crime of endangering state security." Judge Fei Zongyi, a member of the Judicial Committee of the Supreme People's Court, said: "It is inappropriate to apply the counterrevolutionary law in many cases now, such as hijacking, because hijacking has nothing to do with counterrevolution." It did not appear that the new provision would affect imprisonment for political cases. It was not to apply retroactively at all, and as for future cases, Fei said that subversion would still be prosecuted. "For example, if you spread your

aries in Xinjiang's prisons was officially put at 0.32. Were that correct, that would probably put the total around 100, a figure we suspect was well below the actual number of imprisoned dissidents even at that time. Certainly today the number of political prisoners is a great many times that. Furthermore, they have political significance that is far greater than their numbers suggest. However, the term "counterrevolutionary" was very imprecise, and simply meant that there was some political aspect to the "crime" alleged, which may have been violent or simply the advocacy of improper views.

In 1996 the regional party committee called for a "people's war" to deal with violent Uyghur nationalism. "All signs point to ethnic splittists colluding with violent criminal elements. Their reactionary arrogance has grown. Their sabotage activities have become more savage."[204] Still, it is dissension, not crime, that is seen as the main threat to social order. "National separatism and unlawful religious activities are the key problems endangering Xinjiang's stability. ... We must firmly rebuff the arrogant criminal elements who have a background of being national separatists, who have ties with criminal syndicates, and who have committed serious crimes."[205] But in reality, many of those arrested in recent years have been non-violent activists engaged in no activities which could reasonably be deemed criminal.

---

reactionary thinking through propaganda, then you have breached the criminal law." *SCMP*, May 22, 1993.

The law was not actually changed until 1997. In the meantime, though, official figures (which undoubtedly underreport) indicate that the number of imprisoned "counterrevolutionaries" in the country was already declining (from 6,935 in 1988 to 2,678 in 1994). Likewise, the *proportion* of "counterrevolutionaries" to all prisoners declined (from a reported 0.65 percent in 1988 to 0.24 percent in 1993). However, the proportion of "counterrevolutionaries" newly tried under Article 102 of the old criminal law (i.e., for political offenses) was increasing, from 25 percent of all prosecuted "counterrevolutionaries" in 1988 to 86 percent in 1991. See the Human Rights Watch/Human Rights in China report *China: Whose Security? — "State Security" in China's New Criminal Code* (New York, 1997).

As we have noted, it is one of the bingtuan's jobs to overcome such Uyghur nationalism.[206] This is in part because elsewhere in Xinjiang, even Party functionaries have been falling under Islam's spell and find the idea of independence as attractive an option as it proved to be for the neighboring former Soviet republics. According to a recent survey conducted in Turpan, 25 percent (and in some areas up to 40 percent) of Party members have been participating in religious services.[207] While the Party leadership wants Uyghurs to join the Chinese Communist Party, religiosity is considered a danger to Chinese control of Xinjiang.[A] The authorities are deeply worried about separatist tendencies in Xinjiang under "the new historical conditions,"[B] and about the implications of such dissidence for the PRC as a whole. As the director of the party Organization Department (Xinjiang) put it: "The stability and development of Xinjiang bear on the stability and development of the whole country. We must recognize the importance of maintaining stability in Xinjiang from this standpoint. . . . We must completely

---

A. "We must severely punish cadres with Party membership, especially leading cadres, who insist on following religion despite repeated advice; who instill into young people's minds the ideas of nationalistic splittism and religious education; and who publish books, magazines, and audio-visual materials that distort history or publicize the idea of nationalistic splittism and illegal religious thought. Leaders are to be investigated for their responsibility in localities and departments where government orders are not properly enforced, where serious problems concerning stability in their own localities and departments are not seriously handled, or where efforts are not made to crack down on nationalist splittism and illegal religious activities forcefully." (Xinjiang Television, May 23, 1996, BBC Monitoring Service, May 28, 1996).

B. In recent years, there had been a sea change in the political situation in Central Asia, and China's Uyghurs appear to have been able to obtain arms from neighboring states of the former Soviet Union and Afghanistan. A United National Revolutionary Front is based in Kazakstan, claiming more than a million supporters in Eastern Turkestan (Xinjiang), where there are said to be "27 secret organizations." (Agence France Press, May 29, 1996, FBIS, May 29, 1996, pp. 76-77.) In mid-1996 the UNRF claimed that 450 Chinese troops had been killed in clashes with its adherents. (AFP, July 16, 1996, FBIS, July 16, 1996, p. 26.) We consider all such claims highly unreliable.

isolate and crack down on a handful of ethnic separatists and serious criminals of various kinds."[208] Furthermore,

> Ethnic separatism and illegal religious activities are the main dangers to the stability of Xinjiang. . . . In areas or departments where no conscientious efforts are being made to implement the arrangements made by the central and regional authorities for maintaining stability in Xinjiang, where orders are not carried out, where grave problems in maintaining stability are not dealt with in a serious manner, or where no forces are organized to crack down on separatist and illegal religious activities, leaders should be called to account. . . . [Some] Party members and cadres collude with criminals, wink at and shield serious criminals, or are seriously derelict in the crackdown on crime. . . . [209]

So dissatisfied did Beijing become with the nonchalance of regional civilian authorities that they announced a "Three No's" policy ("no concessions, no compromises, no mercy"),[210] and instructed the People's Armed Police to take a more active role, particularly in places like Kashgar — a hotbed of Uyghur separatism.[211] The bingtuan's public security departments have dismantled and closed down many unsanctioned mosques and religious schools, and confiscated offending literature (as well as some firearms).[212] Chinese and Uyghur sources put the number of arrests in the wake of the April 1996 disturbances at 3,000.[213] But the violence continued in 1997, with bloody uprisings in such places as Gulja (Yining), and bus bombings in Urumqi, all resulting in many more arrests.[214]

Even if arrested by bingtuan personnel, political prisoners are generally held in local jails *(kanshousuo)* under the Department of Justice; they are not allowed to mix with and "pollute" long-term laogai prisoners.[215] One of our sources claims that four out of five prisoners in the Gulja-area jails are in some sense "political" (which does not necessarily mean non-violent).[A] Not being sent to laogai camps means

---

A. In international human rights parlance, there are two types of political prisoners, those who have engaged in violence and those who have not. The latter are also known as "prisoners of conscience." The two are entitled to

that, in general, Xinjiang's political prisoners do not engage in labor. With all the mid-1990s arrests, some of these institutions must have been bursting at the seams. As many as 200 prisoners are often squeezed into one of them. At this writing we cannot determine precisely to what extent the current crackdown will affect the size of the prisoner population,[A] but in prisons under the Department of Justice it is surely on the increase.

This must be especially true of political prisoners, the number of whom was already substantial.[B] Examples of political prisoners[216] are (in approximate chronological order of arrest):

> Kajikhumar Shabdan (a/k/a Haji Omar Shabdanoglu, Khajikhumar Shab-danek), elderly Kazakh novelist and poet. According to reports, he was a member of the region's Writers Federation who was arrested in 1988 in Tacheng. Charged with being a member of a foreign spy ring.[217]
>
> Wang Xuecheng, Chinese, arrested in 1989 after spreading "rumors" (based on Voice of America broadcasts) about the political events in Beijing.
>
> Alimjan Karihajim, Abdl Malik, Abdu Kadir Ayup, Abdurahman Abliz, and Omer Khan Mahsun, arrested in 1990 after publishing a pamphlet protesting the closing of a mosque and other restrictions on religion.
>
> Tohty Islam, arrested in 1990. Member of the East Turkestan Party.

---

different levels of international protection.

A. By the beginning of June, 1996, 2,700 were officially reported to have been arrested in the five weeks since the crackdown had begun, 1,700 of them in the last five days of April. AFP, May 16, 1996, FBIS, May 16, 1996, p. 48; AFP, June 3, 1996, FBIS, June 3, 1996, p. 72. Exiles in Kazakstan claimed that 5,000 Uyghurs were arrested around May.

B. However, we remain skeptical of claims by the Kazakstan-based United National Revolutionary Front that between April and July 1996, 18,000 Uyghurs were arrested, mostly in Aksu, but also in Urumqi, Gulja, and Turfan, and in the far northeastern part of the Region. The arrests are reported to have been made by "military and paramilitary" groups — the latter an apparent reference to the bingtuan. (AFP, July 16, 1996, FBIS, July 16, 1996, p. 26; *Hongkong Standard*, July 12, 1996, p. 1, FBIS, July 12, 1996, p. 6.)

Cemal Muhammed, Kurban Cuma, Muhammed Ermin Omer, Rah-
mancan Ahmed, Suleyman Isa, Turgun Abdulkarim, Turguncan
Muhammad. Uyghurs apprehended in 1990 in connection with an
uprising in Baren, near Kashgar.

Namat Abdumat, Muslim "counterrevolutionary" accused of arson,
arrested in 1990 and again in 1991.

Turgun Almas. Noted Uyghur historian and writer. Former member of
the Xinjiang Academy of Social Sciences. Status unclear, but he was
placed under house arrest around 1991 and has not been able to
publish since then.

Xu Zhendong, Chinese, detained in 1992 for "counterrevolutionary
agitation" in connection with his role in the Social Democratic Party
of China.

Abdukerin Kari, Abdukerim Yakup, and Omar Turdi, Uyghur Muslims
arrested in 1992.

Mahmut Alim, Uyghur "counterrevolutionary" student arrested in 1993.

Abuduwayiti Aihamati, a Uyghur sentenced in May 1996 to three years
for writing and distributing materials "with the goal of splitting the
unity of the motherland" and trying to "overturn the rule of the
people's democratic dictatorship." Aihamati, we are told, spread
subversive propaganda not only in Xinjiang, but also in Beijing.
"These actions . . . constituted inflammatory counterrevolutionary
propaganda." However, the Urumqi court gave Abuduwayiti Aihamati
a light sentence (for a crime that carries a maximum penalty of death)
because he was deemed to have shown repentance.[218]

Aisha Awazi, Uyghur imam (prayer leader) of a mosque in Aketao,
strongly critical of the Communists as "pagans." According to the
Xinjiang Legal News, he was arrested in Aketao County in July
1996.[219]

Rabiya, Uyghur businesswoman; member of Chinese People's Political
Consultative Conference. Said to have been held under administrative
detention, but authorities have denied that she is a prisoner.[220]

This list is only a sample. The authorities are pressing ever onward. A
Xinjiang government spokesman declared: "We must expose the violent
activities created by these hostile forces and let the people know their real
face. . . . The enemy's plot must not be realized. . . . "[221] Exiled
Uyghur nationalists claim the existence of 27 secret organizations, and
a million supporters, in their homeland. At the time that we write this,

China is not generally allowing foreign journalists into Xinjiang, even under official escort, and it remains for international human rights organizations to try to piece the story together.[222]

But the fundamentals are easy enough to discern. There are plans to nearly triple the bingtuan's farmland by 2001. That would have to be largely at the expense of traditional animal husbandry, and therefore of the Uyghurs and Kazakhs. This can only happen in the context of political repression, which would mean an increasing number of political prisoners.

Outside Influences

Until 1996, Xinjiang's prisons, especially the bingtuan's, were largely insulated from foreign[A] and domestic influences. The investigators from the Ministry of Supervision appeared to have been largely unsuccessful in effecting improvements. If the central authorities lacked the ability or will to get control of the situation, one could not expect international humanitarian appeals to have had much impact. Still, international appeals do not go unnoticed. Fan Sidong, who as a prisoner provided secretarial services to the bingtuan administrators, has commented to us: "I suppose that the central authorities are too busy with their power struggles to pay attention to such insignificant concerns as prisoners' problems. Only when a case gains international publicity are the authorities apt to take action." Fan went on to recount an interesting story:

A. As we shall discuss in chapter 4, China's persecuted Muslims have received much less international attention than have, say, Tibetans. This may be changing. For example, in 1997 the Iranian media began to take notice of ethnic repression in places like Xinjiang. "The situation has revived separatism and a desire for liberation among Muslims. This phenomenon has led the Chinese government to increase the suppression of the people. The crisis in Xinjiang is the outcome of that government's policies. Whether or not the area becomes further inflamed depends on the government's approach to the crisis." *Jomhuri-ye Eslami,* Tehran, February 15, 1997, p. 16, British Broadcasting Corporation transcript, February 21, 1997, FE/2849, pp. G19-20.

One day an officer brought a document to my attention. He had not paid any heed to the fact that it bore the seal of the procurator's office. He barked: "Who's responsible for this? Who's been claiming that we've engaged in misconduct? Throw this thing out!" When I pointed out that it was an official order, he quieted down a bit.

After studying the document, I realized that it was the response to a critique of a foreign human rights organization concerning the Chinese system of incarceration. The Chinese government had sent its response to labor reform camps all over the country, apparently with the intention of ensuring that prisoners would have some rights with respect to maltreatment.

But this officer was genuinely perplexed. "How can the government produce a document like this? It must be propaganda prepared in consultation with the foreign organization." These cadre police have no concept of human rights. They treat all the prisoners like slaves. These officers are usually in their 20s and 30s; when they were growing up they learned that all prisoners were enemies of the people and should be treated accordingly. So it was seen as perfectly appropriate to treat prisoners as sub-humans.

Yet this incident shows how in recent years the cadres have become increasingly aware of, and defensive about, pressure from international human rights organizations.[223]

Shipping prisoners to other jurisdictions, and even privatizing the process of incarceration, are hardly unique to China,[A] and the number of prisoners in Xinjiang is not remarkably large. Altogether, our estimate of the number of prisoners there is 85,000 ($\pm 5\%$), far fewer than has generally been assumed. And the economy of the Xinjiang laogai turns out to be remarkably unimpressive. Total economic output of the Xinjiang laogai, we believe, is well under one percent of the regional total output.

Rather it is the treatment of the bingtuan prisoners that makes

---

A. In the United States, some states (especially New Jersey, Missouri, North Carolina) send prisoners to states like Texas. In Limestone, Texas, they are incarcerated in a prison run privately by Capital Corrections, Inc.

Xinjiang noteworthy. Prison conditions are among the most inhumane in the PRC, with perhaps only Tibet's being worse.[A] Conditions in the bingtuan are particularly harsh, official claims to the contrary notwithstanding. Our informants report that prisoners rarely enjoy sufficient food. One source estimated that 40 percent of prisoners suffer from malnutrition. Only 10 percent were really well fed — primarily cell bosses, whose diet was comparable to that of the cadres. Some prisons have recently shown signs of improvement; many have not.

One thing one notices about Xinjiang is how great is the tension among institutions: between laogai and non-laogai, and between bingtuan and government. Personnel on all sides perceive little potential benefit from mutual cooperation. In the next chapter we shall see that a quite different situation prevails in Qinghai. Furthermore, whereas before the 1980s the changing policies at the national level had been the main factor determining the increase or decline in the number of prisoners in the northwest, this has not been the case in Qinghai since 1984, when the provincial government decided to cease importing so many convicts. We now turn to the other side of the coin of Xinjiang's receiving so many prisoners.

A. That torture in Tibetan prisons is common has been well documented by the impartial Tibet Information Network. In addition, there are persistent reports of prisoners in Tibet being forced to donate blood. Tibetan blood is highly valued because it is considered "thicker" (higher in hemoglobin) than the blood of lowlanders. See Catherine Field, "China's Vampire Gangs," *Marie Claire,* December 1996, pp. 62-63. On how the famine of the early 1960s was especially hard on Tibetan prisoners in Gansu and elsewhere, see Jasper Becker, *Hungry Ghosts: Mao's Secret Famine* (New York: Free Press, 1996), pp. 186-187.

Chapter 4

Qinghai

It would have been the easy way out for us just to interview a few of the Qinghai laogai survivors, and then present our "findings" as the real history of the province's labor reform system. But the dreadful conditions of the historical laogai in places like Qinghai have already been well described in Western as well as in Chinese works.[224] Just reiterating horror stories from the 1950s would tell us little about actual conditions in the 1990s. As with virtually everything else in this province, as with China as a whole, there have been many changes since the 1950s. What has been missing in the literature is a discussion of how the province's laogai has evolved in recent decades, and why it developed the way it did. This is something that can only be answered by looking, first, at the historical records of the organization in charge of the prisoners, and then the realities of today. Such an investigation will show how today's situation is quite different from what it once was. Thus, unearthing the *current* facts is the researchers' fundamental challenge.

Historical Overview

We shall explain below on a case-by-case basis how in the 1950s pioneer prisoners were assigned to various parts of Qinghai to establish the first laogai camps. After these were established, the prisoner population grew substantially, but there were otherwise no important developments until the end of the decade. Then, however, came the great famine of 1959-1961,[225] which severely damaged the reputation of the bureaucracy that ran the prison system, known as the Qinghai Laogai Bureau *(Laogai Ju)*, within both the government and the population of Qinghai. To put it starkly: Many prisoners starved to death. Then came the "Cultural Revolution." At first, this movement did not have too great an effect on the Qinghai laogai. However, in 1967 general conditions in the province became so chaotic that the central government decided to have the entire Qinghai provincial administration, including the Laogai Bureau, placed under the management of the People's Liberation Army. This turned out to be a gradual process, but in the end the results for the laogai were pervasive and profound. Inasmuch as the PLA was not interested in any competition from a large organization with access to arms and resources, in 1970 it almost seemed to be completely dismantling the Qinghai laogai organization. In Xining, the Laogai Bureau was deprived of three major enterprises,[A] and to the west, it lost its position in the most important city, Golmud, with the army taking over management of two key projects already under construction: the petroleum pipeline from Golmud to Lhasa, and the Xining-Golmud Railway.

Alas, the PLA was not able to completely have its way. In December 1972, former prison units began to be reestablished, and by mid-1973 a semblance of the old Laogai Bureau was back in business. Still, things would never be quite the same. For one thing, the PLA did not disappear from the scene. As late as 1975 soldiers in western Qinghai still outnumbered prisoners, with the once autarkic Laogai Bureau now

---

A. The Qinghai Truck and Bus Factory *(Qinghai Qiche Zhizao Chang)* and the Xining Printing Works during 1970, and in 1975 the Number Two Construction Company.

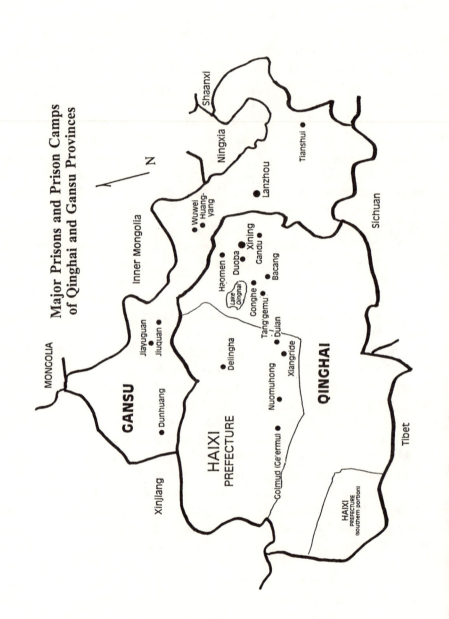

Major Prisons and Prison Camps
of Qinghai and Gansu Provinces

obliged to supply labor and food for the PLA-managed projects. Furthermore, with the carrying out of the Cultural-Revolution plan to build a "Third Line of Defense" against foreign invasions, enterprises from Heilongjiang, Liaoning, Shandong, and Shanghai were moved to Qinghai, and new armament factories and power stations were built. This added a new dimension to the industrial development of Qinghai, with the Laogai Bureau required to help build new plants, but thereafter not being in control of them.

Thus, in the wake of the Cultural Revolution, the authority of the Laogai Bureau, which once had overseen a substantial share of Qinghai's food production, mining, and industry, had greatly atrophied. Instead of being the powerful organ that could command all the scarce commodities and allocate them to other government departments, subsidies now had to be sought just to maintain the large laogai staff. The institution was in a downward spiral.

During the 1980s, just as elsewhere in China, *profit* became the most important criterion by which activity in Qinghai was judged. If an institution was unprofitable, it risked losing its assets. In 1988 there was a serious confrontation between the Bureau and the provincial government. It concerned compensation for land lost by the Laogai Bureau to the new Longyang Xia dam project. The Bureau lost out, and its units that had been involved were dissolved. The political authorities had had just about enough of the laogai, which was now seen as nothing but a money loser. From now on, the Laogai Bureau was excluded from the most promising new industries, such as electricity generation, oil drilling and refining, aluminum smelters, and chemicals.

In recent years, the Bureau has sought to improve its position by making large investments in agriculture. Indeed, in 1995 there was a large increase in laogai area under its cultivation. This, the authorities hope, will make the laogai again self-sufficient in the sense that it would be able to buy necessary supplies with laogai-generated money. Later we shall examine this process, and judge the likelihood of success.

According to an internal source, between 1950 and 1990 a total of 160,000 prisoners were sent to Qinghai from eastern China. Considering that most of them had been sentenced to prison terms of ten years or more, and that many died during the 1950s and 1960s, this number appears to jibe with what we know from other sources about the size of the prison system in Qinghai during this period. At any rate, there can be no question that large numbers of prisoners did arrive, primarily during the years 1955 to 1958, 1964 to 1966, and 1983 to 1984. But the inflow of prisoners was uneven, and at certain times there was actually a reduction in the prisoner population. For example, there was a decline between 1959 and 1961 because of fewer arrivals, and of deaths from famine. From 1966 to 1976, few new prisoners arrived to replace those released, because the Cultural Revolution was accompanied by a general institutional breakdown in the country. From 1980 to 1982, many political prisoners were released, and persons on *jiuye* were able to return home or to obtain local non-*jiuye* jobs. Finally, after 1984, the provincial government decided that it liked the idea of reducing the intake of prisoners from outside Qinghai. As we noted in the last chapter, a side effect of this new policy was an increase in the number of prisoners being sent all the way to the Xinjiang bingtuan, which was now the only entity willing to take prisoners in large numbers from eastern China.

Regarding the number of native Qinghai prisoners,[A] it fluctuated with the various changes in policy. In the 1950s, with the crackdown on Qinghai's former landlords and on obstreperous national minorities, the absolute number of local prisoners reached an all-time high. It fell to an all-time low in the early- to mid-1980s, partly because of the more relaxed policies toward Tibetans. With the phasing out of imported prisoners, by 1995 for the first time since 1950 the majority of prisoners under detention in Qinghai had been sentenced within the province.[226]

A. The exact number of "native Qinghai prisoners" depends on the definition of who should be called "native." Whatever their *hukou,* the Laogai Bureau calls all prisoners sentenced in Qinghai "native prisoners," and we use the same criteria for lack of other data.

Town and Country

Although Qinghai's laogai has never been formally divided into urban and rural sectors, in practice there has always been a division of labor in which one part was responsible for raw materials and food, while the other produced the industrial materials needed to support the laogai system, with any surplus being used to build the "new Qinghai" that the Communists envisaged. Most prisoners toil on prison farms. But it is the provincial capital where the Qinghai laogai got its start.

The Xining Area

The segment of the Qinghai corrections system located in Xining was originally comprised of a group of enterprises, often with the words *xin sheng* (new life) in the name. (Later, in the wake of the great famine, the term became unbearably ironic and was usually dropped.) These were a group of companies which included the huge Xin Sheng Construction Company. By 1958, between 20 percent and 30 percent of the work force of Xining were prisoners from eastern China, busily building the new Chinese capital of this once largely non-Han province. Whereas until 1949 Xining had been a medieval walled town whose gates were locked every night, the Communists drew up plans to quintuple its size and transform it into a city with all the attributes of modernity, including an airport and a municipal water system. While some aspects of the original dream could never be fully realized, the resources and plenty of free labor from the east did ensure that an impressive new city would be built.

In 1949 Xining lacked a normal civilian administration. The People's Liberation Army was in charge of the entire government, including the police and prison administration. The PLA simply began transferring prisoners there from central and eastern China; the soon-to-be-established local civilian government would be obliged to take them on. During the winter of 1949-1950 the new Xining municipal administration was given control over the hitherto PLA-occupied Nantan area just south of the city walls. The city in turn gave it to the newly established Laogai Bureau. For centuries, Nantan had been known primarily as

Xining's cemetery. Now, the graves did not disturb the Laogai Bureau; it was the Bureau that disturbed the graves.

In the course of about three years, a new part of town was built with prison labor on the site of that former graveyard. Nantan came to have several prisons and prison factories, and all the buildings needed to house a large organization in charge of tens of thousands of prisoners. Outwardly, by 1965 it looked about as it does today, though it was then quite remote and outsiders were well-advised to stay away. Since 1970 it has been enveloped by Xining, and can be visited on foot from international hotels in a couple of hours. There are no road signs, however, and often even locals seem not to know how to get there. Mentioned in no travel guide, it probably has the largest concentration of prison-related facilities in any city in the world.

Today, Nantan's prison enterprises include the Qinghai Hide and Garment Factory *(Qinghai Pimao Beifu Chang)*, the Qinghai Fifth Construction Company, the Qinghu Machine Tool Factory *(Qinghu Jichuang Chang)*, the Lumber Works of the Fifth Construction Company, the Qinghai Leather Products Factory, and the Qinghai Brick Factory *(Qinghai Zhuanwa Chang)*. But some of the Nantan enterprises are no longer prison operations. These include the Fourth Team *(Dui)* of the Qinghai Second Construction Company, and the Xining Printing Works.

In the same area is the Xining Detention Center (*Xining Kan Shou Suo,* the local prison of the city of Xining), and the Qinghai Detention Center (*Qinghai Kan Shou Suo,* for criminals detained by provincial level units). All of the female laogai prisoners sentenced in Qinghai work in a special unit of the Qinghai Hide and Garment Factory, called the Female Prisoners Clothing Production Brigade *(Nufan Beifu Shengchan Dadui)*. They produce mainly army uniforms, coats, and quilts, some of which are sold on the open market. (However, we know of no female prisoners being transferred to Qinghai from other provinces in recent decades.) Also in Nantan is the Qinghai Police School *(Qinghai Sheng Renmin Jingcha Xuexiao)* with about 500 students, the most important such institution in Qinghai.

About 15 percent of the area of what is now the central part of Xining (including Nantan) was once owned by the Laogai Bureau.

However, because the city has grown to include its suburbs, the larger new factories (now all non-laogai) have been situated elsewhere, and the Laogai Bureau has had to relinquish a part of its now-valuable real estate holdings in Xining. Furthermore, as Table 14 shows, the Xining laogai's share of the city's total industries has been on the decline. Not only is the value of the industrial output of the Xining laogai now quite small, but because there is little laogai industrial output elsewhere in the province, there is not a great difference between the Xining laogai industrial output and the whole of the Qinghai laogai industrial output. Thus the laogai percentages for the province as a whole would actually be a great deal smaller.

Table 14

Year	Xining laogai factories' gross industrial output	Xining factories' gross industrial output value	Laogai's share of Xining's gross industrial output
1958			30.0% *
1985	RMB 38.9 million	RMB 1,559 million	2.0%
1994	RMB 83.0 million	RMB 4,373 million	1.9%

* Estimate. Industrial statistics in Qinghai began to be compiled in 1973.

Prison Farms

During the 1950s, though the majority of the prisoners were sent to the countryside, they remained under the control of the provincial Laogai Bureau in Xining. Their job was to "reclaim" the fertile lands of the western part of the province that in fact had been used productively by Mongolians, Tibetans, and (more recently) Kazakhs. During the 1930s, Kazakh nomads from Xinjiang captured the most fertile pasture lands. Alas, they were able to enjoy the fruits of victory for barely a decade. Though they resisted mightily, they were expelled by the Chinese Communists in the 1950s. Finally, in the early 1980s, they were "allowed" to leave Qinghai for Xinjiang. Ironically, the original population of mainly Mongolian nomads, having lost their lands in the 1930s, were thereby eventually spared much trouble.

Now, west of the azure lake from which Qinghai derives its name, are the many prisons of what is now officially called the "Haixi Mongolian and Tibetan Autonomous Prefecture." Although it is only one of eight prefectures in Qinghai, Haixi comprises 45 percent of the province's territory. It is sparsely populated, so the 5.2 percent prisoner share of the total population is large compared to other prefectures.[227] In Haixi's Dulan County the portion of prisoners reaches 18 percent — the largest concentration of prisoners of any single county in China.[A] When all laogai-employed or -related persons are counted, the share is more than 45 percent of the county's population. Nonetheless, the prison camps in this area may be the least known in the world. The very concept of "haixi" ("West of the Sea") may suggest how this area has always been perceived as beyond the pale. Since ancient times, the Middle Kingdom considered itself located within "four seas," the northern, eastern, and southern ones, and this "sea" in the west — the briny Lake Qinghai in the northeastern part of the province. Even in the mid-twentieth century, anything west of Lake Qinghai was perceived by Chinese as being very remote.

The roots of the Haixi laogai can be traced to March 1950, when the Military Administration Committee of Northwest China (*Xibei Junzheng Weiyuanhui*) ordered an expedition sent to the Chaidam area, which forms the greater part of the prefecture. The research project lasted the whole summer. The explorers went first to what is today Dulan County, and in the end only got as far west as Delingha to the northwest and Xiangride to the southwest, returning to Xining by the end of October.[228] (See map on page 130.) Their report served as a blueprint for the Haixi laogai. In it they recommended various areas as good for agricultural reclamation, and indeed within the next ten years these

---

A. By "concentration" here we mean number of prisoners relative to the county's overall population, not the absolute number of prisoners, which may be larger in other places.

would all become sites of large prison farms. However, nothing happened very quickly, inasmuch as the PLA was preoccupied with the Korean War and the takeover of Tibet. During these years, supplies and money were limited and the military efforts enjoyed priority. But in late 1952 resources began to become available, and the Qinghai government ordered Dulan District to give full support to the setting up of laogai farms there.[229]

Many of the province's agricultural laogai camps are in this general area of northeast Qinghai; others are scattered farther to the west. Each prison camp is located in a remote desert oasis. The camps are about 2,800 meters above sea level, where the cold winters and dry summers make it impossible to survive independently.

If the two Chinese characters *hai* and *xi* are reversed, they read "Xihai," one of the names for what until 1992 was the Los Alamos of China — where aspects of the country's atomic weapons development took place.[230] This closely guarded town with an original population of more than 10,000, marked on no map, is located just to the northeast of Lake Qinghai in Haiyan county of Haibei prefecture.[A] The existence of this and other important military installations in the area make highly improbable any successful prisoner escape across the desert from Haixi in the direction of the Chinese ethnic areas to the northeast. Furthermore, all labor camps in Haixi are guarded by units of the Third Detachment of the Qinghai People's Armed Police.

Delingha. The first prison camp to be set up was near a barely populated place called Delingha. A team of agricultural experts from the Qinghai Laogai Bureau, headed by one Yang Rongguang, arrived

---

A. Besides the laogai, the atomic experiments are the second perceived mystery of Qinghai. According to Chinese sources the following is known: Built from 1958 to 1963 at an altitude of 3,150 meters above sea level, this base covered an area of formerly 1,170 square kilometers. From the early 1960s to the late 1980s a total of 16 "experiments" were conducted there. The resulting and still remaining nuclear pollution in this as well as neighboring areas is unknown to us. The base was closed down from 1987 to 1992 with most of the staff transferred to a similar base in Mianyang, Sichuan.

in the spring of 1953. During early February of 1954 the first prisoners arrived, all clad in black. During the chilly spring, like the first arrivals in the Xinjiang desert, they had to build their own infrastructure. First they had to build a long road to the chosen site, all the time living in tents. Next, they tilled 547 hectares of land and planted grain, mainly wheat but also some barley. They had no draft animals, much less tractors, to help them. The harvest that year, 2,000 tons of grain, was reported to be barely enough to feed the guards and prisoners for a year and to provide seed for the following year. Finally, in late autumn, the prisoners got around to erecting buildings,[A] as continuing to live in tents would have been virtually impossible during winter.

Year by year, thanks to much hard labor, Delingha became ever larger. By 1959 the cultivated area reached 7,200 hectares, and the harvested grain over 20,000 tons, 1.9 percent of the provincial total. In only five years it had become one of the largest forced labor farms in China. Ironically, its very success would lead to its demise. First, the availability of plenty of food led the Haixi Prefecture government to move the administrative seat to Delingha in 1966. They declared this labor camp a "town" *(zhen)* in 1973, and in 1983 the Qinghai government promoted it to "city" *(shi)* status. By mid-1986, everything that was needed for a normal civilian administration was in place; the Qinghai Laogai Bureau thereupon lost its best farm, receiving no compensation in return. By 1987 the enterprise was already being managed as a large state farm; all employees got paid a wage (commonly RMB 151 a month) and most workers were married. At that time it had a population of 4,012.[231] The prisoners who had not yet died or been released were transferred to other camps in Qinghai. But many former prisoners, including *jiuye* workers, remain in the area.

Thus we see how a laogai farm can become so profitable that the

---

A. However, we know of no case in the northwest where prisoners actually served as architects and planners, as happened at least once elsewhere. Architect Li Maoxiu, while in prison in Hebei Province, was drafted to design and help construct local laogai and other government buildings. Edward Friedman, Paul Pickowicz and Mark Selden, *Chinese Village, Socialist State* (New Haven: Yale University Press, 1991), p. 152.

higher authorities covet the farm. But they rarely covet the laogai. In Qinghai this is not a unique case,[A] but as we shall see in subsequent chapters, neither is it typical in northwest China.

Xiangride Prison Farm. While about half of the Haixi prisons and prison farms from the 1960s no longer exist, some are still there and have adapted themselves to the present circumstances. Xiangride Farm (*Xiangride laogai nongchang*) is a case in point.

This laogai farm had its beginnings in February 1955 with the arrival of a new team from the Laogai Bureau, which began preparations for the camp. In May, fifteen Hungarian-made tractors arrived, together with experienced agricultural staff from the Shayang Labor reform camp in Hubei province. Also, that summer young people from many regions of China were asked to go as volunteers to Xiangride. Up to this point there were still no prisoners. This was an improvement over the method that had been employed in the case of Delingha, where prisoners had been sent to a wasteland with hardly any means to provide for themselves.

It was only in February 1956, a year after arrival of the development team, that Xiangride was formally opened by local government and laogai leaders. At midnight on the evening of the 27th the first group of prisoners arrived. During this first year, 1,330 hectares of land were cultivated, and 1,405 tons of grain harvested. Year after year the yield increased, reaching 2,625 tons in 1960. Then, however, came the great famine, and the province's civilian units and departments virtually confiscated any harvest in sight. Not only did this result in massive starvation in laogai camps, it left insufficient seed for sowing the next spring. The problem was reported all the way up to Beijing, and the

---

A. Another former prison farm that was given to Haixi prefecture by the Qinghai Laogai Bureau is Chachaxiangka, located 45 kilometers north of Dulan County. The transfer took place on January 1, 1987, and since then it has been a state farm under Haixi prefecture. The reason the Laogai Bureau gave it away was evidently that the farm was too small to be efficient; were it to remain inside the laogai system, it would have needed a large investment to upgrade it to a profitable level.

hapless warden of the camp was replaced. In November 1960 two new people from the Ministry of Public Security, Li Yueren and his wife Pan Jiajian, were put in charge. Li and Pan settled right into the camp with their four children, and soon became popular with guards and prisoners. The dismissal of the old warden was thought to be enough to discourage other units from confiscating a harvest, or at any rate to embolden the wardens to prevent them from doing so. In the case of Pan and Li, they would defend the unit's interests right down to the end of the Cultural Revolution.

Still, the winter of 1960-1961 was another hard period for the prisoners, as the main food was a type of turnips normally used to feed the animals. Lack of seed, and the weakness of the surviving prisoners, made the 1961 harvest of 1,200 tons of grain the lowest in the history of the camp. But inasmuch as this time they did manage to save sufficient seed, conditions improved the following year, and continued to do so even during the Cultural Revolution. By 1987 the grain harvest alone was 8,200 tons, of which 4,450 tons were sold to Haixi Prefecture.

In 1988, the warden of Xiangride, now a man named Chen Guangming, found himself in charge of an enterprise so large that it would challenge even a world-class manager. That year he started delegating some of the warden's traditional authority down to the detachment or even squadron level, hoping that the management efficiencies thus achieved would further increase the output. And indeed, in 1989 output rose to 10,700 tons. Alas, Chen had achieved his goal all too well.

If a government agency is considering taking over a portion of the laogai and civilianizing it, that agency will want to know just how productive it is. Likewise, for our purposes in understanding the relative importance of a laogai, we want to ask a somewhat similar question: What proportion of the grain harvest is this of the prefecture (or of the province). Knowing what the proportion is, we can judge the influence of the Laogai Bureau at any level. Table 15 provides the answer for Xiangride. It shows that the farm is very important to Haixi, producing about one-eighth of the prefecture's grain, but not large with respect to Qinghai, of whose production Xiangride accounts for less than one percent. Still, this 10,700 tons make Xiangride one of the most

Table 15

Xiangride Prison Farm's Relative Grain Output			
Year	Xiangride (XRD)	XRD's share of Haixi's	XRD's share of Qinghai's
1987	8,200 tons	11.02%	0.787%
1989	10,700 tons	13.28%	0.965%

productive laogai camps in China.

Now let us compare this to the overall situation at the beginning of 1988 — that is, before Chen Guangming's reforms were instituted. This gives us a rare insight into how a typical large laogai farm functioned over the years. On January 1, 1988, the total population of the camp was 6,961: 569 cadres and guards, 1,108 civilian workers, 402 people on *jiuye*, and 4,882 prisoners. It was organized into 13 brigades that were again divided into 38 squadrons. Of the 13 brigades, only five were old-style prison-farm detachments; the others were various kinds of enterprises (such as a marble factory) that could not effectively use many prisoners but rather depended on a trained and motivated civilian work force.

Some have claimed that Xiangride has had a population of 100,000 prisoners.[232] Actually, even in 1976 Xiangride probably had barely a tenth that. By the late 1980s each of the five prisoner brigades had fewer than 1,000 prisoners (with each squadron in this case having at most 200) altogether with a total of 4,882. During the 1990s, Xiangride has been further downsized, with both the number of prisoners and the number of cadres declining. By 1995 only a total of 4,565 persons were left: 448 cadres, 1,128 civilian workers, and 2,989 prisoners, children, and retired persons.[233] While we do not know the exact number of prisoners, we estimate that only between 2,000 and 2,500 of them remained on this farm by 1995.

How did the ongoing reforms started by Chen Guangming, and the general downsizing, affect the economy of the farm? The answer may be surprising: It turns out that the fewer prisoners the enterprise had, the more productive it was. Today these smaller units are responsible for their own profit and loss, and can make their own decisions. During 1994, Xiangride produced a total of 22,000 tons of grain, more than twice the 1988 harvest, despite (or perhaps because of) the 35 percent reduction in its "personnel." At the same time they sold 17,000 tons to the Haixi grain bureau, more than three times the previous average.[A]

Though it is not mandatory, any surplus grain that laogai enterprises want to sell, they normally sell to the state at the low state price to the local prefecture's grain bureau. Surplus grain could be sold at a higher price to other units, but at least in Haixi this usually does not happen. A labor reform farm lacks the trucks and storage facilities it would need to diversify its markets. Furthermore, doing so could have a negative impact on the relationship between the Laogai Bureau and the Haixi government. While the prison farms belong to the Qinghai Laogai Bureau, the state quota of grain to be produced and sold is set by Haixi. This prefecture-level government sends the numbers to the Justice Department's Laogai Bureau in Xining, and they in turn order the farms to deliver the amount requested. This is very profitable for Haixi; it is considered as a form of rent payment for the land used by the Laogai Bureau. The arrangement guarantees mutual benefits, for the laogai farms in Haixi depend on the goodwill of local governments as well. Compared to what the situation would be for Haixi if the same amount of grain had to be obtained from outside and transported to, as well as distributed within, the prefecture, we estimate the amount saved by the Haixi government every year to more than RMB 10 million for the 1980s and over RMB 20 million by the mid-1990s. It is an excellent deal for

---

A. We calculate the previous average sold to the state at 5,538 tons, inasmuch as the 1956-to-1994 total of grain sold by Xiangride to the state is 216,000 tons. 216,000 ÷ 39 years = 5,538.

In terms of profitability the success has not been so impressive, as agricultural products have to be sold at very low state-set prices. But in 1993 the total value of sales was RMB 10,573,900, which was almost 10 percent of the Qinghai Laogai Bureau total.

everyone except, of course, the prisoners.

Nuomuhong Prison Farm. Nuomuhong is the only other large prison farm remaining today in Haixi Prefecture. Though not as large as Xiangride, it has a much more sophisticated food processing plant.

Founded in November 1955, Nuomuhong's pattern of development paralleled that of Xiangride. By the late 1960s, annual grain output reached 15,000 tons. Although there was a subsequent downturn, by 1993 output returned to the levels of the late 1960s, with 7,500 tons (of the 15,000 tons produced) sold to the state. Still, this did not represent long-term progress. Compared to Xiangride, the yield was considered disappointing by the Laogai Bureau in Xining, which set about to improve the situation. By the end of 1995, the Laogai Bureau managed to invest a total of RMB 22.9 million into upgrading the irrigation system, buying farm machinery, and reclaiming additional land. The result of this upgrading will only be known for sure in a few years' time, but at least it shows that this camp is considered an asset of important potential by the Laogai Bureau.

In 1988, Nuomuhong had a total population of 6,928 persons (prisoners and civilians). By 1993 it had been downsized to 3,293. The total value of production during 1992 was RMB 16.53 million. The total of the grain sold to the state from 1956 to 1990 was 320,000 tons, or an average of 9,143 tons a year. Unlike Xiangride, Nuomuhong sells less to the state now than in earlier years. It prefers to retain as much grain as possible and process it itself, and sells as little to the government as it can get away with. In terms of the value of production, Nuomuhong has so far been the more successful of the two. The main reason for this is that meat, eggs, and industrial products can be sold at a much higher price than grain. Inasmuch as the central government effected large increases in the grain prices in 1995 and 1996, in the future the picture could change and Xiangride may again surpass Nuomuhong.

Ge'ermu Prison Farm. Located in an ethnic minority area, this prison farm was usually known by Golmud City's sinicized name, Ge'ermu. The pattern will now be familiar. First the PLA arrived, followed by prisoners, who built the infrastructure — in this case, roads connecting western Gansu and Tibet. At the beginning of 1957 the total population in the Golmud area was 22,490 (and this was estimated to be many times the 1950 population).[A] Local Kazakhs numbered only 608 persons. (There also happened to be ten Russian advisers in this area — collecting raw material for the Soviet hydrogen bomb.) The total number of persons in the Ge'ermu Labor Reform Farm was 16,000, or well over half of the total population in the area. Even though not all persons in the labor farm were prisoners, the latter then probably comprised the majority of the city's population. After the PLA dissolved the Ge'ermu Labor Reform Farm, no new prisons were built in the area except a local jail. Although the whole city had been mainly built with prison labor, it has now evolved to the point that prisoners play no role in the local economy. Today the Golmud area has a population of around 100,000, with at the most a few hundred prisoners.

In brief, the Ge'ermu Farm had first been used to incarcerate convicts. Then it became a unit of the bingtuan (an institution now primarily associated with Xinjiang — as we discussed on pages 37-50). Finally, it has been converted into a cooperative — essentially a privately managed enterprise. Thus, it provides us in a single setting a rare opportunity to compare these forms of management, and make some judgments regarding the various types of farm systems, all of which are still in use elsewhere in northwest China.

The farm was set up along the lines of Xiangride and Delingha, with the difference that during the early 1960s many prisoners were of non-Han nationality. These included Tibetans who had participated in uprisings against the Chinese Communist regime. But in September 1965, the entire Ge'ermu Prison Farm, then with some 10,000 prisoners, was closed down, and the place was handed over to the PLA.

A. Traditionally, Golmud was a transit point for Buddhist pilgrims making a pilgrimage to Lhasa. However, the name Golmud is actually Mongolian, in the local dialect of which it means "many rivers." The Chinese *pinyin* transcription is Ge'ermu, while in Tibetan it is known as Kermu.

The prisoners were sent to other camps in Qinghai. The Ge'ermu farm, newly manned by demobilized soldiers together with urban youths sent from places like Shandong Province, went into business in 1966. After the hand-over, it was incorporated into the Fourth Agricultural Division of the Lanzhou bingtuan, which had been founded there in September 1965. The following year it was renamed First Regiment of the Twelfth Agricultural Division, still under the bingtuan of the Lanzhou Military Region.

During its sixteen bingtuan years (1965 to 1981), the Ge'ermu farm can only be described as having been a financial disaster. Year after year the losses piled up; in the end the state was out a total of RMB 134 million (without even considering the opportunity costs, had the funds been invested elsewhere). In 1980, for example, the value of the grain output of this farm met only 7 percent of the payroll that had to be paid; the other 93 percent had to be made up by state subsidies. Put in other terms, each ton of grain produced cost the provincial government some twenty times what it would have cost had it been produced elsewhere.[234]

In 1975 all the bingtuan directly under the Lanzhou Military Region were finally dissolved. Now that it had reverted to provincial auspices, it is hardly surprising that the Qinghai government had no interest in perpetuating the farm in anything like its previous form. It was gradually converted into a local cooperative enterprise; to this day it still "belongs" to Qinghai, but these days needs no subsidies.

Even though during the 1960s the prisoners were forced to work far harder than has been true of workers in the 1990s, Table 16 indicates that such effort was not reflected in the bottom line; it also shows the bingtuan phase was even worse. In fact, the 1993 figure would look even more impressive if we took into consideration the total Ge'ermu farm agricultural and industrial production value, which reached RMB 49,713,700. Comparing this amount with the numbers from Xiangride and Nuomuhong, we see that a cooperative farm in Haixi with no prisoners at all can enjoy a per capita total production of up to ten times the value of what a prison farm can.

Table 16

Grain Production & No. of Employees of Ge'ermu Farm			
Period ↓	Organization/ Tons harvested	Employees + prisoners	Per capita kg. output
1964	Laogai: 5,000	16,000	312
1978	B'tuan: 3,513	20,000	176
1988	Coop: 4,592	8,000	574
1993	Coop: 6,272	2,338	2,983

But the important point for our purposes is that though as a laogai farm Ge'ermu was more successful than as a bingtuan farm, it was less successful than as a cooperative. Thus, it should be apparent why these farms in Qinghai are generally no longer interested in having many prisoners. This is quite different from the situation in Xinjiang, where, as we have seen, the authorities have their own reasons for maintaining so many prisoners.

The Haixi Laogai Overall. We now consider the size of the camps and prisons in Haixi taken together, the proportion of the economy for which they account, and their relative significance for the Qinghai Laogai Bureau and for Qinghai Province.

From the perspective of the Haixi administration, the important issue is how much grain the prefecture can obtain from the local laogai bureau. In 1987 the annual quota was 6,350 tons, but since then it is normally supposed to be double that (for all Laogai Bureau farms, and for units that had ever been such). If a year's harvest is poor in a certain area, the farms there are not forced to meet the new quota, but they have to render at least the original quota. The amount of grain actually delivered by Haixi's laogai in 1987 was 12,400 tons,[A] making

---

A. Plus another 4,000 tons from former laogai units. This 16,400 tons was 67.9 percent of the 24,150 tons total bought by the prefectural grain bureau.

the Laogai Bureau's share 51.3 percent. Thus, not only did the laogai farms predominate before 1970, they have remained very important since then.

Inasmuch as the Haixi area is one of the few boom areas in northwestern China, and these laogai units are helping to literally "feed the boom," they have access to financial credit at the provincial and national levels. By the mid-1980s this had already led to a situation where these camps were among the most modern and productive laogai camps in China. In view of the millions of *yuan* in additional loans made available in spring 1995, we can see that even in Beijing they are considered economically important. Few laogai units elsewhere can claim such a distinction.

Back in 1987, the Haixi Prefecture laogai produced 23,202 tons of grain, which was 42.8 percent of the total of the Qinghai Laogai Bureau's 54,252 tons.[235] But this was only 5.2 percent of the grain harvest in Qinghai. Thus, only within Haixi did the laogai play a major role in the economy. There, with economic dominance came a measure of political clout, and indeed the local laogai administration was virtually in charge of Dulan county (the location of the two most important camps, Xiangride and Nuomuhong). But we are only talking about the prefecture level; only there was the laogai a big fish.

How large are the camps in Haixi compared to others in China's northwest, or in China as a whole? In terms of the number of prisoners, they are no longer particularly large; they are just about the size of an average Chinese laogai camp. It is the output of grain that makes them among the most impressive camps in the country. By way of comparison, Xiangride alone produces about three times as much grain as all farms under Gansu Province's Laogai Bureau (which produced 7,586 tons in 1995). Of course, one would expect Xiangride's output to be exceeded by Hubei's Shayang Labor Farm. Indeed, the latter laogai (China's largest) did produce 34,640 tons of grain in 1994, a year in which Xiangride had an output of 22,000 tons. As the entire population of Shayang labor farm is more than ten times Xiangride's, it probably had to retain most of its own grain, so we suspect that the 17,000 tons sold to the state by Xiangride represents the largest amount sold by any labor camp in China. By comparison, the entire Xinjiang bingtuan laogai produced a total of 21,102 tons[236] of grain in 1994, still below the 22,000 tons of Xiangride alone in the same year. Considering that the Xinjiang bingtuan laogai probably operates more than 40 laogai grain farms, the resulting harvest is very poor when compared with Xiangride. (See Table 13, page 105.) While the harvest in Haixi was not particularly good in 1995, the following year was again very successful. As the state allows price increases for grain and these start to affect the profits of the Qinghai laogai, we can expect that the Laogai Bureau will be in a more solid financial condition than ever.

Elsewhere in Qinghai. At about the same time that forced labor camps were established in Xining City and Haixi Prefecture, a number of camps were also established in the same manner elsewhere in the province. Their history since the 1950s is similar to the ones described above, as they were under the same administration and experienced similar changes in policy. As an example of the history and present conditions of such a farm, we will examine Haomen Labor Reform Farm *(Haomen Laogai Nongchang*[237]*)*, located to the north of Xining in Haibei Tibetan Autonomous Prefecture. It is managed by the No. 17 Laogai Detachment of the Qinghai Laogai Bureau. Founded in 1956, the various units stretch twenty kilometers from east to west, and ten kilometers from north to south. In 1990 all this land was divided into nine agricultural and five non-agricultural brigades (the latter rarely using any prisoners). The total population was 5,903 civilians and prisoners, not including the residents of the many ordinary villages scattered among the brigades and which have no relationship to the Laogai Bureau.

In 1956 the Haomen laogai occupied only 1,933 hectares of land. However, in subsequent years it grew markedly, and by 1970 it had expanded to 12,000 hectares. To grow so quickly, they had to confiscate the land of whole villages, with the mostly Tibetan inhabitants forced to find a livelihood elsewhere.[238] As happened in other parts of Qinghai, after 1970 the PLA cut this huge camp down to less than half its previous maximum size, or about 5,000 hectares; the land earlier confiscated by the Laogai Bureau was now returned to the original occupants. During the late 1970s Haomen was further downsized to the point where it had only about 800 hectares under cultivation.

The figures for the Haomen labor camp from 1956 to 1988 can be compared with similar production data of the other labor reform farms discussed in this chapter. In thirty-two years, the camp produced 21,235 tons of grain, and sold 2,973 tons to the state. This means that Haomen's production is very small (compared with that of the large camps in Haixi). In 1990 it owned only 426 cows and horses, 1,209 sheep, and 5,000 chickens. These figures lead us to believe that this camp has been producing mainly enough to feed the employees and prisoners, and that it has not been enjoying sales on a large scale the way other camps have. Otherwise, in terms of its vicissitudes since 1956, it is a typical Qinghai prison camp.

Today, Haomen is used as the prison of Haibei prefecture, and in fact is the only large such institution there. The government cannot close it down, even though it must be losing money. Any other way to maintain a prison would be even more costly.

Duoba: Laojiao. Qinghai's Labor *Reeducation* Administration is organized as a sub-department within the Qinghai Laogai Bureau. At the beginning of 1995 it was responsible for 527 prisoners, a number that has not undergone great variation in recent years. Probably all these prisoners are kept at the provincial *laojiao* camp in Duoba.[239] In 1980, when this camp was first constructed, it occupied a mere 7.8 hectares of land. Unlike the 1950s, now whenever the Laogai Bureau set about to construct a new prison camp it no longer enjoyed the generous supply of land and funds. During the 1980s, some laogai camps as well as prefecture-level administrations did set up their own small *laojiao* squadrons. However, it became too difficult for the people working for the *laojiao* administration in Xining to look after all these little outfits, and so it was decided to concentrate the *laojiao* prisoners in Duoba, where extensive construction of dormitories and classrooms has recently been under way.

In 1993 the total economic output of the Qinghai Labor Reeducation *(laojiao)* system was only RMB 4 million. *Laojiao,* then, is much less important here than it is elsewhere in China. The reason for this is that

Qinghai is the only province in China with a large surplus of prison capacity. It has thus been more practical to sentence prisoners to a laogai term than to build a lot of new *laojiao* facilities. (Just the opposite is true in some other parts of China, such as Zhejiang, where criminals are sometimes sentenced to labor reeducation because the laogai institutions are full.)

The total number of "*laojiao* prisoners" in Qinghai actually includes all the juvenile offenders who are kept under detention in Xining (even though, strictly speaking, juveniles are not *laojiao*). The province's incarcerated juveniles have been numbering below fifty, and sometimes there are as few as six prisoners in the one jail there which is specially maintained for them. Nonetheless, inasmuch as there is a central government regulation requiring each province to maintain separate facilities for juvenile prisoners, Qinghai has no choice but to keep this one in operation.[240]

Sizing Up the Laogai

Of course, a smaller *laojiao* means a slightly larger laogai. We now turn to an overall quantitative evaluation of the Qinghai laogai.

Name Game

One step in determining how many prisoners a province's laogai holds is to count the labor camps. But as we noted earlier, even coming up with a list of camp names is never easy.

This is especially true in the case of Qinghai, due in part to the frequent changes of names. There are at least two reasons for this practice. The first is purely bureaucratic: particularly in the 1950s and 1990s, there have been numerous central government decrees governing the naming of prisons, and local administrators have had to scramble to keep up with the latest in nomenclature. But the second reason would appear to be the desire to maintain secrecy.

During the mid-1950s the Ministry of Public Security issued at least two separate sets of regulations on the subject. The first one was issued on October 8, 1954, and "clarified" how prisons, jails, and enterprises employing prisoners should be named. No sooner had the laogai's many signs been repainted than the second version, with the same title, was sent out (February 17, 1955). Issuing two sets of somewhat contradictory regulations in just over four months led to many changes and a situation where laogai units were often perplexed as to what names they were really supposed to use.

As an example of how prisons are named (and renamed and renamed), we may look at the history of one of the largest laogai enterprises in Xining, known today as the "Qinghai Fifth Construction Company." This company is located in the center of Xining, and in the mid-1980s employed around 1,700 civilian workers and prisoners. The institution may hold the record in name changes for laogai companies.

1952 founded as "Qinghai Construction Labor Reform Detachment" *(Qinghai sheng xiujian gongcheng laogai dadui)*. Renamed in

1954 as "Qinghai New Life Construction Detachment" *(Qinghai sheng xinsheng jianzhu dadui)*. Renamed in

1955 as "Qinghai Local State Owned Construction Company" *(Qinghai difang guoying jianzhu gongsi)*. Renamed in

1956 as "Qinghai New Life Construction Company" *(Qinghai xinsheng jianzhu gongsi)*. Renamed in

1957 as "Qinghai New Life First Construction Company" *(Qinghai xinsheng diyi jianzhu gongsi)*. Renamed in

1975 as "Qinghai Fifth Construction Company" *(Qinghai sheng diwu jianzhu gongcheng gongsi)*.

Even the company's neighbors were hardly able to follow such frequent changes. In fact, the long official names have seldom been used in day-to-day parlance, with various short forms being more popular. Although we believe that until now the Fifth has succeeded in never being discovered by outsiders, one could cite many cases of laogai labor farms known all too well to observers abroad, who unwittingly list them several times.

Also, at any given time an institution can go by multiple names. This makes it difficult to discern exactly where it is located, how many sub-units are involved, and what is the appropriate way to refer to it. Take, for example, a certain labor farm located two kilometers southwest of Gandu township in Hualong county, Haidong prefecture. Its official national name is Laogai Farm 119, but locally it is variously known as:

Gandu Nong Chang (Gandu Farm)
Hualong Nong Chang (Hualong Farm)
119 Nong Chang (Farm No. 119)
Sheng Laogai 119 Nong Chang (Provincial Labor Reform Farm 119)
Sheng Diyi Jianyu (Provincial No. One Prison)
Sheng Jianyu (Provincial Prison)

Furthermore, these names are sometimes intermixed into, say, "Hualong 119 Nong Chang" or "Hualong Laogai Nong Chang," and then intermingled with older names or other extraneous information, resulting in almost hopeless confusion. So it is not surprising that on lists compiled abroad[A] one name has been added to another in the misguided hope of providing insight into the system. Those who have compiled such lists did what they could to sort things out, making the best of a bad situation. But the large number of often obsolete names results in inflated estimates of the number of prisons and prison camps, and this in turn results in greatly exaggerated numbers of prisoners. Below, we try to get at the facts of the matter.

The Number of Prisons

Since the early 1980s, as part of its grand design to shrink the number of prisoners in the province, the Qinghai government has reduced the

---

A. In the 1996 *Laogai Handbook* (p. 75) this farm is mentioned as "Gandu Farm" and "Provincial No. 1 Prison," and the location as "Juhua County," a name for a county that does not exist anywhere in Qinghai. Jean-Luc Domenach (map, page 64) shows it as a camp in Hualong, a county seat indicated far to the north of the actual site. He presumably got this location from one of the many names under which it is known, that is, in this case, Hualong Nong Chang, and has put it on the map with this wrong location. Harry Wu *(Laogai — The Chinese Gulag,* page 185, no. 16-16) described it as "Gangdu Farm (Prov. No.1 Prison) in Xunhua County" with the wrong location, as Xunhua County is to the south of Hualong County. From these Western accounts we can see that even comparing materials for recent years can result in a great confusion.

number of camps by about one-third. They felt compelled to do so for the financial reasons which we have discussed. But there were more than purely financial considerations involved. There was the additional fear that half-empty camps would lead to pressure from other provinces, and thus from Beijing, for Qinghai to accept more prisoners from China proper; this would not be in line with the goal of Qinghai's desire to shed its gulag reputation.

By now there are only nineteen large enterprises (factories and farms) remaining in Qinghai that rely primarily on prisoner labor.[241] In addition to these nineteen, Qinghai has four province-level detention centers, one for adults, one for teen-age delinquents (in Xining), one for children (below age 14), and a special one under the jurisdiction of the railway system. Each county also has its own detention center or jail, as does each prefecture. The prefecture-level jails tend to be somewhat larger, housing several hundred inmates. This adds up to the total of about 55 mostly small jails, used for pretrial detention and sentences of under one year. (For longer sentences, people are handed over to the Qinghai Laogai Bureau.)

The Number of Prisoners

Many foreign estimates of the number of prisoners in Qinghai have been made, ranging up to two million.[242] On the other hand, in a 1984 interview the province's governor, Huang Jingbo, claimed that there were fewer than 20,000 convicts in Qinghai (but he was "unsure of the exact number").[243] He himself had been a political prisoner there for eleven years, and thus had first-hand experience of the provincial laogai system. He claimed that "labor-reform camps helped develop the country," but wished that Qinghai could "lose its reputation as China's prison state." Though such public acknowledgment of a desire to limit the number of prisoners in Qinghai has been rare, the basic policy was indeed realized during the following decade, even if the propaganda battle has yet to be won.

But what are we to make of the figure Huang gave? Curiously, "20,000" is the same number that the Gansu governor mentioned to foreign reporters the same year (see page 32). One has to appreciate the consistency! Inasmuch as the population of Qinghai is only a quarter of Gansu's, the prisoner inflow has certainly had an impact. As we have noted, though, how many prisoners one counts depends to a considerable extent on the definition of who is a "prisoner." To be sure, just living and working at one of these laogais does not make one a prisoner. In many Qinghai units the number of people working around a laogai unit, and attached to it, outnumber the true prisoners. Apparently some prisoners are kept by certain units (like Nuomuhong) just to support the claim that the whole complex is a prison, which obviates the need on the part of even the non-prison enterprises there to pay taxes. But the mere fact that an enterprise is predominantly civilian does not mean that we should overlook such prisoners as are there.

Thus, the counting is not easy. In our judgment, however, the number of prisoners in Qinghai in 1995 can realistically be put at between 22,000 and 24,000. This is based on what we know of the number and size of the camps, as well as certain internal information. Certainly there are far fewer than previous foreign guesses would indicate. Our estimate includes all persons sentenced to any form of detention, including those in the large units of the Laogai Bureau as well as those in aforementioned jails or detention centers and all former drug addicts under detention. This is a "conservative" (maximizing) approach, compared to international statistical practice. Prison statistics in many countries do not include persons in jails, detained drug addicts, and children locked up in some kind of closed boarding schools, but we do include any Chinese counterparts of these. Nor, of course, do foreign authorities include people on parole, and likewise we do not include people on *jiuye* (though the two are not exact equivalents — see chapter 6). When the above range is compared with numbers in other provinces of China or other countries, this is well borne in mind.

Production

The laogai percentage of the Qinghai total production is the largest of any province. Below we examine the agricultural and industrial contributions to this economic output.

Agriculture. As shown in Table 17, in 1987 laogai farms produced about 5 percent of Qinghai's grain. Although most of such grain is normally sold to government agencies at low prices, the managements of laogai farms have developed other sources of income, such as by growing high-value-added foods that they can market themselves. Table 17 illustrates the laogai's share of the market in various agricultural

Table 17

Qinghai and Gansu Laogai Agricultural Commodities[244]

Commodity	Qinghai Laogai, 1987	Percentage of Qinghai 1987 total	Gansu Laogai 1995
Cows, horses (o)	5,000	0.08%	300
Sheep, goats (o)	21,000	0.15%	5,000
Fertilizer (t, u)	9,461	7.57%	1,188
Eggs (p, t)	183	2.29%	148
Wool (t, p)	23	0.15%	5
Apples (t)	565	4.42%	4,272
Grain (t)	54,252	5.21%	7,586
Cooking Oil (r, t)	9,819	9.46%	113

Legend: o=owned, p=produced, u=used, r=rapeseed, t=tons

products in 1987. The 1995 amounts for Gansu are provided for comparative purposes. Gansu, of course, is a much larger province than Qinghai, and yet in almost all cases the laogai output is much smaller than Qinghai's. We do not even try to give the percentages for Gansu, which would be too minuscule to be meaningful.

Since 1987, the Qinghai Laogai Bureau's policy has been to increase rapeseed production at the expense of grain, as the former is more suitable to local conditions, and profits are much more handsome. Thus, the grain harvest in 1992 was only 41,830 tons, but there was a yield of 16,440 tons of rapeseed.[245] Then, because of bad weather, in 1993 the grain harvest declined further to 34,700 tons in 1993. But 1994 was a banner year.

While a majority of the various products are sold within the laogai system, this is not the case with grain and cooking oil, of which the Laogai Bureau has sufficient quantities to sell on the open market. By 1994, more than 70 percent of the grain, and more than 85 percent of the rapeseed, were sold or traded outside the prison system.[246]

When it comes to obtaining supplies, being such a big player gives the laogai an advantage over its civilian competitors, who must also pay the going wages. Not only do economies of scale come into play, sometimes advantageous transactions take place within the laogai. The tens of thousands of workers and guards, as well as (to a lesser extent) the tens of thousands of prisoners, comprise an important market where the workshops, factories, and processing plants enjoy a near-monopoly of sales. Lacking such protection, other producers can hardly compete in this market. The Laogai Bureau can also import supplies from other provinces, if doing so is cheaper; this so is not practical for smaller operators. So business-wise, the Laogai Bureau is well positioned.

Industry. Since 1949, compared to agricultural products, the market share of industrial products and construction has declined even more dramatically.

The Xining laogai, which started with nothing, had by 1958 attained an estimated 30 percent provincial share. They maintained this share until 1965, but it appears to have been on the decline ever since.[247] Unfortunately for us, as laogai enterprises have become less important, the Qinghai Statistical Bureau has not been as interested in them as it is in the large civilian enterprises, so we do not have all the data that we would like.

Since the early 1980s, new industrial development in Qinghai has taken place mainly outside of Xining. Inasmuch as there are no significant laogai industrial enterprises in those areas, the Qinghai figures are not much larger than the Xining figures shown on the table on page 135. Thus, since the Mao era the province-wide share of laogai enterprises has consistently been around or below one percent of the gross industrial output value.

When we look more closely at the laogai's industrial output during the 1980s and 1990s, we see that while the machinery factories[A] have performed poorly (in terms of maintaining the laogai's share of industrial production), the textile and leather factories have done well. The performance of the latter is about on par with that of normal civilian enterprises, which suggests that the management of laogai units is sometimes no worse than that of other state-owned enterprises in China. This is confirmed by the fact that the laogai's share of gross industrial output in Xining, albeit small, declined only slightly during the ten years from 1985 to 1994.

To view the entirety of industrial production under the Laogai Bureau in Qinghai, we must also take into consideration the ancillary industrial output of the prison farms. The farms have satellite units like coal mines that make the word "farm" misleading. In such cases, it is better to use the term "unit," which (in laogai parlance) includes all enterprises under the same management. All such units now have workshops for trucks and tractors, as well as plants for processing cooking oil and flour. Inasmuch as they also do jobs for other units (for which they are paid), those workshops, plants, mines, and transport operations add at least 20 percent to the production value of a unit.

If one includes all of the ancillary "farm" industrial output, the

---

A. Mainly the Qinghai Machine Tool Factory (Number One Labor Reform Detachment), and the Qinghai Water and Electricity Equipment Factory (Fifth Detachment), both in Xining Municipality.

provincial laogai's industrial production reached RMB 104 million in 1992.[248] When this is compared to the total industrial production of Qinghai during the same year, the share is still only 1.52 percent.[249]

Prison Conditions

In China as elsewhere, the quality of life in prisons depends primarily on the priority society assigns to the issue, and only secondarily on the financial resources allocated by the authorities to maintain standards. As our research shows, defining and maintaining minimal standards in these three provinces varies greatly. In the wake of the Mao era, a number of China's leaders at various levels were conscious of how bad conditions were in Qinghai's laogai, for some of them had actually served time there. Huang Jingbo, the aforementioned governor of the province in the 1980s, is a case in point. Thus, the problem of Qinghai's prison conditions enjoyed relatively high priority. And the improvements have been remarkable, especially when we consider that in the mid-1980s Qinghai was one of the poorest provinces in China, and at the same time had, on a per capita basis, more prisoners than any other province. Thus, maintaining adequate standards has meant spending relatively more on the prison system than would have been the case in any other province in China. In those days, the solution was to accept outside convicts, because that was the only way to raise money from the central government for renovating prisons. Each year, however, Qinghai tried to limit the number of arrivals to less than the number of released prisoners, resulting in a steady net decrease in prisoner population.

Qinghai mainly has two types of penal institutions: local jails and laogai prisons (most of which are rural). Compared to the laogai, incarceration in a jail is a great advantage for the inmates, because in the local prison relatives are nearby and can look after a prisoner. The treatment of prisoners by the jail guards is much better, as the latter know they might have to face the former prisoners and the relatives after the end of the sentence. But most of Qinghai's prisoners are in laogai farms. We now turn to the conditions of one such camp, which we shall examine in the context of official policies and the peculiar local geographic features.

The Saga of Tang'gemu. Located in the Hainan Tibetan Autonomous Prefecture south of Lake Qinghai, Tang'gemu Labor Reform Farm is quite large. However, the prisoners there are far outnumbered by non-prisoners (guards, workers, and their relatives). We estimate that there are about 2,000 prisoners there, whereas there are more than 4,000 civilians and around 200 armed guards (PAPs). They all fall under the administration of this laogai camp.

This is an institution of some renown. Harry Wu did some of his filming inside this camp. But the main reason for Tang'gemu's fame is that Beijing dissident Wei Jingsheng, China's most famous political prisoner, was incarcerated there for five years (1984 through 1989). Actually, Wei's was an unusual case. Aside from him, the only other political prisoners there have been former Red Guard leaders, sentenced in Beijing for their part in the Cultural Revolution. Wei was sent there as part of a small group of only fourteen convicts from the capital.[250] (Since then, no other political prisoner from other areas of China or Qinghai itself has been reported to be in Tang'gemu.) The place has been described by a sister of Wei Jingsheng, who visited him there several times.

It is a camp with no real walls around it, as the surrounding desert makes escape without a car or truck impossible.[251] It is not a single camp; rather, the Tang'gemu laogai is comprised of many camps spread out over a vast area, with some units so remote that the main center would be more than a day's walk away. Although Wei was hardly satisfied with the living conditions, he nonetheless readily acknowledged that they were better than in the prisons he had experienced in the Beijing area.[252] His health actually improved after being sent to Tang'gemu. Following his transfer back near Beijing in late 1989,[253] his health declined again, apparently because he now received such bad food (mainly poor quality bread). Also, in Beijing he enjoyed little exercise, whereas in Tang'gemu he had been able to spend a lot of time outside of the prison cell.

This description by a prominent dissident and his family is interesting when compared with contemporary reports about the camp by the Qinghai Labor Reform Bureau, and the changes reported since then. In the mid-1980s the authorities considered Tang'gemu one of the worst camps in Qinghai — a place where the horrendous conditions prompted the prisoners to make a lot of trouble. For example, the Qinghai branch of the Ministry of Supervision reported a large and serious disturbance *(naoshi)* in Tang'gemu during 1987.[254] The situation is confirmed by an article in *Law Daily,*[255] which relates how bad the conditions on this farm were. Aside from this being an unpleasant place for the prisoners, the authorities had their own reasons to be dissatisfied with the institution. The output in agriculture was far below the average of this area. That same year, Xiangride enjoyed more than twice the per-hectare output of Tang'gemu. These reports describe the conditions up to the end of 1987, at which time the Qinghai Laogai Bureau started upgrading Tang'gemu, using its own money as well as funds received from Beijing. These investments resulted in considerable improvement in the living conditions for the prisoners.

Little could be done, however, about the poor natural conditions. For one thing, it is an area of recurrent drought. A disastrous one occurred during the spring of 1995, when it failed to rain for more than seventy days, resulting in a very small harvest.[256] And drought has not been Tang'gemu's only problem.

In 1990, disaster struck in the form of a great earthquake. Its impact on the people of Tang'gemu makes a remarkable story,[257] one that gives a rare insight into life in this camp, and the way in which local leaders react to crisis. By this time there were already new prison buildings in the main Tang'gemu camp; these had been built during the summer of 1989. However, they were all occupied by prisoners; no money had been made available to erect new housing for the guards, civilian workers, and all their families. The result was that whereas the quake caused not a single prisoner fatality, there were more than a hundred deaths among the prison staff.[258]

To understand what transpired, we need to look at how Tang'gemu is organized.[A] As is normally the case, while the Qinghai Laogai

---

A. In Qinghai, a detachment *(zhidui)* under the provincial Laogai Bureau is normally divided into several brigades *(dadui)*, which in turn are divided into up to about 10 squadrons *(zhongdui)* each. In the case of Tang'gemu, there are

Bureau is responsible for operating the camp, responsibility for guarding the perimeter falls to the People's Armed Police.[259] The headquarters of the Qinghai Laogai Bureau unit responsible for operating Tang'gemu, the Thirteenth Detachment, is located right in the main Tang'gemu labor reform camp itself. But the headquarters of this People's Armed Police detachment is 78 kilometers away in Gonghe, the administrative seat of Hainan Tibetan Autonomous Prefecture.

The 1990 earthquake struck at 6:37 in the evening of April 26, and the request to send reinforcements was sent out by the Tang'gemu PAP guards at 7:20. A first advance group of 87 additional PAP soldiers arrived from Gonghe just 90 minutes later and a second group arrived at 11:30 pm.[260] The authorities obviously feared that there would be a prisoner takeover or a mass escape, so the first thing to be done was the dispatching of these supplemental PAPs, and only when they were sure that the situation was under control did they send doctors and relief materials. Claims that one or two hundred prisoners had escaped spread quickly among the local population.[261] While one official insisted that this was unfounded rumor, they were clearly taking no chances, and even more PAP reinforcements were dispatched. They arrived the next day, and patrols were sent out to hunt down any escaped prisoners. An astonishing total of 1,024 PAPs, 834 PLA soldiers, and 1,386 militiamen were sent to the disaster scene.[262] It seems that no prisoner actually made good an escape, not so much because of this massive show of force (which was surely overkill), but because the prisons themselves withstood the earthquake so well. Thus, whereas normally in China the army and the PAP participate in rescue work and cleaning up the rubble after an earthquake, in this instance the priorities of the higher authorities were with security, not with relief. Still, things could have been far worse, and we now come to the most remarkable part of the story.

In Tang'gemu, the prisoners are divided into categories. Depending on how well they cooperate and for what crime they have been sentenced, prisoners are assigned regimes varying from "harsh" (*yan'guan*)

---

just two brigades, numbered One and Two.

to "semi-free" *(ban ziyou)*. Over the course of time, prisoners are normally upgraded, and wind up as semi-free at the end of their terms. This gives prisoners an incentive to cooperate with the prison administration. (As we have seen, this sound practice is quite unlike the practice in camps managed by the bingtuan in Xinjiang.) Depending on their category, prisoners may move around the camp only under guard, move freely inside the camp, or even actually leave the camp during the day.

The PAPs were stationed not far from the center of the camp. Thus, within seven minutes of the earthquake they were able to surround its prison (the wall of which having just been partly destroyed by the earthquake) with guns at the ready.[263] At this point, the prison's desperate administration, which was very short-handed, had the choice of keeping the prisoners locked up, or permitting them out to help dig the personnel out from under the rubble. They decided on the latter course, and released more than 150 prisoners, even including 21 harsh-regime prisoners. During the ensuing hours, teams of around ten prisoners, led by their prisoner cell bosses, dug out many surviving cadres. Long before any of the reinforcements arrived, they had basically finished the job. By 11:00 p.m. the prisoners had been led back to the prison and locked up again.

Needless to say, the cadres were tremendously grateful to the prisoners. Later, a generous "reward" for them in the form of a commutation would be announced by the Hainan Prefecture Court, with 52 men released immediately and allowed to return home, while another 64 had their sentences reduced.[264]

The injuries were not handled so expeditiously. It was too much of a job for the medical staff at the clinic of Tang'gemu Labor Reform Farm (who had suffered their own losses), though they did their best. The severely wounded survivors had to be sent by car or truck to the hospital in Gonghe, where the first casualties arrived within hours of the earthquake. The day after the quake, the Laogai Bureau in Xining sent medical supplies, obtained from various hospitals, the medical university, the hospital of the PAP, the Laogai Bureau hospital, and the PLA's Fourth Army Hospital in Xining. But as for actual doctors, it was only the Xining hospital of the Laogai Bureau itself that promptly sent in any. They arrived 32 hours after the earthquake, and during the next few days treated a total of more than 140 persons.[265]

In most other countries, sufficient medical staff and supplies would immediately have been sent to the disaster area by all the appropriate agencies. In this case, Gonghe even had the potential advantage of having nearby a large military airfield. That, however, was never used for relief work. Medical supplies flown in from as far away as East Germany were actually unloaded in Lanzhou, and then sent by truck to the disaster area, which probably took a couple days. Even doctors from the main provincial hospital in Xining only arrived at the hospital in Gonghe a week after the earthquake. By then the health care situation was under control, and these doctors simply checked to see if it had all been done properly.[266]

Indeed, the only higher government bureau that had managed this relief operation well was the Laogai Bureau headquarters in Xining, which naturally wanted to take care of its own people who were in such a desperate situation. As we have seen, they responded quickly by sending medical supplies and personnel, and thus were the first agency to arrive at the disaster scene. All other government departments, including the local government and the PLA, just waited for orders from their superiors. When, on May 2, the government of Hainan Tibetan Autonomous Prefecture finally asked the PLA of the Lanzhou Military District to send medical staff, some were sent; they arrived in the disaster area more than a week after the earthquake.[267] Once there, the army doctors immediately got to work and treated more than 500 patients on each of the following days. Our guess is that the local population jumped at the chance to get a free check-up and medication, for actual casualties outside Tang'gemu proper were limited to a few deaths and less than a hundred injured.[268] As for the prisoners, it had been very lucky for them that they were being housed in the newly built prison facilities; that is the only reason they all survived. Otherwise, relief would never have arrived in time to do them much good, and the gun-toting armed police (rarely the last word in competence) would not have been much help to them.

Thus, in this whole affair, it was the laogai personnel and the prisoners who acquitted themselves well. Because construction of modern housing for the prisoners had been given priority over any for laogai personnel, the prisoners survived the earthquake while many cadres did not. And, with little help from other agencies, the laogai cadres and prisoners responded to the emergency remarkably well.

The Larger Picture. The commutations for the heroic prisoners of Tang'gemu illustrates one way that rewards are distributed in the Qinghai laogai, and also how easy it is to release even large numbers of prisoners — on those rare occasions when the Laogai Bureau officials think there is a reason to do so. But this system can also work against the prisoners, if, for example, a contrary situation arises, such as a rebellion against the laogai system. Such an incident occurred in the Provincial Prison in Hualong County on November 15, 1986, with 21 prisoners participating. As a result, the nine "ringleaders" were all sentenced by the Haidong Prefecture Court to death or to life in prison.[269] But most prisoners experience neither extreme. Rather, they endure whatever conditions prevail in the Qinghai laogai until the end of their set term. Fortunately, these conditions have changed for the better over the years. Large investments have been made to improve the buildings originally erected during the 1950s. At the same time better food, including more fruit, vegetables, and meat, have become available for prisoners.

During the field research that led to this book, prisoners have been observed over the ten-year period from 1986 to 1996. In the late 1980s one could still see them working outside the camps and prisons looking emaciated and frightened, with the prison cadres appearing in not such great shape either. All this changed markedly during the first half of the 1990s. Revisiting prisoners working outside a prison in Xining in 1996, we thought that the majority seemed, if anything, a bit overweight. They worked casually, and were so relaxed that they joked not only with each other, but even with the guards. The butt of the jokes in these instances were the foreigners observing them. At one time, the presence of foreigners in such company would have been no joke. While none of this means that all prisoners are treated well or that any prisons are nice places to be in, it highlights the vast changes that have taken place in recent years.

One criterion by which prison conditions in China are judged is the annual percentage of deaths among prisoners, excluding those who die from normal causes. This is called the "non-natural death rate," and includes mainly the victims of accidents, suicides, and murder (whether by other prisoners, PAP guards, or cadres). While the guards or cadres in charge of a prison are unlikely to report a "non-natural death" as such if their own people are involved, the others are most likely reported. At any rate, the official "non-natural death rate" in Qinghai in 1994 and 1995 was only 0.06 percent (14 people) and 0.08 percent (19 people) respectively.

We conclude that prison conditions in Qinghai in the 1990s are no worse, and indeed almost certainly better, than is generally the case elsewhere in China. Perhaps the facts that the ratio of prisoners to general population (0.5%)[270] is the highest in China, and that the laogai establishment has been there gathering resources since the 1950s, all helps to ensure that there is sufficient food and other supplies available for the guards and the prisoners. At any rate, the notoriety of places like Tang'gemu is no longer deserved.

Special Populations

In many respects the population of the Qinghai laogai reflects the nature of the corresponding populations in Gansu and the remainder of China. Two groups, however, deserve special discussion.

Non-Han Prisoners. The share of political prisoners in Qinghai as part of the province's total is probably not much larger than elsewhere in China. But the two phenomena of political and minority prisoners are closely connected in Qinghai, as many of the political prisoners known to us are non-Hans.[271]

As is generally true for the country, political prisoners, even though a small minority of all prisoners, receive most of the international attention. This is deservedly the case, because political imprisonment both has a far-reaching effect on the political process and is a transcendent moral issue. Still, the focus of international attention can be erratic and distorting. Thus, although imprisoned Tibetans are the subject of much concern abroad, this does not confirm that Tibetans are the only ones suppressed in a place like Qinghai; it reflects the fact that Tibetans have a support group abroad who document such cases. The Hui (Muslim Chinese), on the other hand, have not generally had any such international support, and so their plight has been little known, at least in the West.[A]

While prisoners from most minority groups in Qinghai are sent to the same prisons to which any other local offender would be, there is a special policy concerning Tibetan prisoners. Whether criminals or political offenders, they are now usually concentrated in the Fifth Laogai Detachment, near Xining.[B] This detachment operates the Qinghai Hydropower Equipment Factory.[272] In 1991 the Fifth had a total of 234 Tibetan prisoners[273] out of a total of more than 900 people (prisoners, workers, prison cadres and regular staff). This prison is heavily guarded, and escaping would be even more difficult than would be the case in a laogai farm in the countryside.

Perhaps surprisingly, this company has been among the most successful laogai enterprises in Qinghai. Its most striking feature in recent years has been the frequent shifts in the nature of the goods produced there. In the new market economy, agility of management and ability to anticipate and respond to the demands of the marketplace are the secret to the success of any enterprise, including those using prison labor. The Hydropower Equipment Factory has shown an uncanny ability to make quick changes in its product line when another item promises better profits. The name suggests that the place is supposed to produce generators and switchboards, and this is indeed still part of

---

A. This lack of international attention may be changing. See page 125, note A.

B. This prison (also known as *Qinghai Shuidian Shebei Zhizao Chang)* is located in the western part of Xining, at 30 South Xichuan Rd. The factory compound covers an area of 761,000 square meters or 0.761 square kilometers. The buildings have a total floor space of 68,900 square meters. With this large area under its control, occupied as it is by fewer than a thousand employees and prisoners, at least space is not the same problem as in many prisons and factories in eastern China.

the product mix, albeit now a modest portion. Such equipment is designed for small, local power stations, which used to be in high demand during the 1960s and 1970s. Now Qinghai goes in more for building huge dams, so villages and townships are not building power stations in such large numbers as before. But this situation does not hold back the Fifth's enterprising managers. For example, in 1996, a new workshop for electric cookers went into production, aimed at the local market. Since around 1990, however, most of the Fifth's profits have derived largely from a fairly modern, semi-automatic brick factory located inside the compound. It has a production capacity of 85 million bricks a year. Inasmuch as few of the Tibetans have enjoyed any training that would qualify them for more highly skilled jobs, it is here, where unskilled labor is needed, that they are normally put to work.

Table 18

Qinghai Hydropower Equipment Factory

Year	Production value*	Qinghai laogai total**	Factory's share of Qinghai laogai	Factory's share of Qinghai
1957	1.600	30	5%	1.536%
1985	6.648	45	14%	0.329%
1995	22.000	120	18%	0.314%

* In million RMB (not inflation-adjusted).
** Provincial industrial output, in million RMB (not inflation-adjusted).

Table 18 illustrates the role of the Qinghai Hydropower Equipment Factory for the Qinghai laogai and for Qinghai province. What we can conclude from the table is that this factory accounts for only a tiny 0.3 percent share of the industrial production of Qinghai, but a fairly impressive 18 percent of the Qinghai laogai's. Again, we see what a small share of the Qinghai economy is derived from the laogai. If we assume that the 234 Tibetan prisoners contribute about a quarter of the

Fifth's output, their labor makes up an insignificant share (0.078%) of the value of Qinghai's industrial output.

Although conditions in this prison are not bad by Chinese standards, it is still true that low priority is given to education. In a survey conducted around 1991-1992,[274] a total of 46.44 percent of the Tibetans (109 men) under detention there were illiterate in any language, while another 32.6 percent (76 men) had only primary education. This means a total of 79 percent were either illiterate or barely literate. As all the prisoners were sentenced to two years or more, and many had spent more than five years there, the extremely low literacy rate illustrates the fact that even in a prison with comparatively good facilities and enough time and money, teaching prisoners is not something that is considered a priority by the management.

The total number of Tibetans under any form of detention in Qinghai is estimated by us to be between 1,200 to 1,500. The majority are in local jails, where they are generally not put to work. That fact, however, does not necessarily make them better off than their brothers in the Fifth Detachment, as work under halfway decent conditions is much to be preferred to the boredom and claustrophobia of life in a jail cell. As for prisoners of Han and Hui nationality, they are often sent to laogai farms in Tibetan- and Mongolian-inhabited areas. The most important farm in an entirely Tibetan area is Bacang[275] Laogai Farm in Guinan County, hundreds of kilometers away from Han areas. Because of its remoteness, it is especially difficult for non-Tibetan prisoners to abscond, as they do not know the language and customs of the population in the surrounding area. Although Tibetans have been known to harbor escaped Han political prisoners, normally relations between Tibetans and non-Tibetans are not particularly good. Such ethnic "exogenizing" appears to be a deliberate policy used by the Qinghai Laogai Bureau to socially isolate prisoners and minimize the likelihood of their escaping.

It is ironic that one result of this "exogenizing" contradicts the official labor reform policy. While serving their sentences, prisoners are, in theory, supposed to learn useful skills. But under the circumstances, Tibetan prisoners are sent to industrial (Han-dominated) Xining, where they learn menial factory skills, even though there will be virtually no factories in Tibetan-inhabited areas for them to return to. Tibetan buildings are seldom made of brick, for which the raw materials do not often exist locally. Han prisoners, in turn, learn to farm on the high plateau, or even to work as yak herdsmen — skills in little demand in places like Xining, not to mention Shanghai. The fact that this situation has not changed for many years shows the priorities of the Qinghai Labor Reform Bureau: security first, output second, and reform a distant third. Still, the priorities are not as skewed as they have been in Xinjiang.

Drug abusers. In the early 1950s, many drug addicts were sent from China's eastern cities to the northwest, where they were forcefully detoxified. Most eventually joined the local population. Then, for three decades, China seems to have had little or no drug problem. Now it is different. Indeed, in Xining, as in so many of the world's cities, the most serious single problem for the police is the use of and trade in illegal drugs, and the attendant crime.

Only in 1988 did the police in this area round up their first large batch of addicts. By 1992, when drug abuse had become a problem in all urban areas of Qinghai, the province had set up three detention centers for addicts, located in Xining, Golmud, and Minhe County. The one in Minhe is mainly for Hui, some of whom have been involved in drug use and trafficking. This is not unrelated to the fact that in Yunnan province, near the "Golden Triangle" to the south, the local Muslim Chinese control a large share of this business. This leads to a number of itinerant Hui being sentenced in various areas, including the northwest, as drug traffickers. Conversely, up to 1993 a total of 81 natives of Qinghai were reported to have been sentenced in other parts of China for this crime.[276]

From 1991 to 1993, an average of only 93 drug dealers were sentenced in Qinghai each year, whereas during 1994 the number rose to 230.[277] A similar increase took place in the number of detained drug addicts. From 1991 to 1994 a total of 3,794 addicts were sent to the three detention centers. Alas, as in Western countries, mere detention of drug addicts has not proven to be a very effective "treatment." In Qinghai, some 80 percent have been returning to the habit after release.[278] During the same four years, a total of 596 drug addicts were sentenced to labor reeducation, mostly for small crimes or prostitution connected with the habit.[A] For the year 1994 the police estimated that 75 percent of Xining drug users committed other (non-drug) crimes. In some Xining districts, drug-related crimes that year made up about 60 percent of all crimes reported. Such crime results from the fact that in order to sustain the habit a drug user needs about RMB 50 a day, an amount very few can obtain legally.[279] Adding up the above figures on Qinghai's drug-related crime, between 1991 and 1994 a total of 4,899 persons were sentenced or detained.[280] Since then, drug-related crimes have further increased, and spread to more areas in Qinghai. In 1995, 3,204 drug users were known to the provincial police, not including those in prisons and detention centers, or those among the "floating population."[B] During 1994 and 1995, more than 2,000 users passed through the Xining detention center, of whom 96.4 percent were aged 35 or below.

For our purposes, what is important is that, inasmuch as the police tend to detain a larger portion of the drug-using population than is the case in most Western countries, the main reason for the increase in the number of prisoners in Qinghai during the 1990s has been drug-related crime. Alas, Qinghai cannot avoid this aspect of "development." Considering the fact that Xining is not one of China's larger cities, it is almost impossible to conceive of the magnitude of the problem for China as a whole; it is known that seventy percent of China's counties

---

A. *Qinghai ribao,* May 23, 1995.

On prostitution in China generally, see Rocca, pp. 247-255. (Our more recent, unpublished information is that in 1992 about 240,000 women were arrested for prostitution, and the number has been rising since. Others, to avoid arrest, often pay protection money to the police. According to some estimates, there are about 20 sex-workers for every one that is arrested.)

In Qinghai as elsewhere, drug users who are also convicted of other crimes are usually first sent to a special camp for drug addicts, and after detoxification are transferred to a laogai or *laojiao* camp.

B. This term refers to people who are not located where the government expects them to be living, but who have migrated (usually in search of work).

and cities have narcotics problems, involving millions of people.[A]

Checking Up on the System

As is typical in China, the Ministry of Supervision maintains a branch in Qinghai which has as one of its responsibilities the job of checking up on the prison system there. How effectively this work is carried out depends on the caliber of the persons in charge of this work locally, and how seriously they take this duty. Beijing, after all, is far away, and the authorities there cannot do much if local inspectors botch their work.

The most difficult part of checking the laogai is convincing the provincial government and the Laogai Bureau that in the long run such supervision is in everyone's interest. Once this concept has been accepted, the real work can get under way, but without local interest and cooperation, a few officials cannot change an organization involving tens of thousands of people. Furthermore, the Laogai Bureau in each province has been there for a long time and is deeply entrenched, with all sorts of "networks of connections" *(guanxi wang)* in place, while the Ministry of Supervision officials are apt to be outsiders and perhaps new to the business of prisons. Nonetheless, such supervisory officials can sometimes be very effective, especially if they have the courage to address problems directly, and to go after the individuals who are not doing corrections work well.

In 1987, the Ministry of Supervision issued detailed regulations on what had to be checked and how, but by 1992 they realized that for various reasons little was happening. Therefore a new order[281] was released by the Ministry with somewhat different and more detailed regulations. This time a clear deadline was included: The new regulations had to be implemented by the beginning of 1995. It seems that again this was ignored in many parts of the country, such as in Tibet

---

A. Security Minister Tao Siju put the figure for 1995 at 520,000, but that is only people actually known to the police. Other estimates run as high as five million (*Far Eastern Economic Review,* May 1, 1997, p. 27). We believe the number of serious drug users to be in that range (not including marijuana consumption, or only occasional use of hard drugs).

and Xinjiang (both bingtuan and Justice Department prisons). But it did have big influence in some areas, and Qinghai was one of them.

Our case in point had its beginning on January 8, 1993, when the provincial head of the Ministry of Supervision in Qinghai, Zhang Jimin, wrote a report advocating that prison conditions be improved. Two aspects of his reasoning are especially interesting. First, he argued that proper prison management, and respecting the constitutional rights of the prisoners, would help put a stop to the human rights campaign by foreign countries against China, and would demonstrate the concern of the Communist Party and the government for the rights of the Chinese people.[282] Hitherto, the standard answer by the Chinese government to complaints about prison conditions by foreign organizations and individuals had always been that this is an internal affair of China, and anyway that prison conditions in China are good. But here we see a provincial official insisting that improvements were not only necessary but would also be an appropriate response to the international public relations problem.

Zhang's second line of reasoning had to do with his analysis of the problem itself. Typically in China, the prisoners have been blamed for all that goes wrong inside the laogai system, while all crimes on the part of the staff, if admitted at all, have been considered as only of secondary importance. Zhang took a different view. He appears to have recognized the problems for what they were, citing cadre corruption and other misconduct, and improper handling of cases, as the main sources of trouble in the system. In this instance, the higher Qinghai leaders (whatever their private thoughts about all this may have been) did not openly raise any objections, and let Zhang's efforts go ahead.

From a variety of sources we know that Zhang Jimin did make progress in dealing with these problems. His own 1994 report did not exaggerate. In the intervening two years, better controls had been put into place, which resulted, for example, in 899 cases[283] being discovered in which persons had been detained for longer than the legal limits; all these cases were corrected. By comparing this figure to the total of 4,494 persons investigated by his agency that year, by this single standard alone we conclude that at least 20 percent of the cases investigated had originally been handled incorrectly.

Illegal detention by the authorities for long periods of time is a problem that is widespread throughout China. This is the only case we know of in which the cadre-police have been forced by a supervisory agency to correct so many miscarriages of justice. Elsewhere, the usual practice has been to ignore the problem,[284] or at best to claim that this happens only in rare cases where the police "make a mistake." In Qinghai, this crackdown by the Ministry of Supervision seems to have showed lasting results: The number of such cases dropped from 899 during 1994 to 304[285] in 1995. It is too early for us to know how such supervisory intervention will affect the province's prison conditions, but at least there are areas in China where problems are addressed for what they are; all the blame is not placed on the prisoners, and "foreign interference" is not simply a cause of resentment.

The above numbers document the true extent that this problem used to represent in Qinghai; we suspect it still to be little better in many other provinces.

Conclusion

Recall our little Nantan tour in the prologue. Although the area still has plenty of prisons, one has to be struck by how many are no longer there. To be sure, the buildings still exist. However, in many instances the buildings having been largely or entirely converted to other uses; as far as the laogai is concerned, they are but old ghosts.

For all of the downsizing that has taken place, the province's Laogai Bureau still oversees a system that is equivalent in size to such an organ in a province with a population three to four times that of Qinghai.[A] But in intraprovincial terms, the provincial laogai and public security apparatus is particularly large only in certain areas: Xining, around Lake Qinghai and in Gonghe and Dulan counties. This means that more

---

A. This is only true for staff of the laogai units in the strict sense, as all other penal bureaucracies are the size one could expect for a Chinese province of this size. There are a total of around 13,000 persons employed by the entire police system of Qinghai. A similar number has to be added for the People's Armed Police (see above, page 81).

than 90 percent of the area of Qinghai has no more prisoners and public security staff than is typical throughout China, even on a per capita basis.

Still, where the laogai is big, it is very big. Altogether, we estimate that the province has 23,000 prisoners ($\pm 4\%$). And the priorities are quite clear. After security, for the Laogai Bureau, economics is "in command." Will the large recent investments that the Qinghai Prison Administration[286] has been making in farming pay off? Probably to some extent. However, we think that overall it will be very difficult to achieve profitability. This is because agriculture will remain largely regulated by the state. Although a big rise in grain prices was permitted in 1997,[287] for political reasons the authorities cannot allow an unlimited increase. Furthermore, a highly bureaucratic organization with thousands of employees to pay and feed may never be able to produce as efficiently as can a comparable cooperative enterprise.

The overall picture is quite varied. If we compare the cases of Xiangride and Nuomuhong labor reform farms, we can see that there is only one policy that both consistently follow: reducing the number of prisoners as much as possible. The managements have concluded that it just does not make much sense to feed and guard too many of them. In a larger sense, the two units do just what most units try to do in China: reduce costs and improve profits. This is the only way to achieve a better life for all people employed in a given unit. But we can see that there are many different ways of reaching this goal.

While we are confident in saying that since 1985 the prison situation in Qinghai has been benefiting from sounder policies, we hasten to add that we do not know everything, and one thing that we do know is that there is still room for substantial improvements on many fronts. That this assessment is shared by Qinghai officials in charge of inspecting the laogai system is an encouraging sign for the outlook in this province.

Chapter 5

Prisons and Human Rights

"No one shall be held in slavery or servitude. . . . No one shall be subjected to torture or to cruel, inhuman or degrading treatment or punishment."

Universal Declaration of Human Rights

In this chapter we shall review and summarize the human rights situation in the laogai, and then comment on the government's international responsibilities in this respect.

Excesses in the Laogai

The laogai has often been a brutal institution. This is especially true in Xinjiang, where at least until very recently, many of the prison camps can hardly have been better than they were during "feudal" times. The government's insistence that all detainees and convicts have been treated in an enlightened manner does not withstand scrutiny.[288] To be sure, there may be some truth to that when it comes to those few Chinese prisons which outsiders are permitted to visit,[A] but not to the prisons

---

A. For practices regarding foreign visits to prisons, see below, pp. 226, 247.

of the northwest, particularly in Xinjiang.

To some extent, China's poor prison conditions have been a matter of simple neglect, but there is also an element of deliberate policy. In 1991, one official frankly stated that if a prisoner's life were very comfortable, there would be no reform. "The standard of living of prisoners should not exceed that of ordinary civilians." He complained that some prisoners (such as those from the countryside who were serving sentences in the city) lived better lives in prison than they had back home. "When their sentence is completed they don't want to return to the countryside." To really transform criminals, he argued, they must undergo the painful process of "being reborn with new bones" *(tuo tai huan gu).*[289]

One former Xinjiang prisoner commented to us that prisoners there have found themselves in an utterly lawless environment. In other provinces, the laws and regulations were not being followed quite so haphazardly. The problem in Xinjiang was only in part the fact that one's fellow *prisoners* were not law-minded (which indeed they were not). Even more fundamental was the fact that the *corrections officers* had no concept of rule of law, much less any sense of obligation to obey the law. Even though they often stole prison property and inmates' possessions and food, we know of no cases of guards being punished for theft from inmates (though there may have been some). Sometimes guards have indeed been disciplined for stealing from prison supplies and equipment, but their punishment was minor compared to that which had been meted out to prisoners for comparable crimes.[A] According to our informants, occasionally guards have even sent inmates out into the local community to engage in illegal activities. The example cadres set every day conveys the message that personal relations, not law, are decisive, and that corruption and exploitation (as described in our Xinjiang chapter) are appropriate conduct. Not only did parolees not

---

A. We were told of one case in which a policeman had stolen a camera lens worth RMB 4,000. He was caught and fired, but ended up working as a civilian employee on the same farm. Our source claimed that in this prison was a man who had been sentenced to 12 years for stealing RMB 16.

learn to be law-abiding and productive citizens, they left prison untrained in any occupation, and there was often no work available for them. As we have noted, they thus tended to revert back to a life of crime.

Even the relatively mild forms of abuse would be unacceptable by the international standards which we shall discuss shortly. According to one former Xinjiang prisoner, if an inmate did not accomplish enough labor, at the end of an exhausting day it was common for him to be forced to jog for hours, or to pull a cart loaded with stones. Another common form of punishment was placing prisoners in tiny, cage-like cells in solitary confinement. Although unpleasant, many prisoners found this not much worse than an arduous day's work, though the punishment is sometimes toughened by shackling the victim to the floor and withholding food. Our informants tell us of other even more brutal treatments. Beatings (sometimes by officials but more often by a cell boss or other prisoners) were a daily occurrence. Beatings were often carried out by a team leader under the supervision of the squad leader (both prisoners), on the instructions, often merely implied, of the corrections officers. This practice afforded the latter "deniability" in the case of outside scrutiny. (On occasion prisoners have been punished for beatings which were later deemed to have been unauthorized.)

Guards preferred beatings as a way to deal with discipline problems at the lowest level; more formal punishment, such as term-extension, would require reporting problems to superiors, which would imply negligence on their part. Beatings sometimes have a sado-masochistic quality, with shirtless cell bosses clubbing naked victims. One man who had spent a decade in Xinjiang's prison camps claimed knowledge of six cases of homosexual rape by cell bosses.[A] In another case, two cell bosses regularly tormented a mentally disturbed inmate, including fondling his genitalia and encouraging others to do likewise, and even in one instance pretending to bury the man alive. This latter case turned

---

A. China has no specific law against homosexual rape, and such cases are dealt with "informally"— especially when inmates are the perpetrators.

out to be a rare[A] instance when abusive guards were disciplined: two were transferred to another prison; the sentences of the prisoners who participated were extended.

In addition, there have been other forms of maltreatment and torture, such as applying electric stun guns to sensitive parts of the anatomy. Methods of physical punishment include requiring a prisoner to stand for hours, or to "fly" (bend at the waist and remain in that awkward position), and forced drinking of urine or eating garbage which had been thrown into the latrine. Some of our sources had even worse stories to tell. For example, we were told of one prisoner who, after a series of escape attempts, was given the normal punishment of being forced to work in leg chains; when the officers discovered that the chains had been damaged, the prisoner was beaten to death. (The death was recorded as a "suicide.") Another prisoner, caught trying to smuggle out a letter reporting the incident, was beaten unconscious. Such violence was no secret; indeed, official publications once flaunted it as a warning to would-be criminals.[290] The only meaningful "rule" has been: a prisoner is not supposed to be beaten to death. Officially, the maximum acceptable death rate at prisons and laogai camps is six per thousand. That is a norm which each prison and prison camp should try not to exceed. We suspect that the death rate is much higher than this in Xinjiang.

Although we have not seriously attempted to evaluate laogai conditions in other parts of the PRC, many Xinjiang prisoners have experienced prison life elsewhere, and they report that Xinjiang's have been the worst, in terms of facilities, regimen, and caliber of administrators and guards. The reforms which the authorities have tried to institute in China's provinces have been in little evidence in this

---

A. The White Paper on crime (cited endnote 12), *Beijing Review,* p. 14, claims that prosecution of guards is not so rare, and that in 1990 and 1991 twenty-four wardens and guards had been imprisoned for "administering unauthorized corporal punishment to a detainee." But no such severe punishments are known to us on the basis of testimony of former prisoners.

region.[A] One prisoner remarked to us: "I had thought that conditions in the prison in [a major eastern city] were terrible, but after I got to Xinjiang I was convinced that the prison back east had been heaven."

Still, even at its worst, the laogai is not, as some have claimed, "the Chinese equivalent of the Soviet Gulag."[291] In our concluding chapter we will make quantitative comparisons. Qualitatively, the only period for which such a comparison comes close was the early 1960s, but that was a time the country in general suffered from famine, with upwards of ten million people (largely civilians) starving to death in a single year.[292] There is conflicting information regarding whether the prisons were hit harder than the rest of society. Surely this was at least sometimes the case,[B] but it should be noted that in northwest China even the nation's most strategically crucial personnel, such as those stationed at the missile and nuclear installations in Xinjiang, were reduced to eating leaves and wild plants.[293] Between 1963 and 1966, the food situation in the prisons improved. Some claim that the reason was that reform-minded policies prevailed in the prisons.[294] In reality, it was the abandonment of radical economic policies in the country generally that ended the famine nationwide, and therefore in the prisons as well. Although the diet would continue to be inadequate, there would not be actual starvation.

As for cadre corruption, at least until 1996 there was little sign that it was declining. Indeed, it was reported that, nationwide, cases of crimes by people within the Justice Department increased by 50.8 percent in 1994 compared with 1993, involving a total of 4,007

A. According to an official report, most of the provinces of western China had instituted rules concerning rewards and discipline of guards, but this had not been done in the case of Xinjiang. *FGY,* 1991, no. 2, p. 48.

B. Gao Ertai, who was arrested as a rightist in 1957 and sent to Gansu's 3,000-inmate Jiabiangou State Farm (27 kilometers northeast of Jiuquan), has reported: "More than 90 per cent of us perished. . . . We were given two bowls of thin gruel every day in addition to an insubstantial bun. . . . Years later, when local peasants wanted to convert the site into a seed farm, they discovered hundreds upon hundreds of bodies." Quoted in Jasper Becker, *Hungry Ghosts: Mao's Secret Famine* (New York: Free Press, 1996), p. 186.

individuals.[295] But this figure may tell us less about the extent of such crime than the degree of attention that the authorities are paying to the problem. Anyway, there was no indication that corruption on the part of corrections officers in the *northwest* has been seriously targeted for prosecution, and we cannot say how much, if any, improvement there has been in a place like Xinjiang. At first the 1994 prison law appeared to be making little difference there. Although none of our interview subjects were in prison after its promulgation, the information which did emerge from the northwestern laogai was *plus ça change, plus la même chose.* But in 1996 we finally began to see a little evidence of progress. According to one letter smuggled from a prisoner in Xinjiang: "since the prison law of 1995 [sic], prison conditions have improved greatly. Now the *duizhang* [wardens] no longer beat prisoners, because they also study the prison law." (Actually, the law had already been on the books for two years, but apparently such intended targets had been unaware!) Likewise, another Xinjiang prisoner noted improvements in conditions. "There is still room for improvement, but there are more rules and regulations, and conditions are getting better. I expect that the legitimate rights and interests of prisoners will be increasingly protected." Wrote another: "Now conditions are different — certainly much better than before 1993. Since the Ministry of Justice's [sic] prison law went into effect, everything has been done accordingly. So the prisoners have benefitted from that law. Team leaders no longer beat prisoners, nor do cell bosses or regular prisoners."

Not all communications from Xinjiang are so upbeat, and it is certainly too soon to make any real judgment on the matter. But as of this writing it appears that conditions have begun to change, at least in part.

But some rights violations pertain to the reasons people are incarcerated in the first place. These generally lie outside the scope of this book, but nonetheless deserve mention in any chapter on human rights. While the mere fact of incarceration, even with mandatory labor, does not in itself always represent a human rights violation, it does if the person does not belong in prison in the first place. The crudeness of China's judicial procedures does result in people sometimes being convicted of crimes by mistake. Thus, some prisoners are innocent and do not belong in custody. Although it is no longer true that detention is tantamount to conviction,[A] China's judicial procedures remain slipshod and subject to extra-judicial influence.

Thus, there is every reason to believe that there are many miscarriages of justice. In China, suspects are under great pressure (sometimes involving torture) to confess, and most of the guilty *along with some innocents* do so. Insisting on one's innocence only exacerbates one's difficulties. ("Lenience to those who confess, severity to those who resist.") Even so, since the Mao era this has changed somewhat. Of those arrested in the crackdown which began in 1983, when local police agencies had to fill arrest quotas, an astonishing 82 percent studied in one sample declined to admit any guilt. "We asked many prisoners why they were in jail, and they didn't know how to answer."[296] In the years following the crackdown, the number refusing to admit guilt dropped to 43 percent. Many of the first group were sent to the northwest, which is further indication that the laogai there contains many innocents. One former prisoner source tells us that while he believes that only 5 to 10 percent of those sent to Xinjiang in the wake of the 1983 crackdown were innocent, half of the total received longer sentences than they should have under the law. In the absence of the quota system since then, he said, only about 2 percent of new arrivals have been innocent.

Still, it must be said that the overwhelming majority of prisoners have been incarcerated for the same reasons they are in other countries: they are believed to have committed a crime. Only a tiny percentage of post-Mao-era laogai prisoners have been sentenced for political reasons.

A. The 1989 *Zhongguo jiancha nianjian* (p. 211) contains some interesting figures on this score from Xinjiang. Of all those taken into custody, 12.5% were released without being formally "arrested." Another 9.78% apparently were arrested, but then were not charged with a crime and sentenced. Probably virtually all of the remaining were convicted, but on appeal 71.4% had their sentences changed.

But when a person is brought to trial, a finding of innocent is rare. Nationwide, in 1995, 1,886 (0.35%) were found not guilty. Ren Jianxin, quoted in *Qinghai ribao*, March 24, 1996, p. 2.

As we write this, the authorities appear to be replacing the concept of "counterrevolution" with a new prohibition of "jeopardizing state security," without any real easing of restrictions on expression or association. Thus, the elimination of the crime of "counterrevolution" does not mean that the concept of political crime is dead. It appears that the step is being taken in part to improve China's human rights image, but also to focus more meaningfully on China's rising crime rate, which of course has nothing to do with "counterrevolution." According to Wang Hanbin, a vice chairman of the NPC's Standing Committee, "Revision of the crimes of counterrevolution is made out of the consideration that China has left the era of revolution to enter the era of construction. . . . Criminal groups have come into being and sometimes commit organized offenses, running amok in neighborhoods, lording it over the people in an area, perpetrating outrages and riding roughshod over and slaughtering people."[297]

Actually, as we have noted, drugs are increasingly becoming the issue. In the urban parts of Qinghai, the most common reason for people to enter into the prison system has to do with the use or trafficking in illegal drugs, and this situation appears to be true of much of China today. For example, in mid-1996 it was reported that "since last year" 6,500 drug addicts had been treated in Chongqing's 25 compulsory rehabilitation centers and 21 voluntary rehabilitation centers. In 1996 the city saw 1,980 drug smuggling cases; 4,400 smugglers and addicts were arrested.[298] Alas, the problem persists unabated;[299] just as the police in Western countries have learned, drug abuse is not solved with more repression or with tougher sentences.

As for the very real problem of people being imprisoned for their beliefs, it is unlikely that recent legislation ending the crime of "counterrevolution" will improve the situation. Still, it should be reiterated that prisoners of conscience represent a relatively low percentage of the overall prisoner population. This marks a change from the 1950s, when vast numbers of China's political nonconformists were sent to the northwest, and subsequent decades (up to 1984) when political offenders continued to be sent there. In Qinghai, especially, the political offenders form a very small group. The same is true for China generally. It is not possible to make an accurate estimate of how many prisoners of conscience (non-violent political or religious offenders) there are in China. In 1996 Amnesty International put out a list of around 2,000 (including some people not actually detained).[300] Presumably that is some fraction of the total, which could conceivably run into the tens of thousands. Except in the Tibet Autonomous Region, however, we doubt that prisoners of conscience comprise as much as one percent of the total prisoner population.

One former political prisoner who used to be imprisoned in the bingtuan laogai reported to us that although conditions in the camps there were harsh, he and the other political prisoners were sometimes treated relatively kindly, at least near the end of their terms and by higher-level corrections officers. Although lower-level officers never made much of a distinction between political prisoners and criminals, the higher-level officers were better informed and realized that after rehabilitation today's outcasts might be tomorrow's officials; they feared retribution (or maybe even looked forward to eventual benefits from *guanxi*). But this has probably not been true for the majority of today's political prisoners in Xinjiang, who are mostly local Uyghur nationalists,[301] and often it is not true for political prisoners elsewhere in China.[302]

Of course, even a small degree of political imprisonment has a deleterious effect on the political life of the nation — its purpose in any country is to keep the current rulers in power. But contrary to what has been said by others,[A] we find that China's labor reform camps are no longer integrally related with China's peculiar political system. Though political arrests are essential to the Communists' retaining their grip on power, this is not the main purpose of the laogai system.[B] Virtually all

---

A. In Harry Wu's view, "Labor reform camps are a necessary product of the Chinese totalitarian State." He indicates that the number of counterrevolutionaries was 400,000, or about 10 percent of the total. Wu, *Laogai—The Chinese Gulag,* p. 19, citing *"Laodong gaizao gongzuo"* (Labor reform work), Beijing, 1985, p. 1.

B. Unlike the laogai, China's most famous prison for political offenders, Qincheng (near Beijing), is not even under the Ministry of Justice.

of the inmates of the labor reform and labor reeducation camps are presumed by the authorities (whether correctly or otherwise) to have committed real (non-political) crimes; they are not there under "pretexts."[303]

Though China's non-violent *political* prisoners are now far fewer than was once the case, the international human rights covenants which we shall discuss shortly permit none at all. While there are surely more political prisoners than the recently admitted 2,679 imprisoned "counterrevolutionaries,"[304] this figure is probably closer to the truth than the 600,000 or so suggested (for the mid 1980s) by one critic.[305] In Xinjiang during the 1980s, we believe that political prisoners comprised well under one percent of the total. In one group of 800 men from the Shanghai area, only three were political cases. Since then it has been the policy not to send political prisoners from China proper to the northwest, but rather to remand them to a local prison designated for the purpose (most provinces have one or two such institutions).[A] Thus, by the early-1990s Xinjiang's political prisoners were almost all from the region itself;[306] an internal report put the percentage at 0.32. The decline in political imprisonment and the concomitant increase in the working-class portion of prisoners have been accompanied by the near abandonment of the devastating "class struggle" rationale for prisoner reform, which itself translates into at least a modest improvement in conditions.

China and the International Human Rights Regime

In the early 1990s the authorities began to rethink China's laogai. This was prompted by the perception that China now faced a "new situation" in four respects. First, the political challenges to the regime which culminated in 1989 had been dealt with effectively, which presented a

---

A. The last time that sending political prisoners to Xinjiang was seriously considered was after the 1989 crackdown. At the time, Wang Zhen urged that thousands who had been arrested be sent there (and also to Heilongjiang), but it was not done.

favorable situation for transforming the penal environment without having to make concessions to liberals. Second, there now existed a large young adult population, the average criminal being increasingly youthful. The third factor (partly a result of the second) involved the precarious security situation in both urban and rural China, due to rising crime. Finally, overseas calls for China to clean up its human rights act could no longer be completely ignored, for China had to protect its international image.[307] It is this latter perception that is of interest to us in this chapter.

There are numerous international conventions proscribing many of the penal practices we have detailed. In 1966 the United Nations (with the PRC still excluded) adopted the International Covenant on Civil and Political Rights, Article 7 of which (reflecting the UN's International Declaration) prohibits "cruel, inhuman or degrading treatment or punishment." By 1976 both covenants had been accepted by a sufficient number of countries to be considered "in force" at least with respect to the ratifying countries, though their applicability to non-signatories[A] like China is a moot point of international law. China has been able, year after year, to prevent consideration of the country's human rights situation by the United Nations Human Rights Commission.[308] China has acceded to the Convention Against Torture and Other Cruel, Inhuman or Degrading Treatment or Punishments (in 1988). Furthermore, for many years now, PRC representatives participated in certain aspects of the work of the Human Rights Commission in Geneva. But China has often been less than forthcoming when it came to reporting on and responding to UN questions about the country's own human rights problems, even when the instruments already acceded to were involved. Still, these commitments represented acceptance of the principle that there are internationally protected *individual* human rights.

A. China has occasionally hinted that it was considering acceding to the covenants. The Chinese authorities apparently want this to be part of a bargain, with the Western countries easing up of their scrutiny of China's human rights situation as part of the deal. *New York Times*, February 28, 1997, p. A-6.

According to Article 2 of the torture convention, authorities have an international obligation to take "effective legislative, administrative, judicial and other measures to prevent acts of torture" in any territory under their jurisdiction. Although China's authorities have sent somewhat mixed signals as to whether such treatment is condoned, the official line is that it is not. Nonetheless, torture has persisted, and it sometimes causes death directly, or from suicide by inmates who cannot withstand the treatment. In one case that has recently come to our attention, an inmate drowned himself in a river because he could not endure the electric shocks and other forms of torture that were being administered to him.[309]

Finally, in 1996 the United Nations (though normally reluctant in the extreme to criticize China's human rights practices) did indeed prod China on the matter of torture. After two days of hearings, the UN's Geneva-based Committee on Torture called on China to change the country's laws and investigate reports of abuse of prisoners.[310] (See text, page 235.) Committee spokesman Peter Burns said the committee had found that "torture may be practiced on a widespread scale in China." The response of China's ambassador to the United Nations European headquarters, Wu Jianmin, was reasonably constructive. China, he said, was working to live up to its obligations under the Convention. However, he expressed concern that the UN body's conclusions were largely based on reports by non-governmental organizations (NGOs), some of which he said were biased and inspired by dissidents' accounts. "If you base yourselves on prejudiced information, and I would call it disinformation, I fear you may lose your objectivity." But the committee was assured that China had stepped up a fight against torture and mistreatment, which it noted was already deemed a "criminal act" and never justifiable under Chinese law.[311]

Thus, the laogai has become an international issue. It is bound to be more so as more foreigners are taken into the system. Foreigners have been detained in laogai camps in various part of China,[312] but not many such cases are known to us in the northwest. We suspect that already some persons from countries such as Pakistan are detained in the three provinces, for such persons have indeed been charged with crimes. In September 1996, seven persons from Pakistan were detained in Qinghai's Gonghe County, being charged with illegal hunting and possession of 2,359 grams of marijuana. Similar cases from another location in Gonghe County and one in Menyuan county involving Pakistanis have been reported. As other foreigners have been incarcerated for possession of marijuana elsewhere in China, it would be a surprise if people such as these Pakistanis got off without any sentence. Thus, these once secluded provinces' laogais may evolve into a prison system where the prison cadres have to learn foreign languages to communicate with some of the inmates.

The issue is becoming internationalized in various other ways. International lending agencies have a problem ensuring that their developmental loans do not go to projects using exploited and abused prisoners. This has become a particularly sensitive issue for the World Bank.[A] Also, international human rights non-governmental organizations such as Amnesty International and Human Rights Watch have repeatedly called attention to problems in China's prisons.[313] Indeed, Wu Jianmin was quite right that UN pronouncements, such as those on pp. 235-238 of this book, are largely based on the findings of NGOs. Still, it is noteworthy that in 1994, the point was made by the PRC minister of justice that the country was obligated to adhere to the United Nations' "Minimum Standards and Regulations for the Treatment of Prisoners," and to the basic requirements of international treaties pertaining to the rights of prisoners.[314] Although China still falls far short of these standards, at various levels of the system there is now some awareness of such international norms. The new use of the term "prison" in place of the old "labor reform" appears to be partly motivated by such concerns. According to the *Legal Gazette,* "Our renaming the laogai helps meet the requirements of our association with the international community, and will advance our international human rights struggle."[315]   As we have noted, even local prison administra-

---

A. Harry Wu has alleged that the World Bank finances projects that utilize prison labor. *Shijie ribao* (New York), October 24, 1995. The Chinese authorities flatly denied the allegations. *Shijie ribao,* November 2, 1995. For our view, see commentary, page 228.

tors in both Qinghai and Xinjiang have occasionally taken note of this latter concern.

Clearly, by the mid-1990s the problem of cadre prison behavior had become an embarrassment to many, and it would appear that Beijing has become somewhat more sensitive to the problem and would like to curb the abuses. Whereas once the authorities had a class-struggle mind-set and routinely blamed the prisoners for all problems, today they increasingly see unqualified and corrupt guards as a major difficulty. Thus, numerous new regulations have been enacted, including proscriptions against corruption,[316] along with provisions for improving the conditions of prisoners (see page 250), but it remains to be seen whether the underlying problems will be broadly and effectively addressed.

Because of the international and the other reasons cited above, China's authorities have become conscious of the need to establish a legal framework for the laogai. Thus, in 1994 the Chinese authorities had the National People's Congress pass the new law on prisons (text, page 252). At the time, there were some in the NPC who thought that the bill, which largely deals with what can be done to prisoners, was still one-sided, and at the last minute they were able to have inserted an injunction against abusive behavior by cadres. (See "Article 15" on page 231, and Article 14 on page 253.) However, those cadres found to have committed a legal offense would only be administratively punished, rather than be treated as criminal suspects.

As we go to press, China's leaders and representatives reject the relevance of international human rights standards for China. When Denmark tried to get the UN Human Rights Commission to take up the issue (with little support from other countries), China's representative blusteringly called such criticism "a rock that smashes down on the Danish government's head."[317] But as China tries to become more integrated into the international community, it will doubtless find itself obliged to be more respectful of such international concerns, which after all are shared by many Chinese.

Chapter 6

The Aftermath:

What Happens upon Release?

> "You prisoners leave at the end of your terms;
> we guards are here for life."
>
> *Northwest corrections officers' lament*

In Qing times when a prisoner completed his sentence (or in rare cases won release through hard work and good behavior), he was usually required to remain in the northwest.[318] This practice has some parallel in recent decades. During the Mao years, when prisoners were "released" they often had to stay in the vicinity of the prison. Occasionally, however, they were actually kept in prison after the expiration of their terms.[A]

A. This situation appears to be improving (at least in two of our three provinces). During 1994, the Inspectorate in Gansu Province found that a total of 293 persons were being held longer than the courts had authorized. This

Jiuye

As we noted earlier, when a convict is sent to the northwest, his *hukou* (residence permit) back home has normally been canceled.[319] Therefore, upon eventual release, the person has had no automatic right to return home. Until the 1980s a majority of released prisoners continued to live and work in the neighborhood of their former prison. In Qinghai, this was true for about three-fifths of released prisoners. The phenomenon is called *jiuye*, which normally means "take employment." However, when used in reference to China's former prisoners, the term is short for *liuchang jiuye*. This, in turn, is a shortened version of the old term *xingman shifan qiangzhixing liu chang jiuye*, meaning "post-release compulsory retained workers." Under *jiuye*, millions of released prisoners used to be given local *hukous*. Under this regime (not entirely without parallel in Western countries[320]), former prisoners are given local jobs. In China, jiuye pay has traditionally been very low (with no pay in the case of those who had been deprived of political rights).

The practice of jiuye began in earnest around 1954, when the policy was "retain more, release fewer."

> The labor reform institutions should organize those whose terms are expiring and are to be released, and arrange for them to continue to work if they wish to be "retained for at-camp employment," or if they have no homes to go back to; otherwise they can be placed as settlers in remote and sparsely-populated areas.[321]

The Ministry of Public Labor Reform explained further:

> Jiuye is mainly aimed at consolidating the security of society and defending national economic construction, so the major targets are counterrevolutionary criminals who are still a danger to society; confirmed thieves and habitual robbers should be retained as well.[322]

In August 1954, the State Council approved a set of more benign-

---

would be far below one percent, indicating that the phenomenon is still a problem, but not nearly to the degree that it once had been. *(Gansu 1995 Yearbook,* p. 118). Regarding Qinghai, see above, pp. 171-173.

sounding regulations[323] concerning jiuye. Upon completion of sentence, a former prisoner was to be eligible for local resettlement and employment if he or she met one of the following three criteria:

1. Willing to remain in the area, and his or her services were needed.
2. Having no home or job to which to return.
3. Having served sentences in sparsely populated areas and wanting to set up a family locally.

If one met any of these conditions, it was to be the responsibility of the local laogai unit to help the former prisoner establish a new life, perhaps set up a new business, and even bring relatives (usually a spouse) from elsewhere if they wanted to come. A local *hukou* was to be arranged. People with skills were to be encouraged to pursue self-employment. People for whom this was not an option might continue to work for the laogai, but were to be properly compensated according to the nature and quality of work performed. In farming areas, land was to be allocated and a collective farm was to be established for jiuye villages.

Doubtlessly this ideal manner of handling former prisoners occasionally occurred. But during the early decades persons consigned to jiuye were at best treated as if they were on probation. Usually the reality was much harsher. Other regulations were quite restrictive (such as a near ban on jiuye people having radios). Indeed, it was later admitted that people had been treated almost as severely as those still serving prison sentences.

> After 1957, due to "leftist" thinking, we did not differentiate among those under retention for at-camp employment, and convicts under labor reeducation, and treated them all as targets of the dictatorship.[324]

Conditions did improve in the mid-1960s, with many jiuye people sent home (primarily those unable to work), and the status of many others converted to regular workers. These steps were part of the pragmatic economic reforms following the economic disaster of the early 1960s. Then, during the Cultural Revolution, the general institutional breakdown meant that few people entered, or left, the jiuye regime. In 1979, the Ministry of Public Security decreed that people on jiuye who had not been deprived of political rights should now be designated "workers" or "farmers," though they generally continued to work at the same workplace.

The original 1954 regulations had left the matter of restoration of political rights up to the local laogai authorities. If such rights were restored, then the former prisoner was supposed to enjoy the constitutionally protected rights of free speech and political participation. In one sense, whether or not such rights were restored would seem unimportant, inasmuch as not even those who had always obeyed the law really enjoyed such rights, the constitution to the contrary notwithstanding. Still, to be officially denied "rights" was socially damning and psychologically debilitating. It meant that one was officially deemed an inferior human being. Thus, the importance of restoration of political rights should not be underestimated.

Although some observers view jiuye as a form of imprisonment,[325] at the very least such people have had some of their rights restored. Even in the 1960s jiuye people were able to marry and raise families. Travel away from the area was usually possible (and is now common). To be sure, during the Mao Zedong years some of the people on jiuye were indeed virtual prisoners.[A] In Xinjiang in 1965 there was actually an uprising of such "free prisoners," resulting in dozens being

---

A. This has been a matter of some controversy. Apparently referring to the early 1970s, Harry Wu describes his own jiuye situation as follows: "Despite the increased measure of freedom given to us as resettled prisoners, we still had to fear arbitrary punishment from the security guards and confinement in the solitary cells that marked the mine not as a regular industrial facility but as a compulsory labor-reform camp. ... Without a work certificate or grain coupons, we could not leave. ... I understood with a crushing finality that my assignment to this labor-reform enterprise offered no possibility of termination, no chance of returning to normal society." *Bitter Winds: A Memoir of My Years in China's Gulag* (New York: John Wiley, 1994), pp. 233-234. But others insist that even at that time former prisoners remained simply because there were no jobs available elsewhere.

killed.[326] But, if anything, the number of people in Xinjiang on jiuye appears to have then increased, and by 1971 the bingtuan had 80,000 such people (including former Kuomintang soldiers, Uyghur nationalists, etc.).[327]

In the late 1970s some thought was given to abolishing the national system of jiuye. Instead, however, in 1980 the State Council ordered only that jiuye should be ended in its existing form. Soon, the whole jiuye regime was greatly relaxed. As early as 1983 it was ordered that the former prisoners whose jiuye status had been effected before the end of 1981 should be released and sent home.[328] Other regulations also signaled an easing of the situation.[329] From now on, with some exceptions, whenever a prisoner was released he was normally supposed to be given the choice of returning home.

But back home to what? One of the first of these decrees stated that, as a general rule, if people had had jobs before being imprisoned, they should regain their old jobs. If they had behaved well in prison, the work unit was supposed to accept them back. And if it was determined that a person had been innocent of charges, the unit not only had to reinstate him, but actually owed the back pay.[330] In 1985 it was decreed that in the case of people who had had no job, or were unfit, they should go to the neighborhood committee, register, and apply for a suitable occupation; it would be up to the neighborhood committee to make arrangements according to production needs.[331] Later, special provisions were enacted for former PLA employees.[A] As for people from rural areas, because of the agricultural reforms they often had no "unit" to return to; it was left to the provinces to decide what to do with such people. Hebei declared that if one's situation had changed back home and a former prisoner had no close relative, so long as he had not lost the ability to work he should still be sent back to his original village. But with regard to people originally from the cities

---

A. Regarding pay and rank for military employees (soldiers and civilians) after release from prison: their unit was to reassess and redetermine the rank. For those who had once made "major contributions," their rank and pay need not be lowered. Joint Decree no. 258 (1989).

who had been "sent down" to the countryside and then arrested, they were to be allowed to go where they had direct relatives, which usually meant back to the city.[332]

Though the change was slow to take place, according to a 1981 decision of the National People's Congress the practice of *mandatory* jiuye was to be continued only in certain limited instances. This was mainly to deal with the growing problem of escapees. In these cases, any original city household registration would be permanently unrecoverable, and the prisoners would be given an extra prison sentence before being released to jiuye. The law on this subject also contains one extraneous sentence that could conceivably allow more general continuance of jiuye: "Criminals who have not reformed after undergoing reform through labor shall remain at the camps for employment after finishing their terms."[333] Although this might appear to be a major loophole in the law, in practice only a small percentage of convicts seem to have been affected. The context and title of this provision suggests that this clause was intended to apply only to recidivists. A 1983 advisory concerning formerly sheltered or reeducated prisoners repeats this ambiguity.[A] However, a 1992 State Council Notification makes it clear that, at least in the case of former labor reeducation prisoners, the apparent loophole is directed at recidivists.[334]

At any rate, all jiuye people are supposed to be either placed in special camps or otherwise separated from the laogai regime. According to a 1981 Ministry of Public Security advisory,

> Retained people should be put in special camps or in special teams in the labor camps and they must be strictly managed and controlled. On the one hand, all of them except those who are deprived of political rights enjoy the rights of citizens, but on the other hand they should be reformed under supervision.[335]

A. "After completing their terms, with the exception of those who have actually reformed, they shall all remain at the camps where they shall be employed and may not return to the large- or medium-sized cities of their origin. Therefore, such persons undergoing reeducation through labor shall be discharged from public employment." *CLG,* September 1994, p. 85.

And indeed, during the early 1980s the jiuye ranks were swelled, at first by a large number of people who were among the many released from laogai during these early reform years, but who were mentally or physically unable to return to normal society. Through the mid-1980s the number of people on jiuye remained high as part of the fallout of the anti-spiritual-pollution campaign. At first, the life was tough. As late as 1984, people on jiuye were under severe restrictions, as implied in the above quotation. If they strayed from their proper venue they could be handcuffed and forcefully returned.[336]

Finally, in the mid-1980s, all this really did begin to change, and in recent years people on jiuye have had much more freedom than before. Although many former prisoners remain on jiuye *faute de mieux,* rather than out of genuine preference, they have their reasons. Perhaps they cannot afford the cost of the long trip east, and even if they can, they may have been away so long (and had been charged with such serious crimes) that they have lost any roots they once had and now lack a *guanxi* network back home. For some former prisoners, life there would be so problematic that, on their release, they really have "chosen" to accept work assignments near the prison.

On jiuye, some effort is made to integrate these former prisoners into a socio-economic "unit" *(danwei)*. In these units, there typically are regular civilian members, including otherwise-unemployed youths, and the offspring of guards and employees, in addition to the jiuye workers. In such remote places it is often impossible to find jobs outside the laogai system, and at the same time it can be very difficult to get a residence permit elsewhere. Thus, there tend to be many civilian unemployed, especially among young adults. Thus, jiuye workers are actually considered lucky compared to many others. Far worse off are the unemployed or even seasonal or contract workers, who have to pay for food and lodging, and who are paid only if there is work available.

To be sure, people on jiuye do not get the best jobs, but virtually any job is better than no job. There is actually much competition for some of the available positions, especially desirable and higher-status occupations like truck driver, landing which may require payment of bribes. There are even stories of jiuye people becoming rather affluent,[A] though we suspect that more typical is a case described in *Xinsheng Bao* who was earning RMB 110 per month.[337] Not all discharged prisoners have it even this good, of course. Often they get caught up in the above-described myriad of regulations and policies concerning the placement of released prisoners.[338] After all, the time has passed when the laogai could simply order a work unit to accept an ex-convict. With the economic reforms, enterprises must heed the bottom line as never before. Today's competitive labor market, both urban and rural, is not very hospitable to former prisoners.

How many people actually remain on jiuye, and how many are able to arrange alternatives? On October 18, 1989, *Xinhua ribao* indicated that 43 percent of Xinjiang's longest-term former prisoners did remain on such a regime.[339] In 1996 it was claimed that 70,000 were serving time on jiuye, while 30,000 had gone "back to society"[340] This phrase usually refers to ex-convicts who return to their old homes or to new ones. Sometimes the new homes are in the same province where the person has been imprisoned. In Xinjiang, there were (by official count) 121,938 reformed "new citizens" remaining there in 1975 (not including jiuye people).[341] The city of Karamai, for example, is said to have resettled 1,306 former prisoners between 1983 and 1991, out of a total of 1,395. The rest were either recidivist (2.6 percent) or apparently settled elsewhere.[342]

The percentage returning east has been on the increase. Often a released prisoner simply turns down the local job offer and joins the "floating population," but usually people are determined to return to their hometowns, which they can now usually manage to do. Sometimes they are even able to have the *hukous* transferred back home. True, for

---

A. According to one Xinjiang prison press account, one welder stayed on after his release, and made a lot of money because the prison outsourced work to him. In eight years he supposedly made RMB 300,000. He also became a small-time landlord, renting out 16 rooms. Li Changxun, *"Zouguo qu qianmian shi ge tian"* (The sky's the limit), *XSB*, March 23, 1996.

some these are not viable options. A person may have no home to
return to (at least not a welcoming one). He may not have what it takes
in stamina and chutzpah to join the floating population — participation
in which often means for these people returning to a life of petty crime.

An internal document has put the number of people placed on jiuye
at "several million" (*shu bai wan*) nationwide between 1949 and the
1990s.[343] But since the mid-1980s, when inmates have been assigned
to work on farms, there has rarely been much supervision, and, as a
practical matter, they have been free to walk away. The "special camps
or special teams" called for in the 1981 advisory rarely amounted to
much. Indeed, as part of the inducement to encourage people to accept
a jiuye assignment, they are given the right to make trips away for
business or pleasure.[344] By 1988 the number of people on jiuye in
China was already down to under 100,000, or only about 5 percent of
the number of actual prisoners.

The de-emphasis on mandatory jiuye has not pleased many eastern
cities, which have often found themselves saddled with large numbers
of former prisoners. As early as the mid-1980s there were frantic
"notices" in places like Beijing declaring that people who were
supposed to be on jiuye were to be returned to their proper units, in
manacles if necessary.[345] But there were many problems with this.
For one thing, except in special cases jiuye was now supposed to be
voluntary, and consistent with the needs of the local economy.[346]
Even in the case of people on mandatory jiuye, the 1981 advisory had
been short on details; it had no provisions for punishing people who
jumped ship. Thus, after the first few people who went AWOL in the
early 1980s got away with it, most others appear to have followed their
example. In one division, of the 6,440 former prisoners who were
assigned to jiuye between 1983 and 1991, only 14 actually remained for
any length of time; most of the others went back home (though some
ended up in a nearby city[A]). For the ex-convicts, China proper, now

---

A. An interesting case of someone who did this was the Nanjing poet Zhang
Xianliang, who served many years in Ningxia prisons and state farms. After his
rehabilitation in 1979 he chose live in Yinchuan. See John Gittings, "The Labor

freer and more affluent, was more attractive than ever. The pull of the eastern cities was so strong that in this same division it was found that 89.47 percent had boarded an eastbound train even before the completion of release procedures. (Released prisoners who do not accept jiuye are supposed to have a "transfer certificate," or *qianyi zheng,* which enables them to return home. But laogai paperwork is rarely handled expeditiously.) In one survey of 75 prisoners from eastern cities, not a single individual was willing to remain on jiuye. One remarked (somewhat hyperbolically) that jiuye was "nothing but a second laogai."[347] Said another: "I'd rather go back and sell bowls of tea on the street than stay one more day in Xinjiang."[348]

While the eastern cities may not be too pleased with the turn of events, the northwestern provinces are generally happy to see these people go. Whereas there had once been a time when the area was so starved for manpower that farms and enterprises were delighted to get any labor they could, this is no longer the case. With easterners free to move about the country seeking their fortunes, local units can go to the labor market, and pick and choose. People on jiuye are hardly prized; after all, these are usually men who have spent years figuring out ways to slacken off without being noticed. Furthermore, any unit accepting jiuye people would have special responsibilities toward them, including helping them reintegrate into society. This is especially a problem with the elderly, sick, disabled, or mentally ill prisoners. Upon completion of their sentences, they are supposed to have the *right* to jiuye, and to get a wage or pension paid as well as food, housing, and medical care. (Otherwise, they would have to depend on relatives or become beggars.) Naturally, the local units are concerned that if they accept these people they would become a burden.

In short, neither the discharged prisoners nor the local farms and industrial units relish jiuye, and the phenomenon has been greatly on the decline.[349]

Camp Memoirs of Zhang Xianliang," *Index on Censorship,* 1991, no. 9, pp. 31-33.

Recidivism

In 1983, when a large number of prisoners were to be sent to Xinjiang, the plan was that after their eventual release they would be given RMB 200 and remain permanently in the region. Xinjiang, however, was appalled at the prospect of having to absorb so many convicts, which is one reason why the policy has not been enforced. A more ostensible reason for the relaxed official attitude toward former prisoners is the assumption that they will have been reformed and are prepared to become good citizens. But what has been the reality?

In China proper, it is claimed that the recidivism (*leifan*) rate was never very high. For example, a study of former Shanghai prisoners indicated not only that the rate had been quite low to begin with, but that it declined quite sharply during the 1980s. Thus, whereas in 1982 it was 18.1 percent, by 1985 the rate was down to 6.8 percent. That was almost the recently acknowledged national average, which today is about 7 percent.[350] The rate is then said to have declined to a remarkable 4.1 percent in 1986, rising only slightly the next year to 4.4 percent.[351] This figure approximates the level that the authorities consider acceptable.[A]

The Shanghai figures are somewhat anomalous because of the fact that they do not include many of the most serious offenders, who were sent off to the northwest. Recidivism among northwestern prisoners is officially admitted to be "conspicuously higher" (*mingxian piangao*) than elsewhere,[352] and is clearly giving rise to concern. Among urban-background people who had served in one detachment that has been studied, 61 percent were found to have returned to a life of crime.[353] This is consistent with the impressions of our informants,

---

A. We base this assumption on the fact that the government has trumpeted the success of Guangxi, where the relapse rate has been put at 4.5-5 percent. *China Daily,* April 4, 1995, p. 3.

This same article has other information about Guangxi. The province has 18 prisons (including one for women and one for juvenile delinquents), holding 50,000. In 1994, 10,184 were paroled, and another 225 prisoners were released on probation. Sentences were increased for 203 people already in prison.

one of whom estimated that half of the former bingtuan prisoners tend to continue with their former illegal activities (which would approximate the American rate[A]). For about 40 percent of releasees, this means petty crime like pimping; if they have connections with corrupt police (which many do) they often find their occupations quite lucrative. About 30 percent of released prisoners turn to more serious crimes (though it is rare for them to commit the most vicious crimes such as murder and robbery). Professor Cai Shaoqing, criminologist at Nanjing University, has observed that many criminal gangs are comprised of former prisoners.[354]

Around the world, there have been published over five hundred research papers on the relationship between prison regimes and recidivism. They generally reach the same conclusion: that the more education and rehabilitation prisoners enjoy, the less likely they are to reoffend after they are released.[355] Chinese authorities are well aware of this wisdom. As noted on page 26, there was once a national ten-year plan to develop prison education, intended to prepare prisoners for post-release employment. By 1991, it was claimed that 71 percent of penal institutions had such programs. But success seems to have been limited to the major eastern cities. There, we are told, most former prisoners have been able to find employment.[B] But even if these figures are accurate, they can hardly reflect the nationwide situation.[C]

A. For example, the recidivism rate for formerly imprisoned serious offenders in New York State is about 50%. The rate among those undergoing non-prison rehabilitation under what is known as the Court Employment Project is 31%. Both figures refer to serious offenders, but apparently exclude "significant drug users." *New York Times*, June 1, 1996, p. 18.

B. Former prisoners' reported employment rates are Beijing, 83%; Shanghai, 79%; and Tianjin, 85%.

C. One problem is illiteracy. A survey made in the wake of the 1983 crackdown found that of inmates born during the 1957-1967 period (i.e., 80% of all prisoners), 45% were illiterate, compared with a claimed 15% for society in general. Curiously the percentages of prisoners who had graduated from senior high was almost exactly the same as in society at large: 18%. (Sun Xiaoping and Yang Jianmin, "Exploring the Laogai Economy in the Wake of

As far as the northwest is concerned, despite some claims of post-release successes,[A] our interview subjects appear to have had little in the way of education in prison (particularly those in the Xinjiang bingtuan), and job prospects have been decidedly meager.[356] Those who return to the east often cannot find work. On rare occasions they might be able to reclaim their old jobs, but in practice they generally have no right to do so. Indeed, in 1988 it was officially decreed that in the case of labor reeducatees, any old labor contract was canceled.[357] While often former Xinjiang prisoners revert to a life of crime, they sometimes return to Xinjiang (where they are often better able to find work, such as in the garment trade, or as shopkeepers). Once they have "made it" out west, they may again try their luck back east. (In a tongue-in-cheek reference to Maoist military tactics, this process is known as "taking the city by first occupying the countryside.")[358] Even if these individuals manage to succeed by one means or another, rarely is anything in their prison experience a contributing factor.

Thus, China has a long way to go before it solves the problem of the re-entry of former prisoners into society.

'Eating Imperial Grain,'" *BLGT*, 1994, no. 5, p. 26.)

Of course, many jobs do not require an ability to read, so illiteracy does not automatically translate into unemployment. Still, in China's modernizing economy there are fewer and fewer jobs available for those without basic literacy and arithmetic skills.

A. One does read in Xinjiang's prisoner newspaper *Xinsheng bao* (May 21, 1994, p. 2) of prisoners learning computer repair. Another issue (May 14, 1994, p. 1) reports of a former prisoner being elected to a township people's congress.

Chapter 7

Conclusion

With ready-made opinions one cannot judge of crime. Its philosophy is a little more complicated than people think. . . . Neither convict prisons, nor the hulks, nor any system of hard labor ever cured a criminal.

Fyodor Dostoyevsky[359]

Conceptions of China's laogai are often rooted in the events of the 1950s, when vast numbers of citizens of supposedly dubious class background or political outlook were rounded up and herded off to prison farms. But much has changed since those days; we have tried to evaluate the contemporary system in the light of these changes.

China does indeed turn out to have the world's largest prison system, but that is not surprising given that it is the country with the largest population. To be sure, in the 1950s the *rate* of imprisonment may have been very high by world standards. But the prisoner population, both nationwide and in the less-populated northwest, which peaked in the late

1950s,[A] has since declined. Table 19 summarizes our findings for the northwest in the mid-1990s.

Table 19

Prison population in the PRC's northwest				
Prisoners' origins ↓	Gansu (±5%)	Qinghai (±4%)	Xinjiang (±5%)	Total (±4%)
Non-northwest	none	15,000	50,000*	65,000
Local residents	33,000	8,000	35,000*	76,000
Total	33,000	23,000	85,000*	141,000

*Including Bingtuan

The total number of northwestern prisoners, about 140,000, compares with about 60,000 for Guangxi,[B] a region with almost exactly the same population as our three provinces combined.

The *rates* of imprisonment, in terms of number of prisoners per 100,000 population, we estimate to be about as follows:

Gansu   127[360]
Qinghai   485[361]
Xinjiang   525[362]

By comparison, the rate for the country as a whole is 166.[363] In Guangxi (where the crime rate is below the national average), it was only 110 per hundred thousand.[364] Xinjiang and Qinghai are far above

---

A. One of the reasons that the prisoner population peaked in the late 1950s was the policy, instituted at the end of 1953, of "releasing few, retaining many" *(duoliu, shaofang)*. "It has been decided that henceforth, for the next four or five years, a policy of many staying and few leaving will be implemented with regard to criminals due for release." The "released few" were generally those who volunteered to settle in borderlands. Dutton, p. 274, citing Xu Juefei, et al., *Gong'an fagui huibian, 1950-1979* (Anthology of security regulations) (Beijing: Qunzhong Chubanshe, 1981) pp. 223-224.

B. The number of people on laogai is 50,000; we have added 10,000 for labor reeducation and others not on laogai.

the national average, owing to the importation of prisoners from elsewhere, and (to a somewhat lesser extent) to ethnic problems.

Although laogai *bureaucracies* are structured quite differently from one province to the next, rough if inconclusive confirmation of the relative size of the prison systems of these provinces can be had by comparing them. The numbers of administrators in the provincial laogai in the late 1980s were as follows.[365]

Sichuan:	512
Xinjiang:	**330** (including bingtuan)
Hubei:	258
Guangxi:	185
Yunnan:	182
Gansu:	**106**
Qinghai:	**57**
Ningxia:	57

The number of administrators in Gansu is about what one would expect considering the province's size. Xinjiang is slightly above the mean, which is unsurprising considering the number of "outsiders" among the prison population. But there is one anomaly. Before researching this, we did correctly assume that Sichuan would be about the largest. But we had also guessed that Ningxia (which has almost as small an overall population as Qinghai and is not believed to have an especially large rate of imprisonment) might be the smallest. In fact, Qinghai turned out to be as small as Ningxia. This is consistent with our view that the Qinghai laogai is much smaller than has generally been presumed, but the figure surprises even us.

Why is the northwestern laogai not larger than it is? Much has to do with politics. Just as used to be the case during the Qing dynasty, prisoners are a mixed blessing for the people who have to supervise them, and for the local society. The officials in Xinjiang and Qinghai have reacted differently to this "mix," but in both there has been a decline in prisoner importation. To return to the Table 19 on page 203, in the mid-1990s we estimate that about 15,000 of Qinghai's, and 50,000 of Xinjiang's, prisoners were from other provinces, representing not much more than half of the two provinces' combined total number of prisoners. In the 1980s, the percentages had indeed been much higher, but in recent years somewhat fewer prisoners have been sent to Xinjiang, far fewer to Qinghai, and probably none to Gansu. Thus, the overall populations in the northwestern prisons have declined, though local offenders, especially those involved in drugs, have replaced some of the outsiders.

As for China as a whole, we estimate that there are today only about 1,250 prison units,[A] probably fewer than half the number that existed in the late 1950s. Determining the size of China's prison *population,* however, is still an inexact science. There are numerous data and methodologies to use in making an estimate. The lowest meaningful figure (the official one) is 1.35 million,[366] but that has to be taken as conservative. (For one thing, it probably excludes non-laogai prisoners.) Internal sources indicate that the overall ratio of prisoners to civilians (guards and workers) is no more than one for every five prisoners,[B] and there are about 300,000 such personnel in the country.[367] This suggests an overall prison population of 1.5 million (excluding people

---

A. There is some confusion as to what should be taken as the official figure. In 1993 China seemed to indicate to the United Nations that there were 1,368 penal institutions, though actually only the component figures were indicated: 684 laogai camps, 155 prisons, 492 rehabilitation centers (labor re-education camps, etc.), and 37 juvenile centers. However, in other internal listings the "155 prisons" were included among the 684 laogai camps. Thus, we take 1,213 as the "real official figure." This is not meaningless, but to that must be added certain institutions which were omitted, namely 36 Xinjiang bingtuan laogai camps, which brings the total to 1249. This still does not include pre-trial detention centers *(kanshou suo),* local jails, prisons for soldiers, or "shelter for investigation centers" *(shourong shencha suo).*
Our estimate is lower than others, especially that of Harry Wu, who "reckons" the number of laogai camps alone at between 3,950 and 5,950. *Laogai — The Chinese Gulag* (Boulder: Westview, 1992), p. 147.

B. This includes both guards and administrators. The ratio of guards inside the camps is seldom more than 1:10, and can be as low as 1:42.

in local jails).[A] From other sources, we are given to understand that the actual total of laogai and *laojiao* prisoners in January 1995 was 1,464,325, or 0.12 percent of the population. Though this does not include all prisoners, the figure is reasonably consistent with what we know of the prison populations of the various provinces studied in this book, and also with recent sentencing patterns there (see Table 20).[B] Allowing for the jail population, the total number of prisoners that year was probably just under 2 million, and (with the increasing crime rate) is now right around 2 million.[368] That indicates an unremarkable prisoner-to-population ratio of 166 : 100,000.[369] Later in this chapter we will place this in international comparative perspective.

Thus, it is not the size of the laogai that is outrageous, but what goes on within its worst prisons. In this book we have concentrated on the northwest. One cannot automatically assume that the situation there reflects the country as a whole. Still, there is plenty of evidence to suggest that the problems we have described are not peculiar to these provinces. Studies by labor reform bureaus, and by the Ministry of Justice, make it clear that the authorities are worried about the laogai. There just is not much *gai* (reform). Prisoners are increasingly defiant; they refuse

---

A. Other observers' estimates are much higher. Domenach, p. 489, hypothesizes 4 or 5.7 million for the mid-1980s (including people on jiuye), and Harry Wu puts the figure at up to 20 million. A U.S. TV network has reported that "8 million people work in slave conditions." NBC Nightly News, June 26, 1995.

B. The information in Table 20 pertains to numbers of people *sentenced* (as distinct from size of prison populations) in 1988-1989, for which we have the most detailed data. However, the national total did not change significantly during the following four years, and we believe that it has continued to average around 500,000. (For 1994 it was officially reported that nationwide 208,267 people were sentenced to five years or more, including the death penalty. *Tibet Daily*, April 11, 1995, p. 4.)

Regarding Xinjiang: To make the provincial population comparable, the 2.2 million bingtuan population has to be deducted from the "15.2 million" population figure. Thus, Xinjiang's "comparable population" is about 13 million. After making this adjustment, the sentencing rate in Xinjiang is revealed as heavier than in any other area in the northwest.

to admit guilt, resist reform efforts, and even engage in criminal activities while still in prisons. Meaningful "mutual surveillance" among prisoners appears to be a thing of the past, and self-criticism meetings are rarely held.[370] Clearly, things have changed since the 1950s. One exacerbating factor is the primacy of economics.

The Economy of the Laogai

There is, in our view, no direct correlation between prison profitability on the one hand, and humanitarian concerns and rehabilitation on the other. We consider it neither highly desirable, nor particularly evil, for a prison to make a profit. Still, in the Chinese literature about the prison system, a common theme has long been the "contradiction" between resocialization and productivity. The tension between the two goals has recently increased due to China's economic reforms. Now, more than ever, economics is in command. True, prison personnel are occasionally reminded of Mao's 1965 injunction that "We should take laogai work very seriously, and should not think about making a profit. Do not be concerned about making money off of the prisoners. The focus should be on reform. . . . Thought reform comes first; production comes second." But although Mao may have made those remarks, he had more realistically implied the operative priorities when he said: "Our prisons are in fact factories as well as schools."[371] From both the documentary evidence,[A] and from our interviews of former inmates, it is evident that labor and production have generally been the priority.[B] By the end of the Mao era, the laogai officials had less human and material capital to work with than ever. By the end of the

---

A. As one commentator put it in 1988, while the policy may have been "first comes reform," the practice was "production first, finance first, food first." Li Junren, "On the Nature of Labor Reform Organs and Economic Reform" (in Chinese), *FGY*, 1988:6, p. 1.

See also Li Yong, "The Significance of the Ministry of Justice's Fifth Decree" (in Chinese), *FGY*, 1990, no. 4, pp. 15-16.

B. However, even that is subordinate to maintaining prison security. Guards' bonuses are tied not only to production, but also to escape prevention.

TABLE 20 (See footnote B on page 206)

Sentences in Northwest China, 1988-89, Compared to National Total

Persons Sentenced To:	Pop. 1990: 4.5 mil. Qinghai 1988	Qinghai 1989	Pop. 1990: Xinjiang 1988 ex-Bingtuan	15.2 million Xinjiang 1989 Ex-Bingtuan	Pop. 1990: Gansu 1988	22.4 mil. Gansu 1989	Pop. 1990: National 1988	1.134 bil. National 1989
Death and For life	140 (4.8%)		231 (3%)	338 (3.71%)				16,607 (3.44%)
10 to 20 years in prison								29,377 (6.08%)
5 to 9 years in prison								119,272 (24.70%)
Total: More than 5 years	892 (30.73%)		1,034 (13.39%)	2,478 (27.20%)	2,191 (30.8%)	3,379 (33.4%)	113,547 (30.79%)	165,256 (34.24%)
Total: Less than 5 years	1,884 (64.9%)		5,270 (68.23%)	6,031 (66.19%)			240,517 (65.22%)	309,770 (64.18%)
Local Jail (Gouliu)			379 (4.91%)				Included Above	Included Above
Suspended Sentence			713 (9.23%)					
Not Sentenced	87 (3%)	42	174 (2.25%)	179 (1.96%)				6,035 (1.25%)
Innocent	40 (1.4%)	9	77 (1%)	68 (0.75%)				
Various			77 (1%)	32 (0.35%)				1,582 (0.33%)
Total	2,903 (100%)		7,724 (100%)	9,111 (100%)	7,113 (100%)	10,111 (100%)	369,779 (100%)	482,658 (100%)

1970s, the amount of prison land under cultivation had actually declined by 60 percent compared to two decades earlier.[372]

True, after that, the downward trend in laogai output slowed; between the rise of Deng Xiaoping in 1978 and the crackdown which began in 1983, total output declined by just 3.3 percent. But in terms of financial profitability, the drop was more dramatic: by 1983 profit had declined 86 percent in the five years. In the wake of the 1983-84 crackdown, productivity did begin to climb, but even increased productivity did not translate into higher profit margins, which never even recovered to 1978 levels.[A] Thus, more prisoners may or may not equate with more output, but certainly they do not equate with profitability. In these respects, Xinjiang probably reflected the national situation. However, as we have seen, the profit motive led Qinghai in a somewhat different direction. Indeed, Qinghai has gone far in resolving the reform-productivity dilemma: it has increased per capita production by *downsizing* the laogai.

Although much has been made of the economic importance of forced labor in China,[373] in fact prison output makes no significant contribution to the gross domestic product. Claims to the contrary tend to be based on erroneous statistics.[374] In 1988 (that is, before laogai production was deemed too sensitive a subject to report on in any detail), the national laogai output was approximately RMB 4 billion,[375] which was only about 0.2 percent of the country's industrial and agricultural output.[376] Official reports since then put the figure at less than half that.[377] Although we do not attach a great deal of credibility to such statistics, it remains true that the laogai has indeed been an insignificant factor in the national economy. Little has happened in recent years to change this situation.[B] Since the mid-1990s, with the civilian economy booming and the laogai economy languishing, the percentage is unlikely to be greater than it was in 1988.

A. 1987 profit was down 54 percent compared with 1978.

B. One 1993 internal document put the laogai's total fixed assets at RMB 10.5 billion, and its annual *liudong zijin* (something like "cash flow") at only "RMB 4 billion or so." See endnote 379.

Let us recall some of our observations about the Qinghai and Xinjiang laogais. Comparing the civilian production figures with the output of laogai institutions such as Xiangride and Nuomuhong, we concluded that a cooperative farm with no prisoners at all makes a per capita total production value of up to ten times that of a prison farm. If the industrial and agricultural production of the laogai in Qinghai is so small compared to the total production, and if we consider that the share in Qinghai is probably the highest of any province in China, then our Qinghai data are further confirmation of how small the share of the prison economy in China really is. In Qinghai (and also Gansu) this share has continued to decline, and is likely to decline further. It is thus clear why these prison farms are no longer interested in having many prisoners, and why only a system like the Xinjiang bingtuan would want to take prisoners. In the case of Xinjiang, many laogai units of the bingtuan have been making a deficit as high as those in Golmud area used to. But the bingtuan, which now has a monopoly on the prisoner-importing business, hopes that the payments for prisoner maintenance remitted by the eastern provinces and central government will make this a business that will help them to survive financially and, not incidentally, make them indispensable politically.

But when it comes to macro-economics, the picture is entirely different. Although the national laogai system was supposedly profitable in certain years, such as 1988,[378] if we use international accounting standards[A] to analyze the return on the investment, hardly any laogai enterprise ever shows a profit. It does have to be said that prison enterprises in Western countries normally make no profit either, so there is a fundamental similarity that should be borne in mind. A profit with prison enterprises is possible when working conditions are extremely primitive and casualties among prisoners are acceptable, or if the enterprise is extremely well run and lean — a rare but, as we have seen in Qinghai, not unknown, occurrence. Even then the profit may be

---

A. The normal international practices are to write off part of the original investment year by year, and to pay interest on borrowed funds; these practices are not generally followed by laogai enterprises.

smaller than would be the case in an otherwise comparable civilian enterprise. That should not surprise us; it is the normal condition in prison enterprises around the world.

Certainly in China, productivity of laogai farms and enterprises is almost always even worse than similar state-managed enterprises. And private or joint venture enterprises would usually require only a fraction of the work force to produce the same output. So it is obvious what has to be changed if the goal of increased productivity in these enterprises is to be attained: they would have to be largely civilianized. The Qinghai Laogai Bureau has read the handwriting on the wall and simply reduced the number of prisoners. As we saw in chapter 4, not only has the number of persons working for the Laogai Bureau declined, but the number of prisoners relative to the area under cultivation has declined even faster, so the per capita area under cultivation has increased. With a greater number of normal workers employed, and fewer prisoners to look after, the productivity of the prison enterprises in Qinghai improved greatly between 1985 and 1995.

But Qinghai is something of an exception. Chinese commentators have lamented that in general the system is a burden on the state.[379] The problem is seen partly as bad management, but more serious has been the autarkic nature of the system; the laogai economy has been sealed off *(fengbi)* from the real world. In the old, more socialist economy, it hardly mattered whether operations were efficient; given the general shortage of goods, the prisons could always find a way to sell their output. But now that the outside economy has been market-ized, it is so efficient that even prison-made products are no longer competitive.

The situation, we are told, has now been exacerbated by "hostile Western forces" who refuse to import prison-made products. Indeed, to export prison products to some countries is against their laws (as is the case with the United States[380] and Britain). Outside the northwest, prison exports are slightly more important than in the cases of our three provinces, and at least until recently were growing fast. During the first half of 1988 (before the authorities realized that this was too sensitive a subject on which to go public), prison exports are claimed to have earned US$150 million, up 65 percent from the previous year.[381] A sales fair of prison-made goods was held in Beijing in 1988, with 2,000 products on display.[382] For obvious reasons, there have not been any more such flagrant promotions. In fact, China now generally denies that its prison products are exported at all, and officially bans the practice. For example, a Hong Kong press report about the export of tea and engines from Guangdong labor reform camps was dismissed as "sheer nonsense."[383] Processed or manufactured products are on occasion still sold on international markets. When such products are exported, it is usually by selling the products to a subsidiary company that then does the actual exporting. The main markets are Southeast Asia and Hong Kong. But such exports make up a minute share of the output of the northwestern laogai, and we believe that it is fairly small for the system nationwide. We estimate the total exports at only around one percent of the total production value of the Qinghai prison system. The national figure is not known, but it is certainly higher.

Chinese who think about the laogai's economic problems have come up with a variety of answers. One cadre's solution is to improve the technology of prison industry, diversify, branch out, and participate in the "tertiary economy."[A] Failure to take such steps, one is warned, would only lead to a further deepening of the "crisis" of the laogai economy.[384] Other writers, while agreeing that the economic performance of the laogai has been poor, have had less far-reaching explanations and remedies. To paraphrase one commentary in an internal bingtuan penology journal, the problem has a lot to do with the way the system has evolved geographically.

> For historical reasons, the laogai has been unable to solve its problems in management and production. In fact, our laogai economy is in very shaky condition. We ought to be granted preferential policies and protection. Laogai enterprises are simply too remote from the markets. And we need not only better access to markets, but also to raw materials. Land used by laogai enterprises should either be free

---

A. This is not quite as fanciful as it may sound. In Chinese, the term "tertiary economy" is often used in a vaguer sense than in English; it can refer to any economic activity that is not strictly industrial or agricultural.

or low-cost. We should be given breaks on taxes paid on land and other resources. And we should be provided with more capital.[385]

Such writers seem to think that laogai enterprises have untapped potential; all that is necessary is to set it up better. But we have seen how the leaders of at least one province, Qinghai, rejected this idea; they saw the laogai assets as simply too valuable to waste on the prisoners, so they virtually confiscated farms and factories from the laogai bureaus.

China does have a few profitable laogai enterprises. These tend to be ones with unusually able management and a large contingent of *civilian* labor. But in general, whereas the size of the national economy has vastly expanded in recent years, we have shown that at least in the northwest the importance of production by prisoners has declined in absolute as well as relative terms.

Although the laogai's economic arrangements still vary from one province to another, this does not necessarily mean that the provincial administrators are free to conduct business any way they want. They are under various constraints, and one of these is indeed central policy. At the time of the market reforms in the early 1980s, it was decided that "market principles" should be applied to the laogai. The new policy was that the laogai had to be self-financing. This meant that the guards were under pressure to maximize the output of the prisoners. For example, a detachment's revenue had to cover all of the expenses of maintaining the prison camp, and the administrators doubtless often felt compelled to use dubious means to achieve this end — such as over-working prisoners, or selling products abroad. It used to be that if at the end of a fiscal year a local laogai authority could not make ends meet, it simply went into debt; this had to stop. Beijing may not have been responsible for the results in the sense of ordering that extreme measures be taken. However, the new overall framework laid down by Beijing inexorably led to such unintended but predictable results. For example, the plan was for the central government to pay for the initial construction of prisons, and then leave subsequent financing to the localities, which few could afford.

Eventually, the central authorities became aware of these realities, and realized that the "self-financing" policy had been a failure. In 1994 it was decided that the government would have to begin funding prisons and the laogai system. Although this was a virtual admission by the center that, in a macro sense, the laogai was uneconomical and could not pay its own way, Beijing still wanted to cut its losses as much as possible. However, by now there was the growing realization at all levels that the old idea of the symbiotic relationship between labor and resocialization was empty myth. Some prisons started experimenting with the practice of "separating production enterprises from reeducation-through-labor." Under this regime, while prisoners are still required to work, in at least some areas the reform and production functions are being disaggregated. According to a report from Hebei:

> The previous system, combining production and correction, seriously affected the development of reform-through-labor and reeducation-through-labor. In the face of this unfavorable situation, in which reform-through-labor and reeducation-through-labor enterprises' economic results were continually decreasing . . . the system has been changed. The new system, characterized by separating production enterprises from reeducation-through-labor groups, has been introduced. . . . Under this system, management and education organs are to exercise macro control over the enterprises subordinate to them, and management and education cadres are free from their dual jobs — managing both production and persons undergoing labor reform — so that they can devote themselves to managing reform-through-labor personnel.[386]

This new system, which is in the trial stages and does not seem to have been thought out very clearly, is claimed to be better both for production and for reform.

In sum, there are not nearly as many laogai institutions as has been widely assumed, and those that do exist are not very productive, just as they have not been elsewhere in the world, or historically in China. Today, the laogai plays a minimal and declining role in the national economy. We have shown how, with some notable exceptions, in most of the northwest these institutions have been poor economic performers.

In reaching this conclusion we have generally relied upon Chinese government statistics (mostly classified), supplemented by interviews with former prisoners. While these official data are often inaccurate, the bias is in the direction of overstating actual output, so the performance is, if anything, even worse than we have portrayed it.

The Laogai in Theory and Practice

It will be recalled from our introduction that the main Western study of law and order in China is Michael R. Dutton's *Policing and Punishment in China*. His highly theoretical post-modernist work covers policing in general, but here we comment only on its relevance to the laogai.

According to Dutton, although the laogai is infected by socialist utopianism, merely injecting individual human rights into the system would be no solution. "Despite certain Western accounts and assertions, the problem is not that 'the gulag' crushes individuality, . . . it actually creates a form of individuality within the collective." Thus, Dutton dismisses the suggestions of Chinese reformers like Su Shaozhi that prisoners should be transformed into self-actualizing individuals.

> There is no reason to assume that Su's idealized concept of a self-actualizing individuality, if operationalized into a programme of trainings, would be any less "repressive" or any less proscriptive than the present system of collective "individuality." The answer, then, is not to construct yet another utopia — this time in the form of a self-actualizing individual — but to examine the structural and institutional conditions necessary to guarantee rights and secure particular and calculated outcomes within a programme of trainings.

We would heartily agree with the latter assertion *if* by rights Dutton meant *individual* rights, that is, if it meant that individual prisoners deserved fairer trials and more humane treatment in prison. Unfortunately, he does not. In the Chinese context (though doubtless not for himself), Dutton seems not uncomfortable with a regime which does not recognize the individual except in the collective context. For his purposes, criminal procedure is unimportant.

> I omit criminal procedure because . . . , quit frankly, for what I
> wanted to demonstrate and plot, which was the shift from patriarchy
> to "the people," it was simply not all that important. Historically,
> criminal procedure simply does not figure in post-revolution China
> until the criminal code of 1979 and, even after that time, it covers
> only some ideas of policing and punishment. . . . If there is no ethical
> investment in the criminal procedure, then the grounds for paying
> undue attention to it diminish.[387]

But for *our* purposes, the grounds *increase*. After all, every instance of
incarceration in the history of the People's Republic has been preceded
by procedures. The problem is that those procedures are primitive,
often reckless, and commonly result in miscarriages of justice.

What is needed to prevent the sending of people to the laogai who do
not belong there is trial procedures that protect the *individual* defendants' rights. Alas, Dutton does not see it this way. "Individuation is
simply one more mode of social classification; it is neither universal nor
the pre-condition for human rights."[388] Individualism, like socialism,
is said to be but an "idyllic dream" to establish a "higher-order
morality," and can never serve as the basis for solving the gulag
problem.[389]

> Can the absence of individuality be treated as an indication of the
> despotic or could we not equally talk of the realm of freedom created
> by the "liberation" of subjects from individual subject forms? As
> rhetorical as this question may be, it nevertheless highlights the need
> for specificity in any assessment of the role of individuation. This is
> not something that will be achieved in theoretical works which "blur
> the lines" between idealist accounts of individuality and the social
> process of individuation.[390]

Not only do we disagree with Dutton's views on trial procedures; we
also part company with him when it comes to the subject of what
happens after prisoners have been convicted and sent to the laogai. In
our view, "socialist utopianism" is not the problem. Many societies
come up with comfortable rationales for consigning prisons to outside
the psychic perimeter, and guards find ways to rationalize abusive
behavior ("class enemies" in China; race in America). That is all highly

relevant to the problem, but it is not *central* to the problem. For one thing, after moving beyond official rhetoric to laogai reality, we see little impact of utopianism. For example, the three-person group, which for Dutton is the quintessence of collectivism, looks to us more like a buddy system in a Western children's camp, except that its main purpose is to prevent escapes. Certainly, it is largely irrelevant to reform. The important thing that is missing is a system of procedures which would protect the generally agreed-upon rights of each prisoner.

In short, Dutton's theoretical study is difficult to reconcile with the results of our empirical research. Anyone reading these two works will have a difficult time relating one to the other. If utopianism ever informed the laogai, it certainly does not today. We found nothing utopian "on the ground," and we find Dutton's theorizing largely irrelevant to the real "gulag" (his term, which itself distorts the reality). Dutton would doubtless say that we have operated in the worst traditions of what he dismisses as "Sinology" in which "scholarship [is] reduced to research reportage,"[391] and (perhaps even worse) exemplify the coterie of "Columbia University critics."[392] But unlike the "Sinology" which he rejects, we do not fear comparisons with other cultures. It could hardly be said of our study that it has been constructed less "out of the desire for academic accuracy" than "at the behest of government agencies and business."[393] In fact, we have no connection with either. On the contrary, we believe that only through accurate reportage and empirical analysis can China really be understood.

Even though Dutton's understanding of the laogai is derived from normative documents rather than from a study of the laogai itself, his writing has some value in terms of explaining what Chinese theoreticians think prisons *ought* to be like. Thus, families, education, and group pressure are said to play important roles in transforming prisoners.[394] But we found that none of these is of much importance, at least not in the northwest. As for his view that the difference between the laogai and the larger socio-political system is one of degree rather than kind,[395] there may have been some truth to this during the Mao years, as one of us suggested at the time with regard to labor reeducation.[396] But much has changed since then. Given the loosening of social controls in the past two decades, civilian life has virtually nothing in common with the laogai. As for the old "bridges" between them, the coercive jiuye has largely disappeared, and there is now often little to distinguish laogai and *laojiao*. The "dynamism" which Dutton professes to see in the laogai is now found only outside it — in the civilian arena.

The Laogai in Comparative Perspective

The Chinese laogai gives rise to interesting comparisons, not only with respect to other countries, but also domestically with respect to other epochs and institutions, and with respect to regional variations.

In Stalin's time, the population of the Soviet gulag averaged around 3 million, or 2 percent of the national population. That was more than ten times the current rate in China.[397] More contemporary comparisons are shown on Table 21, in which various national rates of imprisonment are compared. When referring to this chart, it is important to note that these figures reflect different years, and inconsistent standards as to what is "serious crime." But, while the table should be taken only as a rough guide, we believe that its main point about China is valid, namely that in recent years its prison population, relative to the overall population, has been higher than, but in the same general range as, the world average.[A] It is interesting that the rate is actually lower than the other two ethnic-Chinese states, Taiwan and Singapore. This is explained in part by the fact that many PRC offenders are executed, thereby reducing the pool of potential prisoners, but this is not a major factor. More important is the fact that China, which is less urbanized, also has a relatively low crime rate.[398] It is on the rise, however. In 1995 the number of criminal prosecutions in China was 3.15 percent higher than the previous year.[399] Then, in 1996, came

---

A. In 1995, China handled just over one million criminal cases, an increase of 6 percent over the previous year. About half of these cases involved serious criminal charges. That is 0.4 per hundred thousand population, compared with about 18 per hundred thousand in the United States in FY 1994 (though the definitions of serious crime are not the same). Steven Mufson, "As Rigid Controls Ease, Violent Crime Mounts in China," *Washington Post,* February 13, 1996, p. A-14.

Table 21

International Prisoner Populations (per 100,000 population)

Japan	37[400]
Germany	65[401]
Norway	70[402]
Azerbaijan	80[403]
United Kingdom	80[404]
World average	**105[405]**
(China — official figure	107[406])
China — our estimate (see p. 206)	**166 ***
Taiwan	187[407]
Singapore	210[408]
Russia	335[409]
South Africa	380[410]
U.S. (excluding jails)	440
U.S. (including jails)	614[411]
Dominica	714[412]

---

* Harry Wu implies that the total prisoner population in 1985 was 4 million. Although he does not actually mention this figure, he indicates that the number of counterrevolutionaries was 400,000, or about 10 percent of the total, from which we infer an overall prisoner population of 4 million (roughly 350 per hundred thousand). Although we doubt this figure, it is indeed likely that the prisoner population had just peaked, and has since declined. Wu, *Laogai—The Chinese Gulag,* p. 19, citing "Laodong gaizao gongzuo" (Labor reform work), Beijing, 1985, p. 1.

In 1996 Wu estimated that China had 1,100 prison camps with a population of between 6 and 8 million. That would be 500-667 per hundred thousand. Since 1949, "fifty million" had entered the system, of whom 20-25 million were said to have disappeared.[413]

the second crackdown. This will have some, but not a serious, impact on the rate of imprisonment, which is still far below that in, for example, the United States.

In addition to viewing the prisoner population in relation to the overall population, there is another way to analyze the rate of imprisonment, and that is in relation to a country's crime rate. Although it is not possible to come up with meaningful figures,[A] we believe that the prisoner-to-crime ratio is much higher in China than in almost all other countries. That is, for each serious crime committed, someone is much more likely to be arrested and imprisoned in China than elsewhere. Thus, whereas China's rate of imprisonment is only moderately above average when gauged in terms of the overall population, it seems extremely high when viewed in terms of the number of serious crimes committed. If one were to factor in the number of executions in each country, or adjust the figures to account for China's expanded notion of "serious crime," the international disparities would be even more pronounced.

One thing our research reveals is how different are the policies among and within the various provinces, and how this did not begin with the Deng Xiaoping era. In Qinghai, for example, we have seen a surprising variety of the methods by which camps are managed in this one province. In northwest China generally, such varieties multiply and can only be described one by one. Thus, any general claim regarding how good or bad prison conditions are, or for that matter regarding any other aspect of China, must be limited to actual cases that have been thoroughly documented. Even though we have studied quite a few, we still do not claim to have written the last word on the subject of any province's prisons.

Politics, and now even public opinion, can be factors in determining

------

A. Our efforts to establish data on this subject were not very successful, as comparable statistics are not available. In our attempt, it appeared that the number of people imprisoned per serious crime was 192 for China, compared with 8 for the United States and 2 for Norway. While these results are too extreme to be believed, they do probably point in the right direction.

prison policies. For some years, Qinghai's authorities have identified with popular opposition to any further influx of convicts from the east. On the other hand, given the ethnic sensitivities, the opinions of Xinjiang's Uyghurs are, if anything, stronger on this point. Even within the largely Han bingtuan there is a feeling that the prisoner inflow should not be unlimited. However, the bingtuan authorities (who are overwhelmingly Han) side with the central authorities on this point, and have usually been willing to accept the eastern prisoners. From Beijing's point of view, it is a happy circumstance that there has existed a semi-autonomous bingtuan in Xinjiang's compliant colonial regime that has been willing to accept outside ethnic-Han prisoners for the money that comes with them, and for the virtually free labor that they offer (redolent of England's sending its prisoners to Australia between 1788 and 1839). Thus, Beijing and the bingtuan have a symbiotic relationship; each needs the other for a number of reasons, not least of all so that they can have their way vis-à-vis not-always-cooperative provincial administration, and the downright hostile general population.

The differences among the various provincial prison systems are at least as stark as are the differences between China's overall prison system and, say, those of other third-world countries. China's prisons, after all, serve the same real function as prisons do elsewhere in the world: warehousing convicts and keeping them out of further trouble. For the nation's old revolutionaries, it must come as a disappointment that the laogai is no more than this. They have always had total faith in the potential for reforming people's mentality, including that of prisoners. There was a time when resocialization (even "brainwashing") was an important feature of imprisonment in China.[414] Judging by the situation in the northwest, this is simply no longer the case. As Wordsworth wrote, "Stone walls a prisoner make, but not a slave." We have noted how some prisoners resist even taking the first step: admitting guilt and accepting the "justice" of their punishment. Indeed, the subculture of resistance which develops among the prisoner population has more impact than does the culture of reform that the cadres are supposed to inculcate.[415]

Getting Modern

Prisons are a necessary evil. Every instance of imprisonment is a human tragedy. It represents a human failing, perhaps on the part of the individual, perhaps on the part of society, and very likely of both. In this volume, it has not generally been our purpose to pass judgment on China's handling of people perceived as social misfits. We express no opinion regarding just how many prisoners would be appropriate for China, or for any other country. To be sure, we have called attention to some problems with the way "justice" is meted out, but fairly assigning responsibility would not be easy. Surely we do not place the blame on the uneducated guards on Xinjiang's labor farms for the miserable conditions of the prisoners, much less for any miscarriages of justice that landed the people there. Indeed, our research even uncovered a few personnel, like Qinghai supervisor Zhang Jimin, and Xiangride's Li Yueren and Pan Jiajian, who deserve their reputations as good administrators. But it is a mistake to think of either the problem or the solution as having a great deal to do with the guards. Society at large must shoulder that moral burden. Indeed, the persecution of any human being is a human problem, so all humanity has a role in setting things to right. As Bob Dylan told us, "Some of us are prisoners, the rest of us are guards."

That prison conditions are ultimately a moral issue is further suggested by the relatively good conditions in Qinghai. This impoverished province now manages to treat most of its prisoners tolerably well, whereas relatively affluent Xinjiang falls far short. In general, it can be said that prisoners in China are receiving better treatment than they did during the Mao era. They are no longer viewed as "class enemies," with all of the degradation and deprivation that implies. The law is somewhat more respected, and people have much more of a sense of their rights than had previously been the case. In Qinghai, not only has the number of camps declined, but large investments have been made in the remaining ones. Thus, material conditions (food and housing) have improved there. To an uneven extent, the same is true in Xinjiang, though at least until recently the reason usually seemed to be mainly that prisoners' relatives back home (whether Xinjiang or elsewhere) were becoming increasingly affluent and able to send money.

It has been argued that the main sources of injustice in the Chinese penal system are threefold: lengthy pretrial detention, administrative (instead of judicial) sentencing, and convictions that rely heavily on often-dubious confessions.[416] But our research reveals that there has been another problem that is at least as serious, and that is long-term sentencing to sometimes the remotest regions of the PRC under inhumane conditions.

So what is striking about China's prison system over the years is not its large size or the productivity of the prisons, but the substantial number of prisoners who do not belong there, and the harshness of the conditions in the less well managed institutions. The first of these problems is owed to poorly trained judges, ineffective legal counsel for defendants, and the general highly politicized nature of the judiciary. Punishment must always "placate public outrage," which often means satisfy the whim of the party secretary who calls the shots (often literally) from behind the scene. Indeed, the whole 1983-84 crackdown was largely politics-driven. Crime, especially serious crime, had actually been *declining*. However, there had been some high-profile incidents, such as an airplane hijacking and the murder of a journalist, which galvanized the Party into action.[A]

As for the way prisoners are treated, contrary to official claims that prisoners have been treated humanely[B] we have documented the physical abuses and brutal exploitation which abound in the prison camps. We have also observed the coerciveness of treatment, with Xinjiang among the worst places in this respect. On the other hand, we doubt claims that prisoners used to be treated better in Siberian camps than they have been in China.[417] Certainly we know of no Chinese camp that has compared with Stalin's worst, Vorkuta, where the death

---

A. Rocca, pp. 101-104. Crime appears to have peaked in 1981 at 890,000 cases, a level that was not exceeded until 1989. Ibid, p. 315.

B. According to one Xinjiang prison official, "First of all, we treat the prisoners as human beings. We never mistreat them. Beating, scolding, and physical punishment are forbidden." Xu (see endnote 195), p. 26.

rate was about one percent per day, with about 45,000 men and women dying each year.[418] To be sure, many Chinese died during the great famine of the early 1960s, and the death rate of prisoners was almost certainly higher than the death rate of civilians. It has been a quarter of a century since such conditions existed. China's prisons are still far less humane than Western prisons, but are perhaps similar to those in countries at comparable levels of economic development. This is, however, a matter of degree, for a culture of violence is a common (though not universal) feature of prisons around the world. Although comparisons are irrelevant from a human rights point of view, presumably the prisons of northern Europe are relatively good, with the United States' prisons often having some problem with violence.[419] Prisons are particularly violent places in Turkey and India, which are comparable to most of China's, but are not as bad in this respect as those in Xinjiang and Tibet.

What of the future? It has been said that "The laogai will gain in strength because the government needs it, to increase production and keep totalitarian control."[420] We agree that it will probably grow, but not for these reasons. A modern national economy cannot be built on a foundation of forced labor. Furthermore, some political arrests, combined with other repressive measures, may be enough to enable the Communists to retain control. To paraphrase a Chinese aphorism, it is necessary to kill only a few chickens to scare all the monkeys. If the Communists cannot maintain control in this manner, a higher rate of political imprisonment will not help them.

No, the rate of imprisonment will rise from its present unexceptional figure because of China's ever increasing crime rate.[A] The complicated reasons for that phenomenon are beyond the scope of this book; suffice it to say that until a decade ago ordinary citizens were under such constraints, and poverty was so universal that people had little chance or motive to commit crime. That has all changed. Although the Chinese lack political liberty, they increasingly enjoy much social and economic

---

A. In 1996 serious crime was rising at the rate of 20 percent a year. *New York Times,* July 11, 1996, p. 1.

freedom, and with this comes increased opportunities and incentives to commit crime. It is with these "ghosts," new and yet so old, that China must now contend.

Appendix 1

Authors' Commentaries

Commentary A

The Laogai for Foreign Visitors since 1955: A Chronology

1955

The first regulation published on how to manage foreigners and overseas Chinese wishing to be informed about the prisons and prisoners in China (March 3). The regulation was signed by the Supreme Court, the Ministry of Public Security (Gongan Bu), and the Foreign Ministry.

1979

New Ministry of Public Security regulation ordered an increase in the number of laogai units that receive foreign visitors (April 4). *("Guanyu Zengjia duiwai kaifang laogai danwei de tongzhi.")*

A conference *(Laogai duiwai kaifang gongzuo zuotanhui)* was held between June 26 and July 2 in Jiangsu Province, at the Shezhu Laogai Farm. Responsible for this conference was the Eleventh Bureau of the Ministry of Public Security (which was in charge of the laogai at the time). A total of 59 persons participated in this conference. The fifteen provinces represented were: Beijing, Shanghai, Guangxi, Sichuan, Yunnan, Heilongjiang, Liaoning, Hebei, Shandong, Shaanxi, Jiangsu, Hubei,

Zhejiang, Jiangxi, and Guangdong. Presumably, these provinces were considered to have some comparatively good prisons which could be shown to foreigners. Altogether, by this time 20 prisons had been declared "open." Significantly, none of the provinces in China's far west (Gansu, Qinghai, Ningxia, Xinjiang, and Tibet) managed to be represented. Hunan was also excluded. During this conference the prisons from Beijing, Shanghai, Shenyang, and Shezhu Laogai Farm gave detailed briefings on how they handled foreign visitors.

As a result of the conference the Eleventh Bureau published a report entitled: "Report Concerning the Meeting on Laogai Units Open for Foreigners" *(Guanyu laogai danwei duiwai kaifang gongzuo tanhui de qingkuang baogao,* August 14). It outlined the way foreigners should be shown a prison. Topics included "Prepare yourself well before the prison is opened for foreigners," and "Do the propaganda work for foreigners well." These 1979 regulations remained in force until the new regulations of July 4, 1991, replaced them.

1982

An article by Hu Yaobang[421] published. This article recommended setting up a model prison in each province, where local cadres could be trained. This was after Hu had heard that some foreign visitors had been favorably impressed by a prison in Harbin which they had visited. While Hu Yaobang himself would maintain in public discussions or when meeting foreigners that the prisons in China were good, this internal article showed that he knew the reality: that in many provinces not a single prison was up to proper standards. Hu was determined to improve the situation.

1991

The new draft prison regulations internally circulated for comments and suggestions (early in year).

On April 5, another "Conference by Laogai Units Open for Foreign Visitors" was held, this time in Kunming *(Laogai danwei duiwai kaifang gongzuo huiyi)*. More than 90 participants from the now 33 units open for foreign visitors took part. Responsible for this conference was the Foreign Affairs Bureau of the Ministry of Justice. Leading cadres explained the new regulations to the leaders of the 33 units, and the units exchanged information on how to manage foreign visitors.

1991

Conference of all provincial Justice Department Foreign Handlers *(Sifa Wai Ban)* Bureaus. It was held in Luoyang, Henan province, from October 6 to 9.

1991-1994

More model prison construction. During these years some new prisons in locations convenient for foreign visitors were built. From the beginning they were planned to be "showcase" prisons. Some of the projects were well funded, such as:

Beijing: The Number Two Prison

Shanghai: The prison located in Qingpu Yemabin.

The new prisons built elsewhere received far less in the way of construction funds.

c. 1997

Various foreign dignitaries taken on tour of Chinese prisons, including Finnish Prison Administration Director-general K. J. Lang. Although acknowledging that he had not seen enough to enable him to evaluate the entire system, Lang lauded improvements that had been made in both China proper and Tibet. "What was most impressive in both places . . . was the amount of space reserved for living, for work and production, for education." His views were given much exposure in the international press.[422]

Commentary B

The World Bank and Harry Wu

At a time when the World Bank has been under some criticism,[423] its practices in northwest China have come under particular scrutiny.

The World Bank currently lends more money to China than to any other country. Approximately US$ 23 billion in loans have been granted or promised for 159 projects there.[424] About US$ 90 million (0.4%) went to the Xinjiang bingtuan. The Bank's largesse is controversial because some see it as helping to keep a repressive regime in power. In particular, the Bank has been accused of helping to sustain the "forced labor" system in the laogai camps.

The charges of World Bank wrongdoing come primarily from Harry Wu and his California-based Laogai Research Foundation. The Foundation's underlying allegations are (1) China has far more prisoners than it should, and (2) it is for political reasons that most inmates have been incarcerated. As we have shown in this volume, neither of these assertions withstand scrutiny. However, Wu must be taken seriously because he has been given a platform by the Senate Foreign Relations Committee, run by the ultra-conservative Jesse Helms.

The World Bank is an easy target for Wu and Helms, since it does indeed invest funds in places like Xinjiang. Wu has claimed that labor camps have been utilizing funds from World Bank's project on the edge of the Taklimakan Desert, which was begun in 1991.[425] Wu's foundation has stated that Bank projects have been "supporting cotton and grain production in at least 21 forced labor camps (laogai) as well as 30 special farms controlled by the People's Liberation Army" — an apparent reference to the bingtuan. Wu charges that the Bank "attempts to misrepresent the nature of the XPCC [bingtuan]," that its depiction as an essentially non-military institution is "wrong and a lie."[426]

For its part, the Bank has insisted that the projects were solely for the benefit of the local civilian population, which is predominately Uyghur. The Bank claims to have conducted its own investigation in Xinjiang, on the basis of which it concluded: "The Bank is satisfied that the Xinjiang State Farms Organization [apparently meaning the bingtuan] is implementing Bank projects without the use of forced labor. But, to avoid even the appearance of a link to forced labor, Xinjiang State Farms Organization will serve as an implementing agency for future projects only with a complete separation of its commercial and civilian activities from its other functions, specifically prison management."

Neither Wu nor the Bank win high marks for accuracy and candor. Many of Wu's claims are demonstrably false — such as that the laogai is "the Chinese equivalent of the Soviet Union's Gulag," and that bingtuan is "run by the People's Liberation Army."[427] But the Bank has further clouded the issue by issuing reports which are somewhat disingenuous and seem to reflect a poor understanding of how the bingtuan is comprised and operates. The Bank also understates the role of labor performance in

China's penal system and the role of the People's Liberation Army in Xinjiang, and overstates the role of China's judiciary in managing the bingtuan laogai. It refers to the bingtuan farms as "state farms," which, while this is technically correct, is misleading because they are so different from state farms as the term is almost always used. (See page 38, note A, and page 68, note A.)

While we have no proof, we deem it highly unlikely that no prison labor at all was involved in the World Bank's $125 million Tarim project (the Bank's denials to the contrary notwithstanding). We do have evidence of Bank funds providing the capital elsewhere — for Regiment 134 in the Eighth Division in the amount of RMB 200,000 in 1994 for a waterworks project.[428] As we show in the chart on page 69, the No. 134 Regiment now includes no fewer than three laogai squadrons. Thus, we find misleading the Bank's statement that "no evidence was found of any benefit, direct or indirect, to forced labor camps or military special farms." Indeed, it is virtually certain that they do benefit from these irrigation works. But this should be kept in perspective. Any funds which reach the bingtuan laogai could only be a microscopic percentage of the bingtuan's already minuscule 0.4 percent of the Bank's loans to China.

Furthermore, the issue of candor is quite a separate matter from the question of whether bank funds *should* support the laogai. We do not see this in such sinister terms as do the Bank's critics. Such funds do not exacerbate, and might even ameliorate, the harsh conditions under which prisoners live.

In mid-1996 the Bank appeared to be trying to wind down its involvement with the bingtuan. "We won't use the XPCC [bingtuan] in implementing projects until they separate the military and civilian sides."[429] But soon, either the Bank reconsidered the merits, or was satisfied about the "separation," for at year's end it approved a US$ 150 million loan for the second phase of the Tarim Basin project, which was designed to lift local people out of poverty and ensure better environmental protection.[430]

Appendix 2

Others' Commentaries

Commentary C

Some Proposals to the National People's Congress
Regarding the Prison Law[431]

December 28, 1994

This meeting [presumably of some NPC representatives concerned with the subject] considered the amended draft of the draft prison law on 22 and 23 December [1994]. The members of the Standing Committee felt that the views of the members of the Standing Committee and various quarters on the amended draft of the draft prison law had been rather fully solicited and that this meeting should pass it. They also proposed some views about its amendment. On 24 December, the Law Committee and the Internal Judicial Committee convened a meeting to study each of the articles and make the following amendments in light of the views of the members of the Standing Committee:

I. Article 15 [sic] of the amended draft of the draft provides: "People's Police responsible for prison management may not do any of the following: 1) demand, accept, and secretly seize the property of prisoners and their relatives; 2) extort confessions through torture and mistreat prisoners; 3) impugn the dignity of prisoners; 4) connive with others in beating prisoners; and 5) use prisoners to provide labor for personal profit." Some members of the committee suggested that in addition to the above, provisions should be included regarding conduct in serious violation of the law such as private release of prisoners, private transmittal of letters or things for prisoners, and dereliction of duty to permit others to discharge prison management authority, and that legal responsibility for violations of the above provisions should be clearly prescribed. Therefore, addition of the following provisions are recommended: "private release of prisoners or dereliction of duty leading to the escape of prisoners;" "illegally turning over prisoner supervision and management duties to others for discharge;" "violations of provisions, privately transmitting letters or things for prisoners;" and "other conduct in violation of the law." Another provision was added at the same time, namely: "People's Police in charge of prisons who commit any of the acts covered by the above provisions, thereby committing an offense, shall be held criminally liable according to law. Those found not to have committed a legal offense shall be administratively punished." (Revised draft of Article 14 of the draft law). *[Basically incorporated into Article 14.]*

II. Paragraph I of Article 16 [sic] of the revised draft of the draft law provides: "Prisoners whom a People's Court has sentenced to a two-year suspended death sentence, to life imprisonment, or to a fixed period of imprisonment shall be turned over to a prison within one month of the day that the sentence takes effect for administration of the punishment." The Supreme People's Court has noted that prisoners sentenced to a two-year suspended death sentence, to life imprisonment, or to a fixed period of imprisonment are currently turned over to prisons for punishment by the public security authorities. [If] the regulations provide that a people's court turn them over for punishment, the manpower and material resources of the people's courts would be burdened. Therefore, the following amendment is recommended: "People's courts shall issue written notification and a written judgment regarding prisoners who have been sentenced to a two-year suspended death sentence, to life imprisonment, or to a fixed term of imprisonment, to be sent to the public security agency having custody of the prisoner. Within one month following receipt of the sentencing notice and written judgment, the public security agency shall hand the prisoner over to the prison for punishment." (Revised draft of Paragraph 1, Article 15 of the draft law). *[This suggestion was basically incorporated into Article 15.]*

III. Some committee members noted that sentence reductions and parole for prisoners following sentencing were supposed to be handled strictly according to provisions of the law. Therefore, they recommended addition of the following provision: "Prisoners who do not meet provisions of the law for sentence reduction or parole shall not be granted a sentence reduction or parole for any reason." (Paragraph 1, Article 34 of the revised draft of the draft law). *[This suggestion was basically accepted.]*

IV. Article 44 of the amended draft of the draft law provides: "Upon discovery that a prisoner in custody has fled, the prison shall urgently pursue the fugitive. Should it be unable to capture the fugitive at once, it shall immediately inform the public security authorities, the public security authorities bearing responsibility for the fugitive's apprehension in close coordination with the prison." Some committee members noted the need to provide explicitly that when a prison is able to capture a prisoner whose escape it has discovered, it shall capture the fugitive at once. Should it be unable to capture the fugitive, the public security authorities should become responsible for the fugitive's apprehension. Therefore, it is recommended that this article be amended to read: "Upon discovery that a prisoner in custody has fled, the prison shall immediately recapture the fugitive. Should it be unable to capture the fugitive, it shall immediately notify the public security authorities, the public security authorities taking responsibility for apprehension in close coordination with the prison." (Article 42 of the revised amendment of the draft law). *[This suggestion was basically accepted.]*

In addition, various stylistic amendments were made to the revised amendment of the draft law.

Consideration of the above report is requested.

Commentary D

Report on the Work of the Inspectorate in 1995[432]

The following is from a March 1996 report by Inspector General Zhang Siqing concerning the work of the Inspectorate.

In supervising the trying of criminal cases, counter-appeal work was strengthened in light of problems such as light sentences for serious crimes, pronouncing criminals not guilty, and so on. Counter-appeals were lodged according to law for cases in which erroneous criminal decisions or rulings were made. In the entire year, 1,775 counter-appeals were lodged in accordance with appeal procedures, and 641 counter-appeals were lodged in accordance with judicial supervision procedures. Regarding the violation of law in judicial activities, 2,343 opinions for correction were put forward. Many local procuratorial organs strengthened counter-appeal work in light of problems in probation applicable to economic crimes such as corruption and bribery. The Supreme People's Procurate formulated the "Provisions on Reporting Counter-appeals for Cases to the Standing Committees of People's Congress of the Same Level" for procuratorial organs to conscientiously place themselves under supervision.

In the work of law and disciplinary inspection, cases of encroachment on citizens' democratic rights, crimes involving personal rights, and dereliction of duty were seriously investigated and dealt with. While focusing efforts on investigating and handling cases of favoritism and irregularities, also put on record for investigation were 412 cases of forcing confessions by torture; 4,672 cases of illegal custody; 1,739 cases of illegally searching residences, illegally entering residences, and illegally putting people under surveillance; 87 cases of hindering postal and telecommunications and encroaching upon citizens' freedom of communications; 4,234 cases of dereliction of duty; and 5,052 cases of major accidents due to negligence.

In prison procuratorial work, the Prison Law was rigorously implemented. We have been focusing on correcting [such problems as] the use of money to offset criminal punishments, illegal failure to punish criminals according to law, reducing criminal punishments, and releasing criminals on bail and medical parole. Subpoenas were issued for 4,468 criminals who committed new crimes during their probations. A total of 135,419 opinions on ways to correct law violations during surveillance and reform periods were put forward. Criminal cases involving policemen of prisons, houses of detention, and centers for reeducation through labor, of favoritism and irregularities, corruption, accepting bribes, corporal punishment, and torture, were investigated and responsibility was affixed according to law. By the end of 1995, essentially all of the country's prisons, houses of detention, and labor reeducation centers had inspectors assigned to them.

Commentary E

Decision of the United Nations Concerning China

The following is the official text of the conclusions and recommendations of the Committee against Torture (1996).[433]

China

1. The Committee considered the second periodic report of China (CAT/C/20/Add.5) at its 251st, 252nd and 254th meetings held on 3rd and 6th May 1996 (CAT/C/SR 251, 252 and 254) and has adopted the following conclusions and recommendations.

A. Introduction

2. The Committee welcomes the report of the Government of China as well as its core document (HRI/CORE/1/Add/21). The second periodic report of China dated 2nd December 1995 was due on 2nd November 1993 but since China had presented a supplementary report dated 8th October 1992, the timing of this report is quite satisfactory to the Committee.

3. The second periodic report of China follows the Committee's guidelines and meets them satisfactorily.

4. The Committee also thanks the representative of the State party for his most enlightening verbal introduction to the report and for the way in which he and the other members of the Chinese delegation responded so constructively to the questions asked.

B. Positive aspects

5. The reforms contained in the amendments to the Criminal Procedure Law, to take effect in 1997, are an important step towards developing the rule of law in China and towards that country being able to meet its obligations pursuant to the Convention against Torture and Other Cruel, Inhuman or Degrading Treatment or Punishment.

6. There are instances reported of police officials being prosecuted and convicted for acts of torture in China including Tibet.

7. The various steps taken by the Ministry of Public Security pursuant to its notice of January 1992, so as to educate personnel on the prohibition of torture, are noted with satisfaction.

8. The provision of effective administrative and criminal compensation to victims of abuse is a most welcome development.

9. The Committee notes with pleasure the affirmation of the representative of China that "heads of cells and trusties" in prisons, as alleged by some non-governmental organizations, do not exist in China.

C. Factors and difficulties impeding the application of the provisions of the Convention

10. The Committee acknowledges the sheer size of the task confronting China in policing and administrating a huge land mass with 1.2 billion people at a time of economic and social reconstruction.

D. Subjects of concern

11. The Committee is concerned that according to information supplied by non-governmental organizations torture may be practiced on a widespread basis in China.

12. The Committee is concerned also about the following:

a) The failure to incorporate the crime of torture into the domestic legal system, in terms consistent with the definition contained in article 1 of the Convention;

b) the claims drawn to the attention of the Committee by non-governmental organizations that torture occurs in China in police stations and prisons in circumstances that very often do not result in investigation and proper resolution by the authorities;

c) the claims made by some non-governmental organizations that the Procuratorate has yet to establish its authority over the police, security and prison services when dealing with allegations of torture and cruel, inhuman or degrading treatment or punishment;

d) the fact that some methods of capital punishment may be in breach of article 16 of the Convention;

e) the claims made by non-governmental organizations that the special environment that exists in Tibet continues to create conditions that result in alleged maltreatment and even death of persons held in police custody and prisons;

f) the failure to provide access to legal counsel to persons at the earliest time of their contact with the authorities. Allegations made by some non-governmental organizations that incommunicado detention is still prevalent in China;

g) the important number of deaths reported to the Committee, apparently arising out of police custody.

E. Recommendations

18. The Committee recommends to the State party the following:

a) China should enact a law defining the crime of torture in terms consistent with article 1 of the Convention;

b) a comprehensive system should be established to review, investigate and effectively deal with complaints of maltreatment, by those in custody of every sort. If the Procuratorate is the body which carries out the investigations, it should be given the necessary jurisdiction to carry out its functions, even over the objections of the organ that it is investigating;

c) the methods of execution of prisoners sentenced to death should be brought into conformity with article 16 of the Convention;

d) conditions in prisons should be brought into conformity with article 16 of the Convention;

e) access to legal counsel should be granted to all those detained, arrested or imprisoned as a matter of right and at the earliest stage of the process. Access to the family and to a medical doctor should also be accommodated;

f) China should consider cooperating with the Rehabilitation Center for Torture Victims in setting up a Torture Victims' Rehabilitation Center in Beijing or some other large centers of the country;

g) China should continue with its most welcome reforms to its criminal penal law, and continue to train its law enforcement personnel, procurators, judges and medical doctors to become professionals of the highest standing;

h) China is invited to consider withdrawing its reservations to article 20 and declaring in favor of articles 21 and 22 of the Convention;

i) An independent judiciary, as defined in international instruments, is so important for ensuring the objectives of the Convention against Torture, that the Committee recommends that appropriate measures be taken to ensure the autonomy/independence of the judiciary in China.

Appendix 3

Laogai Regulations

List of Laws Governing Labor Reform in China

Listed in approximate chronological order.
Texts of those in **bold print** *appear below.*

"Interim Provisions for Dealing with Resettling Released Prisoners and *Jiuye* Cases." Approved by the State Council, August 26, 1954. Summarized above, p. 191.

"Labor Reform Provisions of the PRC" *(Laodong gaizao tiaoli)*. Approved by the State Council on August 26, 1954; promulgated on September 7, 1954.[434]

"Temporary Disciplinary Methods for the Release of Criminals Completing Their Terms and for the Implementation of Forced Job Placement." Approved by the Government Administrative Council, August 29, 1954; promulgated September 7, 1954.

"PRC Laogai Regulations" (1956). Described p. 96, especially footnote A.

"Reeducation Through Labor Policies." Promulgated by the State Council, August 3, 1957.[435]

"Supplementary Labor Reeducation Regulations," as amended on November 29, 1979.[436]

"Rules for Prisoners" *(Fanren shouze)*. February 18, 1982. Described above, p. 27, footnote A.

"Detailed Regulations on Prison and Labor Brigade Control and Education Work" (1982). Ministry of Public Security.

"Certain Ministry of Justice Regulations Concerning the Work of Prison Control and Reform" *(Sifa Bu guanyu jiaqiang jianguan gaizao gongzuo die ruogan guiding)*. September 19, 1989. Cited endnote 53.

"Regulations of the People's Republic of China Governing Detention Houses" (March 1990).[437]

"Regulations Guiding the Management of the Reform Environment in Prisons." (1990, no. 11.) Excerpted beginning p. 250.

"Regulations Concerning the Behavior of Criminals Undergoing Reform" (1990, No. 12). Text begins p. 241.

"Behavioral Standards for Labor Reform and Labor Reeducation Cadres" [September 10, 1991; Ministry of Justice, no. 17], *BLGT,* 1992, no. 1, pp. 5-6.

"Regulations Concerning Treatment of Foreign Visitors to Labor Reform Units" (1991). Text begins p. 247.

"Prison Law of the People's Republic of China," December 29, 1994. Text begins p. 252.

"Suggestions Concerning Strengthening Resettlement and Training Work for Released Labor Reform and Labor Reeducation Prisoners" (1995). Zhongyang Zong Zhi Wei (General Political Committee of the Party), and signed by six ministries.

Law of Criminal Procedure (revised 1996).[438]

The Code of Criminal Law. The 1979 version is most relevant to this book. However, as we go to press, a new 1997 version has just been adopted by the National People's Congress.[439]

Regulations Concerning the Behavior of Criminals Undergoing Reform

(November 1990)[440]

Chapter One: Basic Rules

1. Strictly observe national laws and regulations and all sets of prison rules enacted by prison administrations and the labor reform organs, and submit to supervision and education.

2. While serving your term, heed the "ten forbiddens":

i. It is forbidden to oppose the four basic principles and to create or spread political rumors;

ii. It is forbidden to resist supervision and education, to evade reform, to malinger, to injure or maim oneself;

iii. It is forbidden to go beyond security lines or the designated sphere of activities, or to leave the small mutual supervision group and engage in unauthorized actions;

iv. It is forbidden to employ such tactics as [giving] food and drink, talking in a chummy fashion or advocating local ideas as a way of claiming kinship and cementing friendship in order to get help from people or to create contention through gossip;

v. It is forbidden to quarrel or fight, for a crowd to gather and create havoc, to practice martial arts, to manufacture weapons, to tattoo, or to gamble;

vi. It is forbidden to pass on criminal methods, to incite others to commit crimes, to read or pass on reactionary or obscene books and magazines, and to engage in activities related to feudal superstitions;

vii. It is forbidden to conceal money, grain coupons, plain clothes, inflammable or explosive materials, poisons or ropes, clubs or knives, and, unless permission has been given, to wear insulated clothing, shoes, boots or gloves;

viii. It is forbidden to have communication privately with people in the outside world, to seek or exchange money or goods, and to seek out a person to whom to entrust a letter or a message;

ix. It is forbidden to bully the weak and to beat, curse, humiliate, blackmail or frame other prisoners;

x. It is forbidden to disrupt production, to conduct go-slows, and to steal or damage public or private goods.

3. Cherish state property, preserve public facilities, behave in a civilized and polite manner, and respect society's public morals.

4. Increase organization and discipline in participating in collective activities. In special circumstances, obey the instructions of the corrections personnel, maintain good order, and do not follow your own inclinations.

5. When lining up and walking in line, obey oral instructions, maintain the correct form of the line, shout slogans, and sing songs loudly and clearly.

Chapter Two: Rules for Daily Life

6. When the order to arise is heard, get out of bed speedily and tidy up, arrange the bedding in piles with the edges and corners clearly lined up according to the standards on size and height, and arrange it neatly in a uniform manner.

7. Proceed to the bathroom to wash in an orderly fashion, without pushing or shoving.

8. Have meals in an orderly fashion at the designated time, place, and using the proper method. It is forbidden to bang utensils or to play and make a racket.

9. It is forbidden to join together in eating or drinking, or to exchange foodstuffs. It is forbidden to waste grain foods or to throw out excess soup or rice.

10. It is forbidden to set up small cooking stoves or to eat or hoard more than one's share of the collective foodstuffs. It is forbidden to drink alcohol or to smoke in violation of the regulations.

11. During times for rest on festivals, holidays or days off work (or study), pursue healthful and beneficial activities within the permitted scope.

12. When the order to prepare for sleep is heard, speedily sit or stand upright in your designated place and wait for your name to be called. It is not permitted to make a hubbub, to whisper or to move.

13. Before going to bed, make sure you take the time to use the toilet. Wash and prepare your bedding. Place the clothes you take off neatly beside your pillow and arrange shoes in a line below the bed.

14. When the order to go to sleep is heard, immediately lie down in the designated direction. It is not permitted to exchange places without authorization or to sleep with one's head covered. It is forbidden to read or write or to disturb the sleep of others.

15. Report any illness to the corrections personnel and go with them or the designated person to the hospital (or clinic) for treatment.

16. While in the process of having a medical consultation, observe discipline, state clearly the nature of the illness, obey the doctor's decision on how to manage it, and do not make an unreasonable fuss. It is not permitted to ask for specific medicine or to seek a certificate mandating rest.

17. Sick prisoners must actively pursue methods which will cure them, follow the doctor's orders, and take their medicine at the proper time. Those being treated in isolation are not permitted to go outside the designated area. Those who have been given permission to rest should do so at the designated place.

18. Do a good job in personal hygiene and wash and change clothing and bedding frequently so as to maintain cleanliness.

19. Pay attention to hygiene in eating and drinking. Do not eat or drink to excess. Do not drink cold or dirty water and do not eat food which has gone bad. Keep eating utensils undamaged and clean.

20. Prisoners assigned to kitchen work must pay attention to their personal hygiene, must wear their work clothes while working, have physical examinations at the proper intervals, and are strictly forbidden to bring illness into the kitchens.

21. Apart from those prisoners who are due to leave the prison within the month, everyone must wear very short hair or shaved heads. It is not permitted to grow beards or whiskers or long fingernails. Apart from prisoners belonging to ethnic minorities who have special living habits, female prisoners must all wear short hair at ear length, not covering the neck, and are not permitted to have perms, dye their hair, wear wigs, paint their nails, wear lipstick or jewelry, and so on.

22. Clean both inside and outside the room on schedule and keep the surroundings neat and tidy. The decorations of the room should be harmonious and moderate, the door and windows clean, and the washing implements should be arranged in an orderly way.

23. It is forbidden to expectorate or to relieve oneself on the ground. It is not permitted to throw down dirty things, garbage, fruit peels, scraps of paper, or to damage or trample on flowers and trees.

24. Everyone must wear the convict's uniform, with the same designation on it. It is forbidden for individuals to alter the form, the color or the designation on the convict's uniform. In the summer, within the room, it is permitted to wear a singlet or t-shirt provided the designation on it is clear.

25. While working, the appropriate clothing must be worn, with the designation on it.

26. Designations such as "person on duty" issued by the prison or labor reform organs are to be worn in the proper position. It is forbidden to lend, alter, or damage them.

27. It is forbidden to conceal or replace clothing. Clothing which is not permitted or which is temporarily not being worn should be handed over to the corrections personnel for general storage.

28. In receiving and sending letters, receiving funds, or getting parcels or other mail, accept the examination of them according to the regulations. Secrets of the prison administration or labor reform unit should not be disclosed in letters; neither should they disseminate words which will hinder reform.

29. When receiving visits from family members, relatives or friends, it is forbidden to use enigmatic language or to secretly pass over letters, money, and other such items.

30. Listen to the radio and watch television at the times when this is permitted. When listening and watching, sit still and upright. It is forbidden to engage in other activities at this time. It is forbidden to chat or move around, to turn the system on or off, or to choose the channel without authorization.

31. When more than three prisoners are walking along together, they should arrange themselves in a line or keep to the right hand side. They may not go arm in arm, shoulder to shoulder, hold hands, or walk abreast.

Chapter Three: Rules for Production and Labor

32. All prisoners who are able to work must participate in the labor to which they are assigned. Those who cannot work because they are sick should get a certificate of examination from a doctor as well as the approval of a cadre.

33. When the order to go to work is heard, line up at the designated place at the proper time, and in the prearranged order, and wait for names to be called. Give full attention to reporting numbers in a loud and clear voice accurately, and without error.

34. While engaged in production labor, keep to work stations and observe discipline. It is forbidden to move or run around, to make a racket, to joke or create a commotion, or to sleep. It is forbidden to do private work.

35. Diligently study the operating technology, strictly observe the operating rules for tools, do not break the rules for your task, pay attention to production safety and guarantee the quality of the products. Actively develop innovations in technology, work hard to increase productivity, complete production quotas or planned tasks while ensuring quality and quantity. The output of waste or poor quality products may not exceed the level stated in the regulations.

36. Cherish the equipment, tools, and mechanical tools. Strictly enforce thrift and put an end to all loss and waste.

37. Do not damage crops, flowers, fruit trees, or other farm crops or sideline products. Cherish farming implements, the cultivated fields, irrigation works, and other installations in the fields.

38. Do a good job of civilized production. Keep the factory clean and tidy both inside and out. The set management rules of each workshop must be observed and each type of tool and part must be arranged in an orderly fashion.

39. When the order to stop work is heard, quickly clean, put in order, and protect the machines, equipment, and other production tools. Clean the site. If requested to do so, at the proper time hand things over to the next shift.

40. At the command of the cadre escorting the team, form a line at the designated place and return together to the prison dormitory. It is forbidden to take any kind of tool, dangerous goods, or banned articles back to the prison dormitory.

Chapter Four: Rules for Study

41. Actively participate in political study, consciously read the relevant political books and periodicals, connect closely with reality, bravely admit your crime, and repent for it and speed up the reform of your thinking.

42. Participate in political, cultural, and technological study at the scheduled time. Observe discipline in the classroom; pay attention to listening to what is being said; and diligently make notes. If you wish to ask a question, raise your hand to show this, and when given permission, stand up and ask it. Stand up when replying to the teacher's questions. After class, revise diligently, and complete homework at the scheduled time. Observe discipline during examinations and strive for excellent grades.

43. Work hard to study production technology; intensively study scientific knowledge; become skilled through mastering the technical ability required for work stations; and strive to become capable in using production technology.

44. Actively participate in professional technological training and strive to achieve expertise in one area in order to make proper preparations for finding employment, earning a living, and participating in the construction of the "Four Modernizations" when you get out of prison.

45. Sit still and straight when in class. It is forbidden to remove shoes, sit with legs crossed, or to go bare-chested or barefoot. In the winter is it is forbidden to wear a gauze mask.

46. Respect teachers. Stand up and present greetings at the beginning and the end of the class. If entering or leaving the classroom at the same time as the teacher, let the teacher go first.

47. Conscientiously cherish the desks, chairs, and educational tools in the classroom. It is forbidden to carve or draw on them.

Chapter Five: Rules for Civility and Politeness

48. Speak moderately and carry yourself in a civilized manner. Tell the truth and what is real. Do no use coarse or dirty language. Vulgar or obscene actions are not permitted, and homosexual love is strictly banned.

49. When requesting something from someone, use respectful words such as "please" and "you" [polite form]; when expressing regret to someone, use apologetic words such as "sorry" and "please forgive me;" when helping someone, use modest words such as "it's nothing" and *"bie keqi* [don't be polite]." When someone helps you, use grateful words such as "thank you" [polite form] and "sorry to have troubled you."

50. Prisoners should all call each other by their proper names and should not make up names for each other or use nicknames. It is forbidden to call each other brothers or to use appellations of neighbors, relatives, friends, family or clan used in society before entering the prison.

51. Respect state personnel. Personnel who hold positions of leadership should be called by the name of their positions, while personnel whose positions are not clear should be called "team leaders." Workers who participate directly in production should be called "master." When people come from outside to carry out inspections, respond to their questions politely, do not contradict them or get into arguments, or create a commotion for no reason.

52. When corrections personnel enter or leave the prison dormitory, automatically stand up and do not lie or sit down (sick people excepted).

53. When the call of corrections personnel is heard, immediately respond "I'm coming." Quickly go over and stand two meters from them and await their orders. When corrections personnel ask a question, stand at attention while responding (special circumstances, such as being in the middle of operating machinery and being unable to leave it, are exceptions). When the corrections personnel have given their orders, immediately reply "yes." While the corrections personnel are speaking, it is forbidden to interrupt as you wish. When speaking to or replying to corrections personnel, it is forbidden to make indiscreet remarks or criticisms.

54. When you have something you need to tell to the office of the corrections personnel, call out "wish to report" and enter after permission is given. If you have something you must tell the personnel on duty when out in the field, or at the work site, stop five meters distant from them and report.

55. When walking in the same direction as corrections personnel, do not walk shoulder to shoulder with them. If you meet on a relatively narrow path, automatically stop, stand to the side, and let them pass. Put down the tools you are holding in your hands and wait until the corrections personnel have gone five meters beyond you before proceeding.

56. If you encounter guests who have come to look, or leading cadres above the branch level who have come to inspect the prison dormitories, you should halt all activities and stand in attendance. If the guests or leaders ask questions, stand at attention and reply according to the facts. While inspections are going on, it is forbidden to tail after them, to stand around and look, or make remarks about their appearances. If you have not been granted permission, you should not approach them or speak to them unauthorized.

Chapter Six: Supplementary Articles

57. These regulations must be observed as the norm for the words and deeds of prisoners undergoing reform. They are a reflection of the basic content of the prisoner's expression of reform. They are a basic condition for carrying out appraisal, and a basis for determining the issuance of rewards and punishments, and all prisoners must strictly observe them. You must put them into effect.

58. These regulations are in force from the day they are issued.

Regulations Concerning Treatment of Foreign Visitors to Labor Reform Units

Notification from the Ministry of Justice, July 4, 1991.[441]

1. The following regulations are made in accordance with regulations governing external exchanges, for the purpose of promoting friendly exchanges with the outside world, publicizing the achievement building the socialist legal system and the work of supervision and control, and strengthening the exchanges in the fields of judicial circles penal [officers] between China and foreign countries (regions), to help foreign friends and compatriots from Taiwan, Hong Kong, and

Macao and overseas Chinese understand the work of supervision, control, and reform.

2. Before receiving foreign guests, labor reform units need to meet the following conditions: (A) The situation with regard to the supervision, control, and reform must be fairly stable and have a solid foundation. There has also to exist institutionalized management over the supervision, control and reform environment, and over the reform of criminal behavior. There must also be excellent special schools [administered at or] above the provincial level. (B) Leaders and the entire force of cadres must have fairly strong political and professional quality. (C) The internal arrangements must be fairly rational, the environment tidy, beautiful and green [i.e. with trees, etc., having been planted], and living conditions of inmates reasonably good. (D) There should have been steady economic activity [i.e. no major recent changes that would have to be explained to guests], with production proceeding in an orderly fashion, and quality output. (E) The prison must be located in medium and large size cities that are open to foreigners.

3. The labor reform units receiving foreigners must apply for approval from the province-level bureau of justice. With few exceptions, each province-level jurisdiction should have one or two such units. No labor reform units can receive foreigners without approval. Those units which have received foreign guests before the enactment of this regulation should apply for approval in accordance with this new regulation.

4. The Ministry of Justice can suspend the approval in one of the following three situations, and ask the units to make reforms. If no improvements are made, then the certification of these units is to be revoked: (A) The prison is poorly organized. (B) There is a lot of crime in the prison. (C) There have been other major incidents.

5. Foreign guests referred to above, who are to be received by labor reform units, include the following people: Taiwan, Hong Kong, and Macao compatriots, and overseas Chinese: (A) Legal workers, experts, and scholars; and friendly personages from other academic fields. (B) Foreign government delegations, internationally well-known personages, and members of the press, who are the guests of the Ministry of Justice and the department of justice at the provincial level, or the department of external relations at the same level. (C) Personages who have been recommended by political, legal, or foreign affairs departments [at or] above the local bureau level.

6. Laogai units cannot receive foreign guests without approval, and should obtain authorization from the following departments as appropriate. (A) Approval from the Ministry of Justice is required if a ministerial-level delegation is involved. (B) If it is a delegation [at or] below the *ting* level, the approval should come from the provincial laogai bureau or department of justice, and the arrangements should be made by the laogai bureau. The unit organizing the visit should provide the laogai unit with the resumés of the visitors, and with [more detailed] information on the head and main members of the delegation.

7. Those laogai units that wish to receive foreign guests should have materials about their own prison in both Chinese and English. They should also prepare a 20-minute video tape about reform work in their prison for foreign guests to see. Where conditions permit, they should also have a display room showing the history and achievements of their prison.

All these above-mentioned materials and video tape need to be approved by the laogai bureau of the Ministry of Justice. Display objects must be approved by the laogai bureau at the provincial level.

8. There should be an ad hoc reception committee at the laogai unit which expects to receive foreign guests. The warden, commissioner, director of general office, director of reform, and director of education are to meet with foreigners, depending on the level/status of the foreigners. When foreign guests are very senior, leaders from the department of justice or bureau of labor reform may accompany foreign guests. When there are important foreign guests, the local propaganda department should be notified so that they can send reporters.

9. Those people involved with reception should have a basic understanding of relevant policies governing external affairs, and should have some knowledge of world affairs. While receiving foreign visitors, they should be neatly dressed, pay attention to their appearance and etiquette/protocol *(lijie)*. They should be neither arrogant nor excessively humble *(bu bei bu kang)*.

Briefers should observe China's regulations concerning secrecy.

10. There should be an ad hoc security committee. This committee is to be responsible for the safety and security during the visit to the prison by foreign guests.

11. There should be a designated route for the visit, and measures to be taken to temporarily remove prisoners who might hamper the visit, i.e., those who have mental disorders, who might escape, or who may act violently.

12. Visitors may not take photographs, audio or video recordings without prior authorization.

13. With the permission from people on the reception committee, foreign visitors may talk with the inmates, but these inmates should first receive the necessary education.

14. Unless the visitors are the guests of the Ministry of Justice, laogai units that receive foreign guests can charge the unit that sponsors the group a fee of RMB 15 per visitor. The foreigners should not be charged directly. If foreign guests need to have meals at the laogai unit, this unit should make appropriate arrangements in accordance with reception requirements. The sponsoring organization should be billed for the expenses involved.

15. Gifts from foreign guests may be accepted. These gifts should be handled in accordance with relevant state regulations. Small gifts can be accepted by individuals, while expensive ones should be turned over to the public. These laogai units can also give foreign guests souvenirs to return with. Other than these, foreign guests should not take away anything from the laogai unit.

16. For each visit by foreign guests, the laogai unit should file a report to the bureau of justice at the provincial level, to the laogai bureau, [a copy of] which will also be forwarded to the Department of Labor Reform under the Ministry of Justice. At the end of each year, the Bureau of Labor Reform should make a summary report about foreign visits, and send these reports to Department of Labor Reform and the Department of Foreign Affairs under the Ministry of Justice. Matters of major of importance should be reported on a timely basis.

17. These regulations come into effect on the date of promulgation.

Regulations Guiding the Management of the Reform Environment in Prisons

1990 (Excerpts)[442]

Article 16: Confinement cells should be set up inside or outside the living compound of prisoners according to actual needs. The usable floor area of each cell cannot be less than three square meters, the internal height should be not lower than three meters, while the windows should not be smaller than 0.8 square meters; protective equipment should be installed on doors, windows, and lights; measures should be taken to ensure that prisoners' beds are waterproof and can provide warmth; such cells should be well ventilated and brightly lit, and frequently disinfected; areas should be assigned outside the cells to let prisoners out for exercise or to relieve themselves. If conditions permit, televised supervision and control equipment should be installed.

Article 17: Visiting rooms should have both front and back doors, which are respectively linked to roads outside the prison and the confinement area to enable prisoners' families and prisoners to each go their respective ways. There should be propaganda boards inside the visiting room. In order to impose different levels of management on prisoners, strict, conventional, and preferential visiting equipment can be installed. . . .

Article 41: Prisoners are required to take an active part in political study, conscientiously read relevant political books and magazines, closely integrate theory with practice, have the courage to admit and repent their guilt, and speed up their ideological transformation.

Article 42: Prisoners are required to attend political, cultural, and vocational studies on time; observe classroom disciplines; and conscientiously listen to teachers and take down notes. When they have any questions, prisoners are required to raise their hands; after obtaining permission they should stand up and ask questions. They should also stand up when they answer their teachers' questions. After class, they should conscientiously review what they have learned in class and complete their homework at the assigned time. They should also observe examination discipline and strive to achieve outstanding results.

Article 43: Prisoners are required to vigorously learn and master production techniques, endeavor to gain vocational proficiency, skillfully master the production techniques of their own work posts, and strive to become top-notch in production.

Article 44. Prisoners are required to take part in professional and vocational training, try their best to gain proficiency in a particular line of work, and make good preparation for seeking employment and for taking part in the construction of the four modernizations after their release.

Prison Law of the People's Republic of China

(1994)[443]

Passed by the National People's Congress Standing Committee.

Chapter I. General Provisions

Article 1. This law has been enacted in compliance with the constitution for the correct enforcement of punishments, to punish and remold prisoners, and to prevent and reduce crime.

Article 2. Prisons are state organs where punishment is carried out.

Prisoners sentenced to two-year suspended death sentences, life imprisonment, and imprisonment for a fixed period in accordance with provisions of criminal law and the criminal procedure code are punished in prisons.

Article 3. Prisons practice the principle of combining prisoner punishment and remolding and combining prisoner education and labor to transform prisoners into law-abiding citizens.

Article 4. Prisons shall supervise and control prisoners according to law, organize prisoners to take part in productive labor as the remolding of prisoners requires, and carry out the ideological, cultural, and technical education of prisoners.

Article 5. Prison people's police manage prisons according to law, mete out punishment, and conduct activities such as educational remolding under protection of the law.

Article 6. The people's procuratorate exercises supervision according to law over the legality of prison activities in carrying out punishment.

Article 7. Prisoners may not be humiliated, and their personal safety, legal property, and right to a defense, to appeal, to complain, to file reports, and other rights that have not been deprived or limited according to law may not be infringed.

Prisoners must strictly abide by the law and rules and regulations, observe discipline, submit to control, accept education, and take part in labor.

Article 8. The state ensures the funds that prisons need for the remolding of prisoners. Prison people's police expenses, prisoners' remolding expenses, prisoners' living expenses, funds needed for the operation of prison facilities, and other earmarked funds are included in the national budget.

The state provides the production facilities and production expenses needed for prisoner labor.

Article 9. The land, mineral resources, and other natural resources that prisons use according to law, as well as the property of prisons, are protected by law. No organization or individual may confiscate or damage them.

Article 10. State Council judicial administration organs are in charge of prison work nationwide.

Chapter II. Prisons

Article 11. The establishment, disposal, and movement of prisons is approved by the State Council's judicial administration authorities.

Article 12. A prison shall have a warden and several deputy wardens; it shall also set up the number of work organizations actually needed and provide other prison management personnel.

The management personnel in prisons are the people's police.

Article 13. Prison people's police shall strictly abide by the constitution and the law, be faithful in the performance of their duties, enforce the law impartially, observe strict discipline, and be incorruptible and honest.

Article 14. Prison people's police may not do any of the following:

1) Demand, accept, or infringe the property of prisoners and their relatives.
2) Release prisoners without authorization or commit derelictions of duty that result in the escape of prisoners.
3) Extort confessions by torture or corporal punishment and mistreatment of prisoners.
4) Humiliate prisoners.
5) Beat or abet others in the beating of prisoners.
6) Use prisoners to provide labor for personal profit.
7) Privately transmit letters or things for prisoners in violation of regulations.
8) Illegally turn over to others the supervision and control of prisoners.
9) Other behavior in violation of the law.

Prison people's police who commit an offense by performing any of the acts cited above shall be held criminally liable according to law. Those not found to have committed a legal offense shall be administratively punished.

Chapter III. Enforcement of Punishments

Section 1. Imprisonment

Article 15. People's courts shall send enforcement notice and written verdicts on prisoners sentenced to two-year suspended death sentences, life imprisonment, and fixed periods of imprisonment to the public security authorities having custody over the prisoners. Within one month following receipt of the enforcement notice and written verdict, the public security authorities shall deliver the offender to prison for punishment.

When an offender has less than one year of his or her sentence remaining in advance of the turnover, the place of detention shall administer the sentence.

Article 16. At the time that an offender is turned over for imposition of punishment, the people's court in charge of the turnover shall send to the prison a copy of the people's procuratorate indictment and the people's court verdict, enforcement notice, and case conclusion registration form. The prison may not accept an offender for imprisonment unless it receives these documents. Should the above documents not be completely in order or contain mistakes, the people's court that issued the verdict shall put them in order or correct them at once. Should any irregularities in the documents possibly lead to wrongful imprisonment, imprisonment shall not occur.

Article 17. Prisons shall perform physical examinations of prisoners turned over to them for punishment. Should physical examination find any of the following in prisoners sentenced to life imprisonment or to fixed prison terms, they may be excused temporarily from imprisonment:

1) a serious illness that requires release on bail for medical treatment;

2) pregnancy, or nursing of one's own infant.

The people's court that committed prisoners who are excused from imprisonment under the preceding provisions shall decide the temporary sentence to be served outside prison. When the temporary serving of a sentence outside prison constitutes a public danger, prisoners shall be imprisoned. Prisoners temporarily serving a sentence outside a prison will have their punishment administered by the public security authorities in the area of their residence. With the lapse of the circumstances in the preceding provisions that have temporarily precluded imprisonment, the public security authorities will turn the prisoners over to a prison to complete their unfinished sentences.

Article 18. At the time of imprisonment, a rigorous examination will be made of the offender's person and articles carried. All articles not needed in daily life will be placed in custody of the prison or returned to the offender's family after obtaining the offender's approval. Contraband will be confiscated.

Female prisoners will be examined by female people's police.

Article 19. Prisoners may not take children into prison to serve sentences with them.

Article 20. Following imprisonment, the prison will notify the prisoner's family, notification to be issued within five days of the day of imprisonment.

Section 2. Handling of prisoner appeals, complaints, and accusations

Article 21. A prisoner may appeal a sentence with which he or she does not agree. A people's procuratorate or a people's court will handle a prisoner's appeal expeditiously.

Article 22. Prisons will promptly turn over to the public authorities or a people's procuratorate the data that a prisoner has provided in connection with a complaint or an accusation. The public security authorities or procuratorate will notify the prison of their disposal.

Article 23. The prison will promptly transmit appeal, complaint, and accusation data. It may not hold them.

Article 24. In the course of carrying out punishment, should the prison deem, on the basis of a prisoner's appeal, that a mistake might have been made in the verdict, it will request a hearing by a people's procuratorate or a people's court. Within six months of receipt of a prison's statement requesting a hearing, the people's procuratorate or the people's court will notify the prison of its disposition.

Section 3. Serving sentences outside prison

Article 25. Prisoners sentenced to life imprisonment or imprisonment for a fixed number of years who are serving sentences in prison may temporarily serve their sentences outside prison provided they meet conditions for serving sentences outside prison prescribed in the penal code.

Article 26. Temporary serving of a sentence outside prison requires that a prison file a written statement for forwarding to provincial, autonomous region, or directly administered municipality prison control authorities for approval. The approving authorities will notify the public security authorities and the people's court that rendered the original sentence of its decision to approve temporary serving of sentence outside a prison and forward a copy to the people's procuratorate.

When the people's procuratorate deems a prisoner's temporary serving of a sentence outside a prison inappropriate, within one month of the date of receipt of the notice it will provide a written statement to the authorities approving temporary serving of sentence outside a prison. Following receipt of the people's procuratorate's written statement, the authorities who approved temporary serving of sentence outside prison will immediately review their decision.

Article 27. Prisoners temporarily serving a sentence outside of prison will be supervised by the local public security authorities. The prison of original custody will promptly report to the public authorities responsible for supervising the status of the prisoner's remolding in prison.

Article 28. Once the circumstances occasioning temporary serving of a sentence outside prison no longer exist, the public security authorities responsible for enforcing the sentence will immediately notify the prison to imprison the prisoner whose sentence has not been completed. The original prison that had custody will complete release procedures for prisoners whose sentences are complete. Should a prisoner die during the period that a sentence outside prison is being served, the public security authorities will immediately notify the original prison having custody.

Section 4. Sentence reductions and commutations, parole and probation

Article 29. Prisoners sentenced to life in prison or a fixed term of imprisonment who truly show repentance or perform meritorious deeds during the period of their sentence may be granted a reduction or commutation of sentence based on the results of a prison review. Prisoners who perform any of the following meritorious deeds will have their sentences reduced or commuted:

1) prevent another from committing a major crime;
2) report to the authorities the commission of a major crime inside or outside prison that investigation verifies;
3) invent, create, or make a major technical innovation;
4) risk their own life to save the life of another in the course of day-to-day production or daily life;
5) render outstanding performance in fighting a natural disaster or clearing away a major accident;
6) make a major contribution to the country and society.

Article 30. Recommendations for reduction or commutation of sentence will be made by the prison to a people's court. Within one month following receipt of the sentence reduction or commutation recommendation, the people's court will examine it and make a ruling. When a case is complex or the circumstances special, the period may be extended one month. A copy of a sentence reduction or commutation ruling will be sent to the people's procuratorate.

Article 31. When the two-year suspension period has ended for prisoners sentenced to a two-year suspended death sentence who meet conditions set by law during the period of suspension of their death sentence for a reduction of their sentence to life imprisonment or a fixed period of time in prison, the prison in which they are located will immediately recommend sentence reduction, filing the recommendation with the provincial, autonomous regional, or directly administered municipal prison control authorities for examination and approval after which a ruling from the Supreme People's Court will be requested.

Article 32. Prisons will file recommendation for parole or probation with a people's court on the basis of assessment results for prisoners sentenced to life in prison or fixed number of years in prison who meet legal requirements for parole or probation. The people's court will examine and issue a ruling on the recommendation within one month of the receipt of the parole or probation recommendation. When a case is complex or circumstances are special, a month's extension is permitted. A copy of the parole or probation ruling will be sent to the people's procuratorate.

Article 33. When a people's court issues a ruling granting probation or parole, the prison will grant parole probation at the appointed time, and issue a parole probation certificate.

Prisoners on parole or probation will be supervised by the public security authorities. Should the prisoner violate the law, administrative rules and regulations, and State Council public security agency supervisory and control regulations pertaining to parole or probation during the period of their parole or probation, even in the absence of any new offense, public security authorities may recommend recision of their parole or probation to a people's court. Within one month following receipt of a parole or probation recision recommendation, the people's court will examine it and issue a ruling. When a people's court makes a ruling to rescind parole or probation, the public security authorities will turn the prisoner over to a prison for imprisonment.

Article 34. Under no circumstances may a prisoner who is not entitled to reduction or commutation of sentence parole or probation according to provisions of the law be granted a reduction or commutation of sentence or parole or probation.

Should the people's procuratorate deem a people's court ruling of reduction or commutation of sentence or parole or probation to be improper, it will file an appeal within the prescribed period of time according to the provisions of the penal code. The people's court will re-hear cases that the people's procuratorate has appealed.

Section 5. Release and resettlement

Article 35. When a prisoner's sentence is completed, the prison will release him or her at the scheduled time and issue a release certificate.

Article 36. Following a prisoner's release, the public security authorities will complete household registration against the certificate of release.

Article 37. Local people's governments will help resettled released personnel who have completed their sentences.

Local people's government will provide relief to released personnel who have lost their ability to work, who have no means of support, and who have no source of a basic livelihood.

Article 38. Released personnel who have served their sentences enjoy the same rights as other citizens according to law.

Chapter IV. Prison Administration and Management

Section 1. Separate custody and management

Article 39. Prisons will institute separate custody and management of male prisoners, female prisoners, and juvenile prisoners. They will show special consideration for the physiological and psychological characteristics of juvenile and female prisoners when conducting remolding.

Prisons will incarcerate prisoners differently and control them differently depending on the kinds of crime they have committed, the kinds of penalty being given, the length of their prison term, and their response to remolding.

Article 40. Female prisoners will be under direct control of female police.

Section 2. Alerts

Article 41. Prison armed alerts are the responsibility of the People's Armed Police, the specific methods employed to be prescribed by the State Council and the Central Military Affairs Commission.

Article 42. When a prison discovers the escape of a prisoner in its custody, it will immediately capture the prisoner. If it is unable to effect capture at once, it will immediately notify the public security authorities, with the public security authorities then becoming responsible for apprehension in close coordination with the prison.

Article 43. Prisons will establish alert facilities as supervision and control needs require. Prisons will set up an alert isolation belt around the prison into which no one may enter without permission.

Article 44. Government agencies, social groups, entrepreneurial units, and grass-roots level organizations around the prison area and the operations area will assist the prison in the performance of its security alert work.

Section 3. Use of nonlethal and lethal weapons

Article 45. Prisons may use nonlethal weapons under the following circumstances:

1) prisoners seeking to escape;
2) prisoners committing acts of violence;
3) prisoners being moved under escort;
4) prisoners committing other dangerous acts requiring the use of preventive measures.

Once the above circumstances no longer exist, the use of nonlethal weapons will cease.

Article 46. When people's police and People's Armed Police duty personnel are unable to halt any of the following without using lethal weapons, they may use lethal weapons as applicable national regulations allow:

1) prisoners committing mob violence and riot;
2) prisoners escaping or resisting arrest;
3) prisoners possessing weapons or other dangerous goods, committing violence or destruction, and endangering the lives and property of others;
4) seizure of prisoners by force;
5) prisoners seizing weapons.

Personnel employing lethal weapons will report the circumstances as national regulations provide.

Section 4. Correspondence and meetings

Article 47. Prisoners may correspond with others during the period of their incarceration, but the letters they receive and send will be examined at the prison. Should the prison find that the contents of the letters obstruct prisoner remolding, they may withhold them. Prison letters to higher-level prison authorities and judicial authorities are not to be examined.

Article 48. During the period of their incarceration, prisoners may meet with relatives and guardians as regulations prescribe.

Article 49. Articles and money that prisoners receive will be approved and examined by the prison.

Section 5. Living conditions and health

Article 50. State-prescribed prisoner living standards will be set at certain levels.

Article 51. Prisoner bedding and clothing are issued by the prison.

Article 52. The special living habits of minority nationality prisoners will be given consideration.

Article 53. Prisoner living quarters will be sturdy, ventilated, pervious to light, clean, and heated.

Article 54. Prisons will establish medical treatment or organizations and living and health facilities. They will set living and health systems. Prisoner medical treatment and health care is to be a part of the health and quarantine plans of the area in which prisons are located.

Article 55. Should a prisoner die during the period of incarceration, the prison will immediately notify the prisoner's family and both the people's procuratorate and the people's court. If the prisoner has died from illness, the prison will perform a medical evaluation. Should the people's procuratorate have doubts about the medical evaluation, it may make another evaluation of the cause of death. Should the prisoner's family have doubts, it may appeal to the people's procuratorate. Should a prisoner have an abnormal death, the people's procuratorate will investigate at once to make an evaluation of the cause of death.

Section 6. Rewards and punishments

Article 56. The prison will set up a regular prisoner evaluation system, the results of evaluations serving as a basis for prisoner rewards and punishments.

Article 57. Prisons may award commendations and material prizes or record merits for any of the following:

1) observation of prison discipline, making an effort to study, taking part in labor, and demonstrating acknowledgment of wrongdoing and willingness to submit to the law;
2) prevention of violations of the law and criminal activity;
3) overfulfillment of production quotas;
4) achievements in the conservation of raw and processed materials or taking care of public property;
5) definite achievements in making technical innovations or imparting production skills;
6) making definite contributions to the prevention or elimination of damaging events;
7) making other contributions to the country and society.

The prison may permit prisoners sentenced to a fixed number of years in prison who do any of the above to leave prison to visit their relatives provided they have served half or more of their original sentence, have behaved in a model way during the period of their incarceration, and do not pose a threat to society after leaving prison.

Article 58. When prisoners do any of the following things that damage prison order, the prison may issue a warning, record demerits, or place them in confinement:

1) engage in a mass uproar that disturbs normal prison order;
2) revile or strike people's police;
3) bully other prisoners;
4) steal, gamble, fight or engage in fisticuffs, pick quarrels or make trouble;
5) refuse to work or remain passive and engage in slowdowns despite ability to work, refusing to change despite indoctrination;
6) use self-inflicted wounds or self-inflicted disabilities to evade labor;
7) purposely violate operating procedures when performing productive labor or purposely damage production tools;
8) other conduct in violation of prison regulations and discipline.

The period of prisoner confinement for the above will be seven to 15 days.

Prisoners who engage in the first of the above activities during the period of their incarceration, committing a crime thereby, will be held criminally responsible according to law.

Section 7.
Handling of prisoner crimes committed during their incarceration

Article 59. Prisoners who purposely commit crimes during the period of their incarceration will be severely punished according to law.

Article 60. The prison will investigate the commission of crimes by prisoners while in prison. Following completion of the investigation, the prison will write a statement of charges or a statement of no charges, sending it together with dossier data and evidence to the people's procuratorate.

Chapter V. Prisoner Educational Remolding

Article 61. The principles followed in the educational remolding of prisoners are tailoring education to the individual, providing different categories of education, and using reason to persuade prisoners. A combination of group and individual education is used, and a combination of prison education and social education is used.

Article 62. Prisons will conduct ideological education of prisoners in the legal system, morality, and the country's circumstances, policies, and prospects.

Article 63. Prisons will provide education to eradicate [il]literacy and [to provide] primary school education and basic level middle school education that is tailored to the different needs of prisoners. Upon successful examination, the educational authorities will issue commensurate academic certifications.

Article 64. Prisons will provide vocational and technical education for prisoners as prison production needs and post-release employment require. Upon successful examination, the labor authorities will issue commensurate technical grade certificates.

Article 65. Prisons must encourage prisoner self-study. Those who successfully pass examinations will be issued commensurate certificates by the authorities concerned.

Article 66. Prisoner cultural, vocational, and technical education will be incorporated into local educational plans. Prisons will set up needed educational facilities including classrooms and book-reading rooms.

Article 67. Prisons will organize prisoners for athletic, cultural, and entertainment activities.

Article 68. Government agencies, social groups, military units, entrepreneurial units, and people in all walks of life, as well as the relatives of prisoners, will assist prisons in doing a good job of prisoner educational remolding.

Article 69. Prisoners who are able to work must work.

Article 70. Prisons will organize manpower in a sensible way to suit the individual circumstances of prisoners as a means of correcting bad habits, fostering the habit of working, learning production skills, and creating conditions for employment following release.

Article 71. Prisons will enforce prisoner work hours in accordance with government regulations pertaining to work hours.

Prisoners have the right to rest on legal holidays and rest days.

Article 72. Prisons must compensate prisoners according to regulations for the work they perform and enforce government regulations regarding labor protection.

Article 73. Prisons will handle according to applicable government labor insurance regulations the injury, disablement, or death of a prisoner in the course of labor.

Chapter VI. Educational Remolding of Juvenile Prisoners

Article 74. Incarceration of juvenile prisoners will be in a juvenile prisoner house of corrections.

Article 75. Educational remolding must be the matter of primary concern in the incarceration of juvenile prisoners. Labor performed by juvenile prisoners will be in keeping with the capabilities of juveniles, the study of cultural and production skills being paramount.

Prisons will coordinate with educational organizations in the government, society, and schools to provide the necessary conditions for juvenile prisoners to receive compulsory education.

Article 76. When juvenile prisoners become a full 18 years of age and have no more than two years of their sentences remaining, they may remain in the juvenile house of corrections for the remainder of their sentence.

Article 77. In cases where this chapter does not stipulate the control and educational remolding of juveniles, relevant provisions of this law will apply.

Chapter VII. Supplementary Regulations

Article 78. This law will take effect from the date of publication.

Endnotes

For more complete citations, and explanation of abbreviations, see Bibliography.

1. From a collection of Du Fu's poems: Xie Wentong, ed., *She shi xuan yi* (Guangdong Higher Education Publishing House, 1985). Though it is not clear on its face (and it is not usually understood this way), historically this line probably describes the aftermath of Sino-Tibetan wars. Translated by us. — JDS & RA.

2. Short for *liuchang jiuye,* literally meaning "retained workers." The full term used to be *xingman shifan qiangzhixing liu chang jiuye* or "post-release compulsory retained workers."

3. Dong Maicang, deputy chief of Qinghai's Labor Reform Bureau. Quoted in Jan Wong, *Red China Blues: My Long March from Mao to Now* (Toronto: Doubleday-Anchor, 1996), p. 309.

4. For purposes of this book, "China" does not include Hong Kong. As we go to press, the former British colony has just reverted to Chinese control. On prison conditions prior to the handover, see the Human Rights Watch/Hong Kong Human Rights Monitor report *Hong Kong: Prison Conditions in 1997* (Vol 9, no. 5 (C), June 1997.

5. Stephen B. Davis, "The Death Penalty and Legal Reform in the PRC," *Journal of Chinese Law*, 1987, I:303, pp. 304-334; Andrew Scobell, "The Death Penalty in Post-Mao China," *China Quarterly*, September 1990, pp. 503-520; Jasper Becker, "PRC: Legislation Allows Sentence of Death by Injection," *South China Morning Post,* April 10, 1996, p. 8; U.S. Foreign Broadcast Information Service, *Daily Report: China* (hereafter: FBIS), April 11, 1996, pp. 46-47; *New York Times,* July 11, 1996, pp. A-1, A-8; and various Amnesty International reports, including index nos. ASA 17/15/94, ASA 17/17/95, ASA 51/02/95, and ASA 17/14/97.

6. The most recent study is *Opening to Reform.* (See Bibliography.)

7. On this problem, see *XSB,* February 26, 1993, p. 1.

8. Even English-language publications can contain good information, though it must be used carefully. For example, on Guangxi see *China Daily,* April 4, 1995, p. 3.

9. Among the best materials on Tibet are those from the Tibet Information Network. These and other materials are available at the following World Wide Web site: gopher://gopher.cc.columbia.edu:71/11/clioplus/scholarly/SouthAsia/Tibet.

10. Unnamed "European newspaperman" quoted in A. Doak Barnett, *Communist China: The Early Years, 1949-1955* (New York: Frederick A. Praeger, 1966), p. 60.

11. Most relevant is Jia Lusheng and Feng Shuo, *Zhongguo xibu da jianyu* [Major prisons in West China] (Nanjing: Jiangsu wenyi chubanshe, 1986). More recent are Jean-Luc Domenach, *Chine: l'archipel oublié* [Fayard: n.p. (Paris?), 1992], which contains an extensive bibliography; and Harry Wu's three books (see Bibliography). Among the classic literature are: Duan Kewen, *"Zhanfan" zishu* [A "prisoner of war's" own account] (New York: World Journal Press 1973); Jean Pasqualini (Bao Ruowang), *Prisonnier de Mao* (Geneva: Éditions Famot, reprinted 1977), trans: *Prisoner of Mao* (New York: Coward McCann, 1973); Lai Ying, *Les Prisons de Mao* (Paris: Raoul Solar, 1970); and Peng Yinhan, *Dalu jizhongying* (Concentration camps on mainland [China]) (Taipei: Shibao wenhua chubanshiye).

12. There have been two relevant "white papers:" State Council, "Criminal Reform in China," FBIS, August 11, 1992, pp. 13-23 (also appeared in *Beijing Review,* August 17, 1992, pp. 10-25); and State Council, "Human Rights Progress in China," December 25, 1996, FBIS, June 10, 1996, especially pp. 28-31.

13. See the writings of Harry Wu (listed in Bibliography), and also various reports of Amnesty International (London), such as *Torture in China* (1992), and *People's Republic of China: Torture and Ill-Treatment— Comments on China's Second Periodic Report to the UN Committee Against Torture* (1996). See also *Detained at Official Pleasure,* pp. 19-22.

14. Dutton (see Bibliography), p. 5.

15. Ibid., p. 301.

16. Ibid., p. 317.

17. Ibid., p. 353.

18. For example, in the "PRC Laogai Regulations" of 1956, which called for special living allowances for these three provinces.

19. 1994 figures, from *1995 Statistical Yearbook,* translated in *Provincial China: A Research Newsletter* (Sydney), p. 37. Xinjiang: 109.93% of national average; Qinghai, 77.64%; Gansu, 50.58%.

20. For more on the subject of women prisoners in China, see p. 86, and also: *Fighting for Their Rights: Chinese Women's Experiences Under Political Persecution* (New York: Human Rights in China, 1995); *People's Republic of China: Women in*

China: Detained, Victimized, but Mobilized (London: Amnesty International, 1996); and Saunders, chapter 14 ("Sexual Reform and Pseudo-Boys: Women in the *Laogai*").

21. Dutton, especially pp. 100-128.

22. Waley-Cohen (pp. 29-31) points out that the reported figures of transferees are unreliable, but puts the number of slaves as at least 600 in 1797.

23. At the height of the Qing period, military expenses far exceeded tax revenues in Xinjiang. Joseph Fletcher, "Ch'ing Inner Asia *c.* 1800," in John K. Fairbank, ed., *The Cambridge History of China,* vol. 10, pt. I, p. 37.

24. Waley-Cohen, pp. 27-28, 160, 174.

25. See Derk Bodde and Clarence Morris, *Law in Imperial China: Exemplified by 190 Ch'ing Dynasty Cases* (Philadelphia: University of Pennsylvania Press, 1967), pp. 85-91; Waley-Cohen, passim.

26. Dutton, pp. 157-184.

27. Ibid., p. 177.

28. A less precise term for China proper is *neidi,* which roughly means "heartland" (but is often mistranslated as "the interior"). The term, which is still common parlance, dates at least from Qing times, but its meaning has shifted over time. See Waley-Cohen, chapter 3.

29. *FGY,* 1991, no. 2, p. 30.

30. "On the People's Democratic Dictatorship," *Selected Works of Mao Tse-tung* (Beijing: Foreign Languages Press, 1961), v. 4, p. 419.

31. Jia (cited endnote 11), p. 2.

32. *The Writings of Mao Zedong, 1949-1976* (Armonk, New York: M. E. Sharpe, Inc., 1986), vol. 1, pp. 191-192.

33. *People's Daily,* September 7, 1954.

34. See Dorothy H. Bracey, "Corrections in the People's Republic of China," in Ronald J. Troyer, John P. Clark, and Dean G. Rojek, eds., *Social Control in the People's Republic of China* (New York: Praeger, 1989), pp. 159-187. For an official account, see the State Council's report "Criminal Reform in China," *Beijing Review,* August 17, 1992, pp. 10-25.

35. E.g., Dutton, though he uses the word in a curious, non standard way.

36. Harry Wu, quoted in the *Sunday Times* (London), November 3, 1996, p. 2. Earlier, Wu had put the figure at somewhat less: from 30 to 40 million. Quoted in the *London Daily Telegraph*, May 10, 1995.

37. English translation in *Chinese Law & Government,* September 1994, pp. 61-62. Later, more detailed guidelines (1982) can be found on pp. 68-83 of ibid.

38. On labor reeducation, see Martin King Whyte, "Corrective Labor Camps in China," *Asian Survey,* March 1973, pp. 253-269; and Amnesty International, *China — Punishment Without Crime: Administrative Detention* (London: 1991), pp. 28-53.

39. The portion varies greatly over time and from place to place, but generally it is at least 60 percent.

40. Such a meeting is described in Li Zijing, *"Zhonggong neibu zhiyi 'laojiao' zhidu"* (Internal Chinese Communist [document] questions "labor reform" system), *Zhengming,* November 1996, pp. 14-16. Although we do not accept the authenticity of the claimed document, much else in this article (such as the report of the meeting) has the ring of truth.

41. See *Detained at Official Pleasure,* pp. 7-8.

42. See endnote 380.

43. See Lynn White III, "The Road to Urumchi: Approved Institutions in Search of Attainable Goals During the Pre-1968 Rustification from Shanghai," *The China Quarterly,* vol. 79, September 1979, pp. 480-516.

44. See *Death by Default: A Policy of Fatal Neglect in China's State Orphanages,* and *Chinese Orphanages: A Follow-Up* (both New York: Human Rights Watch, 1996).

45. Prison statistics in other countries often do not include persons in jails, detained drug addicts, and children locked up in some kind of closed boarding schools. We do include people in ordinary jails.

Although it does not substantially affect our overall findings, there is a slight difference in the way we count imprisoned juveniles and drug offenders in the various provinces. In the case of Qinghai, we take a "conservative" (maximizing) approach, and include juveniles and drug offenders.

In the case of Gansu, we include juveniles. We also include those drug offenders who have been sent to *lao (gai, jiao)* institutions or to prisons. We do not include people sent to detoxification centers. (Drug abuse is lower than elsewhere. During 1992, only 970 drug offenders were sent to drug rehabilitation centers.)

In the case of Xinjiang, our estimates are too rough for these statistically minor considerations to matter.

46. E.g., Shenyang Radio, May 14, 1984, *BBC Summary of World Broadcasts, Asia-Pacific* (hereafter: *SWB),* May 17, 1984, FE/7645/BII/6.

47. Wang Tai, "Shilun laodong gaizao de jiben lilun yiju" (Tentative discussion on the basis of the fundamental theory of labor reform), in Zhou Mingdong, Xu Zhangrun, and Zhu Ye, eds., *Laodong gaizao faxue gailun cankao ziliao* (Reference materials on the general legal theory of labor reform) (Beijing: Central Television Publishing House, 1987), pp. 247-248. Our translation is based on p. 42 of Tanner (cited p. 16, n. A), whose article is recommended for additional information on the theory and practice of prisoner reformation. Emphasis in original.

48. Li Yong, "The Significance of the Ministry of Justice's Fifth Decree" (in Chinese), *Fanzui yu gaizao yanjiu,* 1990, no. 4, pp. 15-16.

49. Quoted in Barnett (see endnote 10), p. 65.

50. See Public Security Bureau notice of November 30, 1981, in *Zhonghua Renmin Gongheguo falü guifanxing jieshi jicheng* (A collection of standard interpretations of the laws of the People's Republic of China). Jilin: Jilin People's Publishing House, 1990. Also, Hu Yaobang, in recommending the establishment of showcase prisons, made clear that he realized the reality and wanted to improve the prisons generally. *Guonei dongtai qiyang* (Drafts of domestic trends), June 4, 1982, vol. 718.

51. *XSB,* January 22, 1994, p. 1.

52. *XSB,* January 22, 1994, p. 3.

53. Article 5 of *Sifa Bu guanyu jiaqiang jianguan gaizao gongzuo de ruogan guiding* (Ministry of Justice regulations concerning the work of prison control and reform), September 19, 1989. This hitherto-unknown set of national regulations appeared in the Xinjiang internal bimonthly *Bingtuan laogai gongzuo tongxun* (Bingtuan laogai work bulletin), 1990, no. 1, pp. 9-10.

54. *Zhongguo Jiancha Nianjian 1989* (Beijing 1991), p. 10.

55. Indeed, in 1997 there were complaints about the cavalier attitude of Gansu government and party personnel in this respect. Yan Haiwang, secretary of the provincial party committee, complained of such attitudes as "we have no secrets to protect,'" "it is difficult to protect secrets," and "it is useless to protect secrets;" he called for great efforts to protect sensitive information. *Gansu ribao,* March 30, 1997, *SWB,* FE/2893, pp. G/7-8.

56. Namely, farms number 85, 104 and 149.

57. Now there is also Provincial Number Three prison, located on Shengli Road in Wuwei city.

58. The precise number depends on how, in this context, one conceives of and defines a single prison camp.

59. The prison factories are: Lanzhou Keche Zhuangpei Chang, at 311 Dashaping Street; and Lanzhou Famen Chang at 315 Dashaping Street.

60. On Jianshe Road. (In most provinces, at least one of the prisons for juveniles is located in the provincial capital, as is the case in Xinjiang and Qinghai.)

61. *Gansu 1995 Yearbook*, p. 119.

62. Ibid.

63. *Gansu 1996 Yearbook*, p. 100.

64. These are basically 1994 figures, but in view of the drop which took place the next year, the figures have been rounded downward.

65. *The Guardian,* August 29, 1984.

66. *Gansu 1995 Yearbook,* p. 120.

67. Ibid, p. 357.

68. *Gansu 1994 Yearbook,* p. 292.

69. *Gansu 1995 Yearbook,* p. 685.

70. *Gansu 1985 Statistical Yearbook,* p. 182.

71. *Gansu 1995 Yearbook,* p. 133.

72. Ibid., p. 688.

73. Ibid, p. 698.

74. Ibid, p. 700.

75. *Gansu Farm Village 1994 Statistical Yearbook,* pp. 216-350, passim.

76. Provincial Party Secretary Li Ziqi, "We Must Not Lose the Tradition of Plain Living and Hard Struggle," *Qiushi,* September 1, 1989, p. 25, US Joint Publications Research Service, October 24, 1989, CAR-89-105, p. 15.

The quality of government does not appear to have greatly improved. In 1997 the former director of the Gansu Public Security Department was convicted of corruption. Zhongguo Xinwen She news agency, May 1, 1997, *SWB,* FE/2909, p. G/1.

77. This is the number reported by the Party secretary of Lanzhou University.

78. This is inferred from a comment by Political Commissar Li Zhuanhua, who called for "taking a clear-cut stand in resisting the influence and penetration by hostile forces on the army units, and obeying the orders of the Central Military Commission." Lanzhou Radio, June 21, 1989, FBIS, June 22, 1989, p. 60.

79. On arrests after the 1989 disturbances, see *DCT,* pp. 150-151.

80. *Dissidents Detained Since 1992: Political Trials and Administrative Sentences* (Amnesty International, 1994), passim; and *Women in China: Detained, Victimized but Mobilized* (Amnesty International, 1996), p. 39.

81. Earlier, it was common for political prisoners from the Tibet Autonomous Region to be shipped to Gansu, as confirmed by an interview with Tanpa Sopa (conducted for us by Tseten Wangchuk). In late 1959, Sopa and some two thousand Tibetan prisoners were trucked to Liuyuan in northwestern Gansu. There, the Chinese officials divided the prisoners into smaller groups and sent them to various labor camps in the province and also in Xinjiang. Sopa's cohort had 74 people, most of whom had been Tibetan government officials under the Dalai Lama; they were put in a cargo train and taken to Changjiao Nongchang near Jiuquan, Gansu. Sopa recalled that there were altogether about a thousand prisoners in that camp. After a few years of hard labor most of the Tibetans there died; only about twenty of them ever returned to Tibet.

82. This is based on 33,000 prisoners and a population of 23.52 million on January 1, 1995.

83. This is the date used in contemporary publications, such as *XSB,* August 20, 1994, p. 4.

84. UPI dispatch, April 12, 1996.

85. Our sources give a range of 30,000 to 50,000.

86. Altogether, Xinjiang had 450,000 urban youths (5.2% of the population). Thomas Bernstein, *Up to the Mountains and Down to the Villages: The Transfer of Youth from Urban to Rural China* (New Haven: Yale University Press, 1977), pp. 191, 234.

87. Quoted in ibid, p. 343, note 110.

88. Xinjiang Party official Duan Tonghua, quoted in *Xinjiang ribao,* January 16,

1996, p. 7, FBIS, February 10, 1996, p. 57.

89. The bingtuan prefers that the organization be called a "corporation" in English. However, it is not a corporation in the sense of a private, limited-liability company.

90. It is difficult to say which of these motives was more important. The "integration" rationale was a selling point for the communes, but the leadership (control) angle may have actually been the real motive of Mao Zedong, who said: "The People's communes are the best system after all. They have the advantage of combining industry, agriculture, commerce, education, and soldiering all into one, thus facilitating leadership." (Quoted in *Zhengming,* October 1966, p. 16.) As far as the bingtuan is concerned, streamlined leadership has probably been deemed most important.

91. See Henry G. Schwarcz, "Chinese Migration to the Northwest China and Inner Mongolia, 1949-1959," *The China Quarterly,* December 1963, pp. 62-74.

92. For the bingtuan's role among Kazakhs, see Moseley, chapter 4.

93. Press release of the Laogai Research Foundation, October 23, 1995. (Actually, except for the militia, only during times of war or martial law would the PLA control the bingtuan.)

94. Xinjiang Television, June 3, 1996, FBIS, June 4, 1996. (The "100,000" doubtless refers to "militia" in the broadest sense, including former soldiers who can be called up in an emergency, but have not had recent training.

95. John Wilson Lewis and Xue Litai, *China Builds the Bomb,* pp. 179-180.

96. Lewis, p. 179.

97. Testimony of Teresa Buczacki before the U.S. Senate Committee on Foreign Relations, July 25, 1996, p. 2.

98. *China Daily,* April 12, 1996, p. 2.

99. Quoted in Thomas Bernstein, *Up to the Mountains and Down to the Villages: The Transfer of Youth from Urban to Rural China* (New Haven: Yale University Press, 1977), p. 70.

100. *Bayinguoleng tongji nianjian* (Bayangol statistical yearbook), 1996, p. 136.

101. Speech by bingtuan deputy commander Hu Zhaozhang, *XSB,* March 16, 1996, p. 1 of special feature.

102. Wang Lequan, quoted in *XJRB,* April 5, 1996, pp. 1-2, FBIS, May 1, 1996, p. 83.

103. Xinjiang Television, May 6, 1996, FBIS, May 7, 1996, p. 72.

104. Xinjiang Television, May 6, 1996, FBIS, May 9, 1996, p. 42.

In May 1997 the Party issued instructions that the bingtuan was to redouble its efforts to combat separatism. "Since the corps was established, the party and state have endowed on it the historical mission to open up wastelands and garrison the frontier region ... it not only has become an important force for Xinjiang's economic construction, but also an important force for maintaining nationality unity and social stability, for strengthening frontier defense, and for defending the motherland's unification. The corps not only has made economic contributions to the state and the autonomous region; but also, more importantly, it, as an important anti-aggression, anti-splittism, anti-infiltration, and anti-subversion force, has played a role that is difficult for other organizations to play in several major political and military struggles in the past. Comrades should clearly understand, and never waver nor be ambiguous on the diversified functions and special role of the corps. Moreover, we should realize that the corps' role and position have not been changed in the slightest degree under the new historical condition, except that its mission has become even heavier and more arduous. Corps cadres at large, leading cadres in particular, should consider problems from a strategic height, bearing in mind, under all circumstances and in the face of all adversities, the special historic mission entrusted upon us by our party and government. ... [W]e should continue to attach equal importance to both development and stability, centering around economic construction. ... Jin Yunhui said: Under no circumstance should we lower our guard against national separatists, religious fanatics, and terrorists who have never ceased their subversive and sabotage activities against the corps ... While paying close attention to the corps' internal improvement and the maintenance of stability, we must, in accordance with the regional party committee's unified plan, go all out to support and coordinate with local party committees and governments at various levels in their intensive drive to maintain public order in key areas and the strike-hard special campaign ... ensure a good job of the corps' internal improvement but, more importantly, we must take up the task of improving public order in key areas throughout the region by bringing into play the corps' special function. ..." Report of a bingtuan party committee work meeting held in Urumqi, April 28-29, *XJRB,* May 2, 1997 pp. 1, 3, FBIS no. 96 (electronic version).

A "top secret" Central Committee document (the authenticity of which we are unable to confirm) insists that the bingtuan "has to improve its administrative functions." "Along with the fundamental changes in the economic system, the function and structure of the bingtuan has to be reformed properly, but its duty of unifying labor with military affairs, opening of new lands and the developing of border regions shall not change. . . . Seizing the opportunity to develop southern Xinjiang; our country should expand the bingtuan in southern Xinjiang." Chinese Communist Party Central Committee, Document no. 7 (1996), translated from the Uyghur.

105. *XJRB,* May 7, 1996, p. 1, FBIS, May 22, 1996, p. 74.

For more on the bingtuan in the 1990s, see Song Hanliang, speech to 1991 Regional Party Congress, *XJRB,* March 23, 1991, pp. 1-3, FBIS, April 12, 1991, especially pp. 78-79.

106. Laogai Gongzuo Ju, located on Xi Hou Jie in Urumqi.

107. Strictly speaking, we should say "maintained," because the word "prison" now has broader usage. The prison referred to here still exists, but now it is one of many institutions called "prisons."

108. Theoretically, the smallest unit would be the *pai,* but this term is only used for civilian farms.

109. *Xinsheng bao*, March 16, 1996, p. 2.

110. On the financial relationship, see Lai Zhengyong, "In Developing the Bingtuan Laogai, Relying on Agriculture Is a Good Way" (in Chinese), *BLTG,* 1992, no. 5, pp. 34-35.

111. Xu Guishan (a cadre), "Nong Qi Shi laogai jinji zouchu digu" (The Seventh Division has bottomed out), *XSB,* April 18, 1992, p. 1; and *XJLG,* December 1995, no. 6, p. 24.

112. Headquarters: Laogai Chu, 91 Huanghe Street in Urumqi.

113. For example, between April 24-29 alone, 189 "criminals" were arrested in Urumqi, Changji, and Bayinguoleng (Bayangol). Xinjiang television, May 2, 1996, FBIS, May 3, 1996, p. 82.

114. Fox Butterfield, *China: Alive in the Bitter Sea* (New York: Bantam Books, 1982), p. 367.

115. Bingtuan Laogai Ju. Address: 17 Xin Tiyuguan Lu, Urumqi.

116. Commonly termed "pocket hukou" people, meaning that their official residence was in their pockets (i.e., fictitious). Jia (see endnote 11), p. 55.

117. "An Investigation of Prison Guards in the Nine Western Provinces" (in Chinese), *FGY*, 1991, no. 2, p. 50.

118. *BLGT,* 1990, no. 1, p. 10.

119. See Tanner (cited p. 16, n. A), p. 61.

120. Domenach (cited endnote 11), p. 334, citing a Taiwan source.

121. Low cadre morale, and suggestions for dealing with the problem (better perks) is discussed in Lu Qiaolin, *"Dui laogai danwei shenhua zhengzhi sixiang gongzuo de sikao"* (On deepening of the political thought work among laogai units), *BLGT,* 1990, no. 1, pp. 11-12.

122. *FGY,* 1991:2, p. 49. Also relevant is Zhang Wenhua, *"Jiaqiang ganjing . . . "* (It is imperative that we improve the quality of rank-and-file cadres), *BLGT,* 1990, no. 1, pp. 4-7.

123. In Chinese, *Yujing,* meaning "prison police."

124. This is a point repeatedly made in Jia and Feng (see note 11).

125. This was first effected in 1982 in Jiangsu Province. In some areas (e.g., Tibet) this step appears not to have been taken for another couple of years.

126. "June fourth" was, of course, considered disastrous by the government for different reasons than most others so consider it. For the government, it was a political disaster; for most, it was a humanitarian disaster.

127. Statements by PAP commander Yang Guoping and political commissar Xu Yongqing. New China News Agency (hereafter: NCNA), March 7, 1996, FBIS, March 7, 1996, p. 41.

128. *New York Times,* February 20, 1997, p. 11.

129. Integrating provincial PAPs into the national system was a problem in other provinces as well. Regarding Shaanxi, see Xian radio, April 5, 1996, FBIS April 11, 1996, p. 54.

130. E.g., Xinjiang Television, May 24, 1996, FBIS, May 29, 1996, p. 76.

131. The regular army is also involved in anti-poverty work. See "Xinjiang Military District Takes Measures to Help Impoverished Areas Through Intellectual Resources: More than 2,000 Villages Lifted Out of Poverty, of Which Over 1,000 Have Become Rich," *Renmin ribao* (Overseas Edition), February 24, 1996, p. 1, FBIS, March 21, 1996, pp. 39-40.

132. Interview with Li Jizhou, vice minister of Ministry of Public Security, in Hong Kong *Xingdao ribao,* March 11, 1996, p. A5, FBIS, March 11, 1996, pp. 58-

59. This source says the PAP was expected to grow to a million by the year 2000, and that the regular police would also expand by 500,000 during the same period.

Officially, the PAP had 696,000 personnel in 1995. Some claim that it is larger. *South China Morning Post,* March 5, 1996, p. 8, FBIS, March 5, 1996, p. 74.

Based on various reports in *Renmin wujing bao,* the force size in Gansu is estimated at 14,000-27,000; Qinghai: 13,500-25,000. (The size of the Xinjiang force is unknown but certainly large.). Tai Ming Cheung, "Guarding China's Domestic Front Line: The People's Armed Police and China's Stability," *China Quarterly,* June 1996, p. 531.

133. "My Perspective on How to Prevent Recidivism" (in Chinese), *BLGT,* 1992, no. 5, p. 4.

134. *"Yunyong mubiao guanli . . . "* (Targeting our management: improving anti-escape work), *BLGT,* 1990, no. 1, p. 17.

135. *XSB,* April 30, 1994, p. 1.

136. Xu Guishan, *Nong Qi Shi laogai jingji zouchu digu* (The Seventh Division has bottomed out), *XSB,* April 18, 1992, p. 1.

137. Zhang Xuejing, *"Ji wang kai lai. . . . "* (Assure the future by building on the past; work hard to propel bingtuan laogai work into a new era of institutionalized development), *BLGT,* 1992, no. 2, pp. 6-7; and *"Gaohao jian guan. . . ."* (Do a good job in prison control and reform, and make a contribution to overall stability), *BLGT,* 1990, no. 1, p. 1.

138. *"1992 nian bingtuan laogai gongzuo yaodian"* (Wish list for 1992 bingtuan laogai work), *BLGT,* no. 2, 1992, pp. 4-5.

139. Zhang Wenhua, "It is imperative that we improve the quality of rank-and-file cadres" (in Chinese), *BLGT,* 1990, no. 1, p. 4.

140. Justice Minister Xiao Yang reported a 28 percent decrease in escapes in 1996 compared with 1995, but no actual figure was given. *China Focus,* April 1997, p. 4.

141. On homosexuality in China's prisons, cited Jia and Feng (see endnote 11), p. 40. On official (quite level-headed) attitudes toward the subject, see *"Zuifan biantia xinli ji qi jiaozheng"* (Corrections, and aberrational psychology among criminals), *BLGT,* 1992, no 2, p. 37.

142. Tanner (cited p. 16, n. A), p. 54.

143. Zhang Yongping, "Some Suggestions for the Reform of the Criminal Law" (in Chinese), *Bingtuan laogai gongzuo tongxun,* 1993, no. 1, p. 5.

144. Xinjiang is one of 16 provincial-level units receiving "fixed-sum subsidies" (*ding'e buzhe*). See Jae Ho Chung, "Beijing Confronting the Provinces: The 1994 Tax-Sharing Reform and Its implications for Central-Provincial Relations in China," *China Information,* Winter 1994-1995, p. 5 and passim.

145. Quoted in June Teufel Dreyer, "The PLA and Regionalism in Xinjiang," *The Pacific Review*, 7:1, 1994, p. 52.

146. "Outline of the Ninth Five-Year Plan of the Xinjiang Uyghur Autonomous Region's . . . ," *XJRB,* April 8, 1996, pp. 1-2, FBIS, May 2, 1996, p. 60.

147. See chapter 6 of Shao Mingzheng, *Zhongguo laogai faxue lilun yanjiu zongshu* (Studies on the legal theory of China's labor reform) (Beijing: Zhongguo Zhengfa Daxue Chubanshe, 1992).

148. State Council, "Criminal Reform in China," FBIS, August 11, 1992, pp. 13-23.

149. For a claim that education is emphasized even in Xinjiang, see "Xinjiang Prison Terms 'Jail Term into a School Term,'" NCNA dispatch of April 9, 1997 (propaganda aimed at a Hong Kong audience), *SWB,* FE/2893, p. G/4-5.

150. *Chinese Law and Government* (quarterly published by M. E. Sharpe, Inc.) special fall 1988 issue, *Cadre Accountability to the Law.*

151. Quoted in *The Human Rights Watch Global Report on Prisons* (New York, 1993), p. 137.

152. For an idealized description of prison life in China in 1960, see Edgar Snow, *The Other Side of the River: Red China Today* (New York: Random House, 1961), pp. 365-375, 547-548.

153. In general, China has had a low rate of recidivism, but this may be changing. See Tanner (cited p. 16, n. A), pp. 68-70.

154. *FGY,* 1991, p. 51.

155. *SFXZ,* March 1992, p. 6.

156. Xu (endnote 195), p. 26.

157. Domenach (cited endnote 11), p. 395.

158. Zhang Xuejing, *"Ji wang kai lai . . . "* (Assure the future by building on the past; work hard to propel bingtuan laogai work into a new era of institutionalized development), *BLGT,* 1992, no. 2, p. 8. (The source does not make it clear exactly what size unit or administrative level was involved.)

159. Luo Xiaojun, *"Yifa guanli, bianhua xianzhu"* (Management in accordance with law), *BLGT,* 1990, no. 1, p. 23. (The "RMB 20,047" applies only to 1989.)

160. Zhang Wenhua, "It is imperative that we improve the quality of rank-and-file cadres" (in Chinese) *BLGT,* 1990, no. 1, p. 4.

161. Tanner (cited p. 16, n. A), pp. 62-64.

162. On Xinjiang's cotton production, see *Renmin ribao,* September 20, 1995, p. 1, FBIS, October 23, 1995, pp. 88-89.

163. On the reed (*weizi*) business in the bingtuan's Second Agricultural Division, Second Detachment, see *XSB,* January 15, 1994, p. 1.

164. *XSB,* April 30, 1992, p. 2. In the Eighth Bingtuan Division, these reforms were instituted in 1987.

165. Data in Tables 12 and 13 come from *XBN,* p. 127, *XBTN,* p. 28, and other sources.

166. This is based on a total bingtuan farmland size of 958,500 hectares (*XBN,* p. 12).
In 1992 a smaller figure for laogai bingtuan farmland was given in *XSB* (May 2, 1992, p. 1): 259,000 mu, which is presumably 23,933 hectares; we do not know exactly what the size of the bingtuan farmland was then, but we believe that it was fairly stable during those years. If one assumes no change, that would indicate a laogai portion of 3.5 percent.
On April 12, 1996, *China Daily* (p. 2) implied that the bingtuan had only 360,000 hectares of arable land (1.03 million projected total 2001, minus a planned increase of 670,000 hectares), which would mean that there was only about half the farmland that had existed in the 1960s. This we consider unlikely. However, were the *CD* figure correct, the laogai portion would be about 7 percent.

167. Percentages are based on 1991 figures. Zhang Xuejing, *"Duoqu laogai gongzuo xin shengli"* (New victory in laogai work), *BLGT,* 1992, no. 4, p. 8.

168. Between 1989 and 1992, the Seventh Detachment of the First Agricultural Division is reported to have transmitted RMB 2.9 million to the higher levels. In 1993, the detachment's total profit was RMB 500,000. *XSB,* January 15, 1994, p. 2.

169. *Xinsheng bao,* May 2, 1992, p. 1.

170. *XBTN,* 1995, p. 128.

171. *Xinsheng bao,* May 2, 1992, p. 1.

172. *XBTN,* 1995, p. 128.

173. Figures from U.S. Defense Intelligence Agency "Information Paper," July 12, 1996, p. 1.

174. *CD,* April 12, 1996, p. 2.

175. Xu Guishan (a cadre), "Nong Qi Shi laogai jinji zouchu digu" (The Seventh Division has bottomed out), *Xinsheng Bao,* April 18, 1992, p. 1.

176. Wang Huimin, *"Gaohao bingtuan laogai gongzuo bixu zuodao ba ge jianshi"* (In doing good laogai work, adhere to the eight principles), *BLGT,* 1992, no. 4, p. 12.

177. *Bayinguoleng tongji nianjian* (Bayangol statistical yearbook), 1996, p. 136.

178. Domenach (cited endnote 11), p. 107. More information on the value of these public works can be found in Jia (cited endnote 11), p. 3.

179. See, for example, *XSB,* April 30, 1994, p. 2.

180. On water works, see *XSB,* May 7, 1994, p. 2.

181. Our information on prison mines on Xinjiang is based on interviews with former bingtuan judge Ablajan Laylinaman (Baret).

182. Variously rendered in Chinese as "Bianliqi" or "Buliqi."

183. When Harry Wu was a prisoner, he worked in a mine in Shanxi Province, where he was nearly killed in a mine accident. *Bitter Winds,* p. 254.

184. For example, the Bingtuan No. One Prison Xishan Trading Bazaar, near Urumqi.

185. See also p. 212, below. Useful materials on this subject are contained in various provincial yearbooks. For example: "Reform-Through-Labor Work," *Guangxi nianjian 1987,* October 1987, pp. 258-259, FBIS, CHI-91-096, pp. 23-24; and "Reform-Through-Labor Units Improve Economic Performances," *Yunnan nianjian 1986,* December 1986, p. 112, U.S. Joint Publications Research Service, CHI-91-096, pp. 22-23.

186. This is inferred on the basis of a total volume of exports of the region of $763 million in 1995. "The export of key products like cotton yarn and cotton cloth rose considerably over the previous year." "Statistical Communiqué of the Xinjiang Uyghur Autonomous Region Statistical Bureau on 1995 Economic and Social Development," *Xinjiang ribao,* January 27, 1996, p. 2, FBIS, February 14, 1996, p. 57. It is not clear whether the above figures include the bingtuan, whose data appear to be broken out separately. The bingtuan's two-way foreign trade in 1995 was worth RMB 201 million, up 43 percent from the previous year. Ibid, p. 61.

187. Shangmao Gongsi (Commercial Trading Company), bingtuan's Fourth Agricultural Division, Sixty-fourth Regiment, at Korkadala.

188. In our view, it is the living and laboring conditions that raise the moral issue regarding China. Requiring prisoners to perform labor, and even marketing their products, is a widely-accepted practice internationally. In America, 29 states have laws which require most inmates to work, and other states generally have similar policies. See endnote 380.

189. Figures from U.S. Defense Intelligence Agency "Information Paper," July 12, 1996, p. 1.

190. Domenach (cited endnote 11), p. 638, n. 26. The figure given is "161,000," being the number of prisoners who had been sent to Xinjiang. Inasmuch as such prisoners tended to be long-termers, probably none had been released by 1955, though some doubtless had died.

191. Domenach (cited endnote 11), p. 466, citing Jia (see endnote 11), p. 2. (However, we do not find that information there in the edition of Jia that we had available). We are assuming that there were another 30,000 prisoners outside the bingtuan system.

192. Jia (cited endnote 11), p. 11, says that in one *qudui*, the number/ages were: 2,509/17-25, 1,053/26-30, 5,21/31-35, 229/36-40, and 100/over 40.

193. This is in addition to 900 recently arrested Regional prisoners. Associated Press, December 26, 1986, citing NCNA, December 24, 1986.

194. *SFXZ,* March 1992, vol. 1, no. 1, p. 2.

195. Quoted in Xu Yulin, "Reform Farm Provides New Lease on Life," *Beijing Review,* August 19, 1985, p. 25.

196. For example, Hangzhou Radio, May 12, 1984, *SWB,* FE/7645/BII/5, May 17, 1984.

197. Jia (cited endnote 11), p. 6, says that the crime rate dropped by 36.4 percent, the meaning of which is not altogether clear, but it gives some sense of the authorities' perceptions.

198. Number of articles submitted to *Xinsheng bao* (20,755) divided by the average number of submissions (0.61). *XSB Tongxun,* February 25, 1996, p. 4.

199. Margin of error: ±8 percent.

200. Margin of error: ±10 percent.

201. Yu De, *"Qianjiang chengshi zuifan gaizao zhi wojian"* (My view of reforming urban criminals sent to Xinjiang), *BLGT,* 1993, no. 1, p. 30. (An almost identical article had appeared under a different name in the same journal, 1992, no. 4, p. 34.)

202. *Xinjiang ribao,* May 10, 1996, p. 1, BBC Monitoring Service: Asia-Pacific, June 6, 1996.

203. *Xinjiang ribao,* May 18, 1996, p. 1, FBIS, May 24, 1996, p. 82.

204. *XJRB,* May 1, 1996, p. 1, FBIS, May 17, 1996, p. 59.

205. Xinjiang Television, May 6, 1996, FBIS, May 7, 1996, pp. 70, 72.

206. Party Standing Committee member Wang Chuanyou, quoted in "Production and Construction Corps Holds Meeting, Calls on Cadres and Workers of All Nationalities to Contribute Toward Xinjiang's Stability and Development," *Xinjiang ribao,* May 9, 1996, p. 1, FBIS, May 24, 1996, p. 81.

207. *Xinjiang ribao,* cited in *Far Eastern Economic Review,* January 30, 1997, p. 21.

208. Chen Demin, quoted in *XJRB,* May 10, 1996, p. 1, FBIS, May 29, 1996, p. 72.

209. Unattributed report, "Regional Discipline Inspection Commission and Regional Supervision Department Call on Discipline Inspection and Supervision Organs Across Xinjiang to Strictly Enforce Political Discipline and Maintain Overall Stability." *XJRB,* May 22, 1996, p. 1, FBIS, June 7, 1996, p. 83. Another article indicating how seriously religious dissent is taken is Wang Wenheng, "On Stopping Illicit Religious Activities and Enforcing the Party's Policy on Religion," *Xinjiang ribao,* May 7, 1996, p. 8, FBIS, July 11, 1996, pp. 25-27.

210. Discussed in Zhang Chuan, "Shots Ring Out on the Northwestern Border," *Zhengming,* May 1, 1990, pp. 15-16, FBIS, May 1, 1990, pp. 50-51.

211. Tan Daobo, "The Armed Police Corps Takes an Active Part in Crackdown," NCNA, June 5, 1996, FBIS, June 7, 1996, p. 26. Areas other than Xinjiang were involved; in all the PAP participated in "10,000 instances of crackdown."

212. Based on Xinjiang Television, June 7, 1996, 13:30 GMT (BBC Monitoring Service, June 11, 1996).

213. *New York Times,* February 28, 1997, p. A6.

214. Ibid., and CNN and Reuters reports, summarized in China News Digest (Internet), February 11, 1997.

215. But efforts to exclude such influences seem to have been unsuccessful. In 1997, Li Fengzi (regional Party Committee member and secretary of the Political and Legal Affairs Commission) warned: "Xinjiang's prisons must continue to act firmly to stop ethnic separatist activities and unlawful religious activities from infiltrating prisons and sabotaging prisons. We must be constantly alert to the grave situation created by the enemy and the new trends in prisons." Xinjiang Television, Urumqi, April 5, 1997, *SWB,* FE/2887, April 8, 1997, pp. G/7-8.

A "top secret" Central Committee document (the authenticity of which we are unable to confirm) indicates that political conditions in the laogais, especially in southern Xinjiang, leave much to be desired. "We must strengthen the management of labor camps and prisons in Xinjiang, and guarantee stability in them." Chinese Communist Party Central Committee, Document no. 7 (1996), translated from the Uyghur.

216. Unless otherwise indicated, the following information is from *China: Repression in the 1990s — A Directory of Victims,* London: Amnesty International, 1996. (The report also lists an additional 28 cases as "situation not known.") See also Amnesty's *Secret Violence: Human Rights Violations in Xinjiang* (1992), pp. 7-12, and *Religious Repression in China* (1996), pp. 23-27, and *People's Republic of China — Xinjiang: Trials After Recent Ethnic Unrest* (1997).

217. International PEN, Writers in Prison Committee, *Half-Yearly Case List to 30 June 1996* (London).

218. *XJRB,* May 15, 1996.

219. AFP, July 10, 1996, FBIS, July 18, 1996, p. 65.

220. "Xinjiang Uighur Autonomous Region Vice-Chairman Denies Rumour on Rabiya Being Detained for Pursuing Splittist Activities." *Wen wei po* (Hong Kong), April 11, 1997, p. A1, *SWB,* FE/2891, pp. G/7-8.

221. Li Fengzi, quoted in *Xinjiang ribao.* Agence France Presse, May 19, 1996, FBIS, May 20, 1996, p. 17.

222. The first (doubtless of many) is contained in Human Rights Watch's "China: The Cost of Putting Business First" (New York, 1996), pp. 15-17.

223. E.g., Peng Shengjun and Tang Dingxuan, "Shei shuo qiufan wu renquan?"

(Who says prisoners lack human rights?), *XSB,* March 23, 1996, p. 2. The first author of this article (in the Xinjiang prison newspaper) is identified as a cadre (*ganjing*); the second as serving a sentence.

224. A good description of the conditions in the Qinghai laogai during the 1950s and 1960s, and how prisoners toiled on such infrastructure projects as roads, is Pu Ning's *Red in Tooth and Claw.* Inasmuch as Han Wei-Tien, who recounted his personal experiences to Pu Ning, was only involved in building the eastern section of the road from Xining to Golmud, he does not describe the construction of the western section near Golmud and the road from there to Dunhuang. But the living conditions for the prisoners were probably not very different in the various sections.

225. For one version of how the famine affected prisons in Qinghai and elsewhere, see Jasper Becker, *Hungry Ghosts: Mao's Secret Famine* (New York: Free Press, 1996), chapter 12.

226. What has been written in the West about Qinghai is in most cases outdated, despite the fact that the area has been open to foreigners since 1989. The best publication with a history of the development, natural resources and population transfer to this area is *HZZ.*

227. The percentages are for 1988. Since then the number of prisoners has declined and so has their share of the local population.

228. *Chaidamu Pendi dongbu keken qu kaocha baogao* (Research report on the possible agricultural reclamation area in the Eastern Chaidam Basin).

229. Haixi prefecture was not founded until 1954; Dulan District was already in charge of this area in 1953.

230. The cover name of this base was: Qinghai kuangqu 221 chang (Factory 221 of Qinghai mining district). The short version was just "Factory 221."

231. Not "80,000" as given as its "population" in the 1993 (p. 58) and 1994 (p. 67) editions of the *Laogai Handbook.* However, buried in a paragraph under "remarks" both handbooks say "No longer a prison." The 1996 edition (p. 73) simply gives a 1959 figure, for which year a "population" of 200,000 is claimed.

232. *Laogai Handbook,* 1996, p. 74.

233. *Qinghai Sheng nongye yu nongcun jingji zonglan,* p. 128.

234. Liu Xiaomeng, pp. 585-587.

235. *Qinghai Sheng shehui jingji tongji nianjian 1988* (Qinghai 1988 statistical yearbook), p. 159.

236. *XBN,* 1995 edition, p. 127.

237. Renamed Menyuan Prison *(Menyuan Jianyu)* in 1995.

238. Another laogai labor farm was set up as a branch — the Jintai labor farm.

239. The *Sheng laojiao suo,* located 25 kilometers west of Xining.

240. On juvenile delinquency in China generally, see Rocca, pp. 165-299, 315-319.

241. As of 1995.

242. Domenach cites various estimates, ranging from several hundred thousand to two million.

243. *Far Eastern Economic Review*, September 20, 1984.

244. *Qinghai 1988 Statistical Yearbook,* pp. 159 ff.; *Gansu 1995 Yearbook*, p. 698.

245. *Qinghai ribao,* March 1, 1993.

246. Ibid., March 23, 1995.

247. We have only precise figures for 1985, and depend on estimates for the years since then.

248. *Qinghai ribao,* March 1, 1993.

249. *Qinghai 1993 Statistical Yearbook,* p. 223.

250. *Kaifang* (Open Magazine), Hong Kong, January 1, 1996, p. 21.

251. Ibid.

252. *New York Times,* February 18, 1996.

253. *Kaifang,* January 1, 1996, p. 21.

254. Qinghai branch of the Ministry of Supervision, report of January 20, 1988. *Zhongguo Jiancha Nianjian 1989*, Beijing 1991, p. 197.

255. *Fazhi ribao,* December 10, 1988. Cited by Domenach, page 631.

256. *Qinghai ribao,* July 31, 1995.

257. Told in the book *Mian dui da di de zhenchan* (Facing the great earthquake). Xining: Qinghai People's Publishing House, 1990.

258. *Qinghai ribao,* November 14, 1993.

259. In this instance, the Seventh Squadron of the First Brigade of the Qinghai PAP's Second Detachment.

260. *MDDZ,* p. 214.

261. Ibid, p. 215.

262. Ibid.

263. Ibid., p. 228.

264. Ibid., p. 231.

265. Ibid., pp. 223-226.

266. Ibid., p. 226.

267. The PLA units that sent medical staff to the disaster area were: the 25th Section of the Logistics Department of Lanzhou Military District, the Logistics Department of Qinghai, and the Tibet Garrison of the General Staff and the military hospital of Unit 80306.

268. *MDDZ,* p. 227.

269. *Zhongguo Jiancha nianjian 1989,* p. 197.

270. Prisoners: 24,000; provincial population: 4.6 million.

271. For information on religious, pro-democracy activist, and ethnic minority prisoners, Amnesty International's *Repression in the 1990s: A Directory of Victims* is the most recent publication. On the case of Yu Zhenbin (a provincial archivist convicted as a "counterrevolutionary" for his 1989 activities), see AI report ASA 17/20/97/cor (May 19, 1997).

272. This institution was originally set up in 1956 under another name, and in 1966 was given the name still in use today.

273. *LS,* 1992, no. 3, p. 20.

274. Ibid. (The literacy figures for these prisoners is not very different from those for the Tibet Autonomous Region.)

275. This farm was renamed Guinan Prison *(Guinan Jianyu)* in 1995.

276. *Qinghai ribao,* July 5, 1993.

277. Ibid., May 23, 1995.

278. Ibid.

279. Ibid., October 20, 1995.

280. Ibid., May 23, 1995.

281. Number 19, dated October 7, 1992.

282. *Qinghai ribao,* February 4, 1993, p. 2.

283. Ibid., March 5, 1995, p. 3.

284. See James D. Seymour, "Cadre Accountability to the Law," *The Australian Journal of Chinese Affairs*, January 1989, pp. 1-27.

285. *Qinghai ribao,* April 25, 1996, p. 2.

286. During 1995, the Qinghai Provincial Laogai Bureau was renamed the Qinghai Provincial Prison Administration Bureau *(Qinghai Sheng Jianyu Guanli Ju)*.

287. NCNA, April 24, 1997, *SWB,* April 30, 1997, FE/2906, S1/3.

288. State Council's White Papers, cited endnote 12. For critiques, see "China: Political Prisoners Abused in Liaoning Province as Official Whitewash of Labor Reform System Continues" (Asia Watch, September 1992), and "China's Laogai: Comments on 'Criminal Reform in China'" (The Laogai Research Foundation, September 1992).

289. *FGY*, 1991, no. 2, p. 30.

290. See, for example, *Zhongguo xibu da jianyu* (Major prisons of western China) (Jiangsu Literature and Art Publishing House, 1986), pp. 49-52, in which violence and degrading treatment among prisoners, and the use of stun guns by guards, is described in graphic, even sensational, terms.

291. Press release of the Laogai Research Foundation (Milpitas, California), October 23, 1995.

292. Chu Han, p. 57.

293. John Wilson Lewis and Xue Litai, *China Builds the Bomb*, p. 178.

294. "More on the Reform of the Economic System" (in Chinese), *FGY*, no. 6, June 1990, pp. 1-8.

295. "Zuigao Renmin Jianchayuan gongzuo baogao" (Work report of the Supreme People's Procuratorate), *Tibet Daily,* April 11, 1995.

296. *FGY*, 1990, no. 5, p. 26.

297. *New York Times,* March 6, 1997, p. 10.

298. *China Daily,* May 31, 1996.

299. In 1997, Tian Chengping, secretary of the provincial party committee, admitted that "the increase in the number of narcotics-related criminal cases has not effectively been curbed." He called for "paying attention to attacking opium poppy growers, drug makers, drug traffickers, and drug abusers." The provincial Party Committee thereupon decided "to especially wage a large anti-narcotics struggle across the province and to mobilize all social forces and all people throughout the province to join the anti-narcotics battle." *Qinghai ribao,* April 11, 1997, p. 1, *SWB,* FE/2905, p. G/19. See also similar report in *Qinghai ribao,* April 16, 1997, p. 1, *SWB,* FE/2909, pp. G/9-10.

300. *China: Repression.*

301. Reports of the arrests of such people (often in large groups) are common. See, for example, *Eastern Express,* September 28, 1995, p. 13, FBIS, September 28, 1995, pp. 22-23.

302. In mid-1997, China's most prominent political prisoner, Wei Jingsheng, told a visiting relative that he had been beaten by fellow inmates, apparently at the behest of prison authorities. Wei was being held in a prison 100 miles east of Beijing. *New York Times,* June 27, 1997, p. A2.

303. It is implied to the contrary in the 1994 *Laogai Handbook,* p. 1.

304. Reuters, January 27, 1995, citing an anonymous Justice Ministry official.

305. Wu, *Laogai,* p. 19. Wu quotes a 1985 "internal document" as follows: "Of those currently detained, counter-revolutionaries comprise almost 10 percent; those with a historical counter-revolutionary background comprise only 1.6 percent of the total inmates." Wu follows the quotation immediately with this sentence of his own: "This 400,000 figure [the first time we have seen this number] does not include those imprisoned under the auspices of RTL [reeducation through labor]; the number of RTL convicts is probably not much less than 400,000. RTL is very convenient for dealing with counter-revolutionaries and 'anti-socialist elements.'" This seems to imply that Wu considers a large portion (perhaps half) of labor reeducation inmates to be political cases, implying an overall total of more than 600,000 political prisoners.

306. Some may also be from Tibet, though in many cases they are people who are considered to have illegally crossed the border into Nepal. See page 115, footnote B.

307. Mao Sen, "Two Justice Ministry Documents," *Jiushi niandai*, January 1, 1992, pp. 76-77; FBIS, January 17, 1992, p. 20.

308. On how the issue played out at Geneva in April 1997, see *New York Times,* April 16, 1997, p. A-11.

309. Zhang Wenhua, "It Is Imperative that We Improve the Quality of Rank-and-File Cadres" (in Chinese), *BLGT,* 1990, no. 1, p. 4.

310. In 1995, China reported to the UN on the torture situation (its 1989 report having been found inadequate). See *Second Periodic Reports of State Parties Due in 1993. Addendum. China.* CAT/C/20/ADD.5, 20 February 1996. For Amnesty International's response in 1996, see *People's Republic of China: Torture and Ill Treatment— Comments on China's Second Periodic Report to the UN Committee Against Torture* (ASA 17/51/96).

311. Reuters dispatch, May 6, 1996.

312. Dutton (p. 315) describes them as receiving very favorable treatment.

313. See, for example, Amnesty International's *China: Torture and Ill-Treatment of Prisoners* (London: 1987), and *Torture in China* (London: 1992). See also Saunders, chapter 4.

314. Xiao Yuan, "Explanation of 'People's Republic of China Prison Law (Draft),'" presented to the Eleventh Meeting of the Eighth NPC Standing Committee on October 21, 1994," *NPC Standing Committee Bulletin,* no. 8, December 31, 1994, pp. 16-19, FBIS, May 5, 1995, p. 29.

315. January 7, 1995, quoted in *Laogai Handbook*, 1996, pp. 4-5.

316. "Behavioral Standards for Labor Reform and Labor Reeducation Cadres," September 10, 1991, Ministry of Justice, no. 17, *BLGT,* 1992, no. 1, pp. 5-6.

317. Associated Press dispatch by Elaine Kurtenbach, April 15, 1997 (Internet).

318. The main exceptions were (1) exiled officials who had completed their terms or whose sentences had been commuted, and (2) any prisoners who had served at least ten years and were too old or disabled to work; such people were sent home. Waley-Cohen, pp. 6, 194.

319. E.g., Shenyang Radio, May 14, 1984, *SWB,* May 17, 1984, FE/7645/BII/6.

320. Some Western countries, such as Holland, impose a somewhat analogous regime. A person can be held for an unlimited time under detention, even after the sentence has been served, if he or she is considered a danger to society.

321. Article 62 of the Regulations on Labor Reform, as translated in *Detained at Official Pleasure,* p. 15.

322. Labor Reform Document (1955) no. 35, translated in ibid.

323. *Laodong gaizao zuifan xingman shifang ji anzhi jiuye zhexing chuli banfa* (Interim provisions for dealing with resettling released prisoners and jiuye cases). Approved by the State Council, August 26, 1954. Text circulated internally.

324. Ministry of Public Security report, September 9, 1981, translated in *Detained at Official Pleasure,* p. 16.

325. Harry Wu, *Laogai — The Chinese Gulag* (Boulder: Westview, 1992), pp. 6, 13-14. "Because of this system," Wu writes, " . . . very few prisoners have actually been released" (p. 14).

326. Domenach, p. 256 (citing *Xingdao ribao,* January 16, 1968).

327. Liu Xiaomeng, p. 344.

328. Gonganbu directive 1981, No. 135, issued by the Eighth National Laogai Conference, May 4, 1983, *SFSC,* vol. 2, p. 734.

329. For example, on January 23, 1983, it was ordered that all returned overseas Chinese who had been on jiuye be released. All such measures were a follow-through on the 1980 State Council document Guo Fa 239.

330. Document no. 12, 1985, Laodong Renshi Bu.

331. Zhong Fa, No. 67, State Council, 1980.

332. Issued by Hebei province, Ji-gong No. 40, 1983.

333. "Decision of the Standing Committee of the National People's Congress Concerning the Handling of Persons Undergoing Reform Through Labor or Reeducation through Labor Who Escape or Reoffend (1981)," translated in *Chinese Law and Government,* September 1994, pp. 66-67. (Escapees were also to have up to seven years added to their prison sentences.)

334. "Notice of the State Council Concerning the Transfer and Issue of 'Trial Measures on Reeducation through Labor' from the Ministry of Public Security (1992)," *Chinese Law and Government,* September 1994, p. 81.
It is possible that the most recent official statement on the subject (the actual text of which we have not seen) deals with the ambiguities mentioned above. That advisory, issued under the auspices of Zhongyang Zong Zhi Wei (General Political Committee [of the Party]), and signed by six ministries, is: "Suggestions Concerning

Strengthening Resettlement and Training Work for Released Labor Reform and Labor Reeducation Prisoners." From what we have heard, it would appear that the "Suggestions" do not entail any major departures from past practices.

335. Summary of the Eighth National Conference on Labor Reform Work, translated in *Detained at Official Pleasure,* p. 17.

336. See official notice (dated November 16, 1984) to this effect in *Xingfa fabian* (Administrative law compilation), pp. 1596-1597.

337. February 15, 1992, p. 2.

338. For summary, see *XSB,* October 15, 1994, p. 2.

339. Domenach, p. 638. These figures refer to prisoners incarcerated before 1956, of which there had been 161,000, with 70,000 now remaining on jiuye. It is not clear whether 161,000 is the total number of pre-1956 detainees (in which case some would have died), or whether it is the number remaining alive.

340. Speech by Hu Zhaozhang, bingtuan deputy commander, *XSB,* March 16, 1996, p. 1 of special feature.

341. Jia (see endnote 11), p. 2.

342. Yang and Shen, p. 230.

343. Jin Fuhai, "Methods of Enforced Jiuye" (in Chinese), *FGY,* 1988:6, p. 28.

344. Qu Fanqi, *"Dui qianjiang fan xinmang liuchang jiuye de diaocha yu fenxi"* (Investigation and analysis of the jiuye situation with regard to inmates sent to Xinjiang), *BLGT,* 1992, no. 5, p. 22.

345. For example, Notice No. 572 (November 16, 1984) from the Supreme Court, Ministry of Public Security, and Ministry of Justice.

346. See Gonganbu directive 1981, no. 135, *SFSC,* vol. 2, p. 734.

347. Yu De, *"Qianjiang chengshi zuifan gaizao zhi wojian"* (My view of reforming urban criminals sent to Xinjiang), *Bingtuan Laogai Gongzuo Tongxun,* 1993, no. 1, p. 30.

348. Qu Fanqi, *"Dui qianjiang fan xinmang liuchang jiuye de diaocha yu fenxi"* (Investigation and analysis of the jiuye situation with regard to inmates sent to Xinjiang), *BLGT,* 1992, no. 5, p. 22.

349. Ibid.

350. *China Daily* (April 4, 1995, p. 3) put the "national average" at "6 to 8 percent." The same was reiterated by Justice Minister Xiao Yang in 1997. Reuters, May 15, 1997.

351. Former prisoners were tracked for three years. The number tracked were: 1982: 2,418; 1983: 2,364; 1984: 2,750; 1985: 3,684; 1986: 4,542; 1987: 3,507. *BLGT,* May 22, 1993, p. 1, editorial.

352. *SFXZ,* March 1992, vol. 1, no. 1, pp. 1-2.

353. Survey of bingtuan's Eighth Division, a squadron in the First Detachment (not otherwise identified). Of 254 prisoners, 109 were classified as *dingju.* Sixty percent of these were recidivist. Yu De, *"Qianjiang chengshi zuifan gaizao zhi wojian"* (My view of reforming urban criminals sent to Xinjiang, *Bingtuan Laogai Gongzuo Tongxun,* 1993, no. 1, p. 30.

354. *New York Times,* July 11, 1996, p. A-8. Gangs are also comprised of unemployed youths.

355. *The Economist,* November 16, 1996, p. 60.

356. *XSB,* January 22, 1994, p. 1.

357. "Reply Letter of the Ministry of Labor and the Ministry of Justice Concerning Whether Labor Contracts Shall Be Terminated Where Workers under the System of Labor Contracts have Completed Reeducation Through Labor (1988)," translated in *Chinese Law and Government,* September 1994, pp. 86-87.

358. *XSB,* June 11, 1994, p. 2.

359. *The House of the Dead (Prison Life in Siberia),* Everyman Edition, part I, chapter 2. ("Hulks" refers to prison ships.)

360. This calculation is based on a population of 23.52 million and 33,000 prisoners on January 1, 1995.

361. This calculation is based on a population of 4.74 million and 23,000 prisoners on January 1, 1995.

362. This calculation is based on a population of 16.20 million and 85,000 prisoners on January 1, 1995.

363. Explained on page 206.

364. Based on a provincial population of 44,380,000, and 50,000 prisoners (a number reported in *China Daily,* April 19, 1995, p. 3, and confirmed by internal documentation).

365. *Zhongguo Renmin Gongheguo sheng, zizhiqu, zhixia shi dang zheng ji guan zuzhi jigou gaiyao* (General outline of the organization of provincial-level party and government organs in the PRC). Beijing: China Personnel Press, 1989, pp. 330, 354, 364, and passim.

366. Minister of Justice Xiao Yang, quoted by Reuters, May 15, 1997. At other times, the more rounded figure of 1.4 million has been cited. *China Focus,* April 1997, p. 4.

This indicates a 9 percent increase compared to the 1.286 million reported in the State Council's "Human Rights Progress in China," December 25, 1996, FBIS, June 10, 1996, p. 29. A slightly lower figure (1,285,000) had been given by Justice Minister Xiao Yang, quoted in *South China Morning Post,* February 15, 1995, and Reuters, January 27, 1995. The total since 1983 was put at 3.84 million. Since 1949, 10 million were said to have been imprisoned, though we believe the figure should be between 20 million and 25 million.

367. Reuters, May 15, 1997 (Internet) and otherwise confirmed.

According to internal sources, in 1992, the total number of prison cadres *(renmin jingcha)* in *lao* prisons and camps (including the Xinjiang bingtuan) was 257,906. Of these, 126,168 were *jingsi,* 109,352 were *jingdu,* 20,426 were *jingyuan,* and 1,960 were *jingjian* (top officials). The category *ganjing* (cadre police) normally denotes *jingdu* and/or *jingsi.*

368. For both years, margin of error $= \pm 10\%$.

369. This calculation is based on a population of 1.2 billion and 2 million prisoners.

370. The previous sentences in this paragraph are drawn from Tanner (see p. 11, note A), whose analysis is based on two articles in *FGY* (4:1, 5:25).

371. Quoted in Lan Wubin and Lin Zhengju, "On Human Rights, Criminals' Rights, and the Special Characteristics of China's Labor Reform System" (in Chinese), *BLGT,* 1995, no. 5, p. 6.

Actually, this policy had been originally identified with Liu Shaoqi, who had advanced the idea in 1956.

372. *FGY,* no. 6, p. 3.

373. "The labor reform camps . . . constitute an integral part of the economy of the socialist society." Wu, *Laogai,* p. 49.

374. This is true not only of propagandists; even reputable scholars have erred. For example, an otherwise excellent article in a distinguished journal contained the following statement: "Altogether, labor reform is a huge business. In 1993, the system was reported to have RMB 105 billion in fixed assets *(guding zichan yuanzhi)* and over RMB 40 billion in circulating funds *(liudong zijin)." (China Information,* Winter 1994/95, p. 43.) The author, who has acknowledged his error to us, was off by a factor of ten, due to a translation error; the correct numbers are a much more modest RMB 10.5 and 4 billion, respectively.

375. This is based on a reported RMB 2.06 billion for the first half of the year, an increase of 300 million over the previous period. *China Daily,* August 5, 1988.

376. In 1988 prices, the gross value of industrial output was RMB 1,822 billion; gross agricultural output RMB 587 billion. *(Tongji nianjian, 1992,* pp. 329, 406.) If one assumes that the laogai figure is comparable to these (i.e., includes the same degree of "gross" double-counting), the laogai percentage of the combined total is 0.17. If one assumes that there is little or no double counting in the laogai figure, then to make it comparable the laogai figure should be adjusted to about RMB 6.5 billion (gross), increasing its percentage to 0.25% (which we believe to be the largest conceivable percentage).

Note that the 0.2% figure is about in line with our estimates for the number of prisoners as a percentage of the national population.

377. The laogai's output in 1990 was said to be "2.5 billion yuan, which is about 0.08 percent of the nation's total industrial and agricultural production output value for the year." State Council, "Criminal Reform in China," *Beijing Review,* August 17, 1992, p. 16.

378. It is indicated that during the first half of 1988 "profits and taxes handed in amounted to 330 million yuan." *(China Daily,* August 5, 1988.) If one assumes that the laogai did not incur any expenses for the state (which we can hardly say), then that would mean that the system had been profitable.

379. Wang Zengze, *"Jiefang sixiang, juaju jiyu; jiaqiang fazhan disan chanye"* (Liberate thinking, grasp opportunities, accelerate the development of tertiary economy), *FGY,* 1993, no. 2, p. 10 and passim.

380. However, it is common for prisoners in the United States to be required to work, and it is not against American law to *export* US-made products, which is often done. For example, jeans (marketed as "Prison Blues") made by Oregon prisoners are popular in Asia. For a detailed report on prison labor in the United States (examined in the context of the debate about human rights in China), see Paul Blustein, "Prison Labor: Can U.S. Point Finger at China," *Washington Post,* June 3, 1997, pp. C-1, C-4).

381. *China Daily,* August 5, 1988. (We consider these figures to be inflated.)

382. Based on plans described in *China Youth News,* subsequently described in *China Daily,* August 5, 1988.

383. FBIS, December 17, 1991. Actually, it may well be that a substantial amount of tea is exported. See *Kuai bao* (Express news, Hong Kong), October 31, 1994, p. 12, excerpted in *Inside China Mainland,* January 1995, pp. 25-26.

384. Wang Zengze (see endnote 379), pp. 10 and passim.

385. Sun Xiaoping and Yang Jianmin, "Exploring the Laogai Economy in the Wake of 'Eating Imperial Grain,' " *BLGT,* 1994, no. 5, pp. 25-27. "Eating imperial grain" refers to Beijing's new policy of financing the prison system. The authors are cadres in the Heilongjiang prison system (Qiqihar), but their views are doubtless equally applicable to the other provinces.

386. Wu Yiliang, director of Shijiazhuang's reeducation-through-labor reformatory, Shijiazhuang Radio, February 2, 1996, FBIS, February 6, 1996, p. 82.

387. Dutton, "One Story, Two Readings" (see p. 11, n. A), pp. 309, 313.

388. Ibid., p. 349.

389. Ibid., p. 353.

390. Ibid., p. 12.

391. Ibid., p. 204.

392. Ibid., p. 311. (The "Columbia critics" charge would be highly unfair to one of us, but the other might have to plead guilty.)

393. Ibid., p. 204.

394. Ibid., pp. 255-262, and 314-315, respectively.

395. See page 7 of this book.

396. James D. Seymour, *China: The Politics of Revolutionary Reintegration* (New York: Thomas Y. Crowell Co., 1976), p. 102.

397. Alan Bullock, *Hitler and Stalin* (New York: Random House, 1993), p. 284. The disparity is even more stark if one were to compare death rates.

398. In 1992 the crime rate was said to be "2 per thousand per year." State Council,

"Criminal Reform in China," *Beijing Review*, August 17, 1992, p. 11.

399. In 1995 China had a reported 545,162 defendants; 219,922 (40.34%) of them received sentences of 5 years or more or the death sentence. Ren Jianxin, quoted in *Qinghai ribao*, March 24, 1996, p. 2.

400. *Time* (Asia Edition), October 28, 1995, p. 21.

401. *The Economist*, June 8, 1996, p. 24.

402. 1987 figure. Norway is the lowest of the Scandinavian countries. *Nordisk statistisk arsbok* (Yearbook of Nordic statistics), Stockholm: Nordic Council, 1989, p. 337.

403. Figure for 1993 (shortly after the dissolution of the Soviet Union). *The Human Rights Watch Global Report on Prisons* (New York, 1993), p. 225.

404. Derived from *The Human Rights Watch Global Report on Prisons* (New York, 1993), p. 241.

405. Rough estimate for 1986. Ibid., p. 127.

406. The official Chinese government figure for the 1994 prison population was 1,286,000, or "10.7 per 10,000 people." State Council, "Human Rights Progress in China," December 25, 1996, FBIS, June 10, 1996, p. 29.

In 1993 China reported to the UN that there were "about 1 prisoner per 1,000 inhabitants," i.e., 100 per 100,000. It appears that 107 has been rounded downward, a common practice.

407. Based on year-end 1995 figures, supplied to the authors by the Taipei Economic & Cultural Office (unofficial consulate), New York.

408. *The Economist*, June 8, 1996, p. 24. *The Human Rights Watch Global Report on Prisons* (New York, 1993), p. 126, gives a figure of 144.

409. Figure for 1993 (shortly after the dissolution of the Soviet Union). *The Human Rights Watch Global Report on Prisons* (New York, 1993), p. 222.

410. *The Economist*, June 8, 1996, p. 24.

411. According to U.S. Justice Department statistics, in June 1994 there were 100,000 prisoners in the United States federal prisons, one million in state prisons, and 500,000 in local jails. (*New York Times*, December 4, 1995, and July 7, 1996). The population of the U.S. at the time was 260,714,000.

A more recent figure for the number of incarcerated Americans is 1.6 million for the end of 1995. NPR, August 19, 1996.

412. *The Human Rights Watch Global Report on Prisons*, p. 126.

413. Interview, radio station WNYC (New York), November 15, 1996.

414. See Robert Jay Lifton, *Thought Reform and the Psychology of Totalism: A Study of Brainwashing in China* (New York: Norton, 1961); Edward Hunter, *Brain-Washing in Red China* (New York: Vanguard, 1953); and Edgar H. Schein et al., *Coercive Persuasion: A Socio-Psychological Analysis of the "Brainwashing of American Civilian Prisoners by the Chinese Communists"* (New York: Norton, 1961).

415. On these two cultures, see Tanner (cited p. 16, n. A), especially pp. 51-53.

416. Quoted in *The Human Rights Watch Global Report on Prisons* (New York, 1993), p. 137.

417. Wu, *Laogai,* pp. 3-5.

418. In Vorkuta, about 500,000 died between 1946 and 1954. See Aleksandr I. Solzhenitsyn, *The Gulag Archipelago* (New York: Harper and Row, 1979), parts III and V, passim. (In 1981 in China this work was translated into Chinese. It is available in the internal libraries of the Ministries of Justice and of Public Security.)

419. Matthew Purdy, "Prison's Violent Culture Enveloping Its Guards," *New York Times*, December 19, 1995, pp. A1 and B8 (a feature-length article primarily about the prisons of New York State).

420. Harry Wu, quoted in *Financial Times,* November 25, 1995, p. xxii.

421. Published in *Guonei dongtai qingyang* (Drafts of domestic trends), April 6, 1982, vol. 718.

422. Reuters dispatch by Mure Dickie, May 15, 1997 (Internet).

423. See Jeffrey A. Winters, "Down with the World Bank," *Far Eastern Economic Review,* February 13, 1997, p. 29. (This commentary, which does not mention China, focuses on the way that bank funds feed corruption in Indonesia, and socialism in Vietnam.) On the bank's efforts to meet the criticisms that have been launched against it, see *New York Times,* February 21, 1997, pp. D1 and D3.

424. *Washington Post,* December 21, 1995, p. 41.

425. Reuters report, October 23, 1995, by Jim Wolf.

426. Harry Wu, testimony before the U.S. Senate Committee on Foreign Relations, July 15, 1996, p. 4.

427. Both statements made in Laogai Research Foundation press release of October 23, 1995.

428. XBTN, 1995 edition, p. 227.

429. Bank spokeswoman Lauren Ptito, quoted in *Far Eastern Economic Review,* August 8, 1996, p. 25.

430. Agence France Presse, December 29, 1996, citing NCNA, carried by China News Digest (Internet), December 31, 1996.

431. "Report on Views About Amendment of the Prison Law (Amended Draft of the Draft Law)," submitted to the National People's Congress on December 28, 1994. U.S. Foreign Broadcast Information Service, CHI-95-087, May 5, 1995, pp. 20-21.

432. Extract from a report by the inspector general, Zhang Siqing, concerning the work of the Jiancha Yuan in 1995. Source: *Qinghai ribao*, March 25, 1996.

433. UN Doc. reference: CAT/C/XVI/CRP.1/Add. 5, pp. 8-10.

434. *GFH.*

435. *GFH.*

436. *GFH.*

437. NCNA, March 23, 1990, FBIS, April 16, 1990, pp. 34-36.

438. As revised by the National People's Congress, March 17, 1996. Articles 214-225 concern imprisonment. NCNA, March 23, 1996 (Chinese); FBIS, April 9, 1996, pp. 24-47 (translation).

439. The section most relevant to human rights problems (articles 102-113) appears as Appendix B of the Human Rights Watch/Human Rights in China report *Chinese Legal "Reforms" Have Serious Implications for Hong Kong,* April 29,1997, pp. 50-55.

440. Internal Ministry of Justice document no. 12, November 6, 1990. Translation from Human Rights Watch, "The Price of Obscurity in China: Revelations About Prisoners Arrested After June 4, 1989," *Xin Zhongguo Sifa jieshi daquan* (New China encyclopedia of judicial explanations), Beijing: Zhongguo Jiancha Chubanshe, 1992, pp. 44-48. We have made minor revisions in the translation.

441. This is our own translation of an internal document.
Somewhat related is "Circular on Visits by Foreign Business People to Labor-Reform Enterprises to Inspect Ordered Goods, and Related Problems," issued by the Ministry of Public Security, November 27, 1979, in *A Collection of Standard*

Interpretations of the Laws of the People's Republic of China (in Chinese), People's Publishing House of Jilin Province (Jilin 1990), pp. 1577-1578, translated in Asia Watch, "Forced Labor Exports from China: Update No. 1," September 10, 1991, pp. 7-8. According to Article 5, "During their visit, effective supervisory measures must be taken and control must be strictly exercised in accordance with the principle of 'internal repression, outward relaxation' *(neijin waisong)*. . . ."

442. Ministry of Justice Order 1991, No. 11. Our text is taken from Mao Sen, "Two Justice Ministry Documents," *Jiushi niandai*, January 1, 1992, pp. 76-77, FBIS, January 17, 1992, pp. 20-21.

443. This law was passed by the Eleventh Meeting of the Eighth National People's Congress Standing Committee on December 29, 1994, and was published in the *National People's Congress Standing Committee Bulletin,* no. 8, December 31, 1994, pp. 5-16. Our translation is taken from FBIS, May 5, 1995, pp. 21-27.

Bibliography

Periodicals:

BLGT: Bingtuan laogai gongzuo tongxun (Bingtuan laogai work bulletin). Bimonthly published by the Xinjiang Production and Construction Bingtuan Labor Reform Work Editorial Office. N.p. (Urumqi?)

CD: China Daily. Beijing.

CLG: Chinese Law and Government. Armonk, N.Y.

FGY: Fanzui yu gaizao yanjiu (Studies on criminals and reform). Beijing.

FBIS: U. S. Foreign Broadcast Information Service, *Daily Report,* People's Republic of China (hard-copy version unless "electronic version" is indicated).

Gansu fazhi bao (Gansu legal news). Lanzhou.

Gansu laogai bao (Gansu Province labor reform news). Gansu internal newspaper no. 2114. Editions per year: 36. Circulation: 10,500 (prisoners: 7,000, guards: 3,500). Employees: 279 prisoners, 300 others.

ICM: Inside China Mainland (Taipei).

LLLY: Laogai laojiao lilun yanjiu (Studies on labor reform and labor reeducation). Beijing.

Laogai laojiao yanjiu gongzuo (Labor reform and labor reeducation study). Xinjiang publication for guards.

LS: Laogaixue yu shijian (Labor reform study and practice). Xinjiang publication for guards.

Qinghai laogai gongzuo bao (Qinghai Province labor reform work news). Qinghai internal newspaper no. B-033. Editions per year: 26. Circulation: 7,500 (primarily guards). Employees: 80 prisoners, 40 others.

Qianshao (Front line). Hong Kong.

Qinghai fazhi bao (Qinghai Legal News). Xining.

QHRB. Qinghai ribao. (Qinghai daily). Xining.

Qinghai xinsheng bao (Qinghai Province new life news). Qinghai internal newspaper no. B-033. Editions per year: 26. Circulation: 7,500 (primarily prisoners). Employees: 80 prisoners, 40 others.

Renmin jingcha (People's police). Shanghai.

SCMP. South China Morning Post (Hong Kong).

SFSC: Sifa shouci (Handbook for the administration of justice), Jilin: 1983, People's Court Publishers.

SFXZ: Sifa xingzheng (Law Administration). Beijing (Ministry of Justice).

SWB: BBC Summary of World Broadcasts, Asia-Pacific.

XJLG: Xinjiang jianyu laogai gaizao yanjiu (Xinjiang prison laogai reform studies).

XJRB: Xinjiang ribao. (Xinjiang daily). Urumqi.

Xinjiang xinsheng bao (Xinjiang new life news). Xinjiang internal newspaper no. 0072-B14-0026. Editions per year: 24. Circulation (prisoners): 6,100 Chinese-language, 3,000 Uyghur.

XSB: Xinsheng bao (New life news). Xinjiang internal newspaper no. 0071. Founded in 1954. Editions per year: 26. Circulation: 10,000 (primarily bingtuan prisoners). Employees: 100 prisoners, 59 others. Editions per year: 26. Employees: 100 prisoners, 59 others.

Xinjiang shenpan yanjiu (Xinjiang adjudication studies). Quarterly.

Books:

Amnesty International. *China: Repression in the 1990s — A Directory of Victims.* London: Amnesty International, 1996. See also publications cited in endnotes 5, 13, 20, 38, 80, 216, 310, and 313.

Bayinguoleng tongji nianjian (Statistical yearbook of Bayangol Prefecture), *1996.* Beijing: China Statistical Press, 1996.

Bernstein, Thomas. *Up to the Mountains and Down to the Villages: The Transfer of Youth from Urban to Rural China.* New Haven: Yale University Press, 1977.

Bodard, Lucien. *La Chine du cauchemar.* Gallimard: Paris?, 1961.

— . *Chinas Lächelndes Gesicht.* Hamburg: Fischer Bücherei, 1961.

Chu Han. *Zhongguo, 1959-1961 — San nian ziran zaihai chang pian jishi* (China, 1959-1961: Record of three years of natural disaster). Chengdu:

Sichuan People's Press, 1996.

CJCC. Lawyers Committee for Human Rights. *Criminal Justice with Chinese Characteristics: China's Criminal Process and Violations of Human Rights*. New York: 1993.

Cohen, Jerome Alan. *The Criminal Process in the People's Republic of China, 1949-1963: An Introduction*. Cambridge, Mass.: Harvard University Press, 1968.

Cutting off the Serpent's Head: Tightening Control in Tibet, 1994-1995. Tibet Information Network (London), and Human Rights Watch, New York, 1966.

Deng Youtian, ed. *Laodong gaizao zuifan de lilun yu shijian* (Theory and practice of labor reform of criminals). N.p.: Falü Chubanshe, 1987.

Detained at Official Pleasure: Arbitrary Detention in the People's Republic of China. New York: Human Rights in China, 1993.

DCT. Detained in China and Tibet: A Directory of Political and Religious Prisoners. New York: Human Rights Watch, 1994.

Domenach, Jean-Luc. *Chine: l'archipel oublié*. [Fayard: N.p. (Paris?), 1992].

Duan Kewen. *"Zhanfan" zishu* (A "prisoner of war's" own account). New York: World Journal Press, 1973.

Dutton, Michael R. *Policing and Punishment in China: From Patriarchy to "the People."* Hong Kong: Cambridge University Press, 1992.

Epstein, Edward J. *Legal Documents and Materials on Administrative Detention in the People's Republic of China*. *CLG* (special issue), September 1994.

Gansu nianjian (Gansu yearbook). Beijing: China Statistical Publishing House. Various editions from 1985 to 1996. The 1995 edition was primarily used.

Gansu nongcun jingji nianjian (Gansu farming village economy yearbook). Beijing: China Statistical Publishing House. Primarily used were the 1994 and 1996 editions.

Ge'ermu juan (Golmud volume). Beijing: China Encyclopedia Publishing House 1992.

GFH. Gongan fagui huiban, 1950-1979. Beijing: Legal Press, 1980.

He Weimin. *Jianming zuifan gaizao xinlixue* (Concise studies on psychiatric criminal reform). Harbin: Heilongjiang Renmin Chubanshe, 1987.

HZZ: Haixi zhou zhi, juan yi (Historical records of Haixi prefecture, volume 1), Xining: Qinghai People's Publishing House, 1995. (Also available in Mongolian.)

Hsia Tao-ti. *Forced Labor in the PRC: Report to the Congress*. Washington: Library of Congress, 1990.

Jia Lusheng and Feng Shuo. *Zhongguo xibu de jianyu* (Major prisons in West China). Nanjing: Jiangsu wenyi chubanshe, 1986.

Kang Shu-hua et al. *Nü xing zuifan lun* (On female prisoners). Lanzhou: Lanzhou University Press, 1988.

Lai Ying. *Les Prisons de Mao*. Paris: Raoul Solar, 1970.

Laodong gaizao faxue jiaoxue cankao ziliao. (Educational materials concerning labor reform). Beijing: Institute of Political and Legal Studies on Labor Reform, 1985.

Laogai Handbook (latest year: 1996). Laogai Research Foundation, P.O.B 361375, Milpitas CA 95036, USA.

Lewis, John Wilson, and Xue Litai. *China Builds the Bomb*. Stanford: Stanford University Press, 1988.

Li Kangqin, general ed. *Laodong gaizao faxue yanjiu zongshu* (Researches on labor reform legal studies). Beijing: People's University Press, 1993.

Liu Xiaomeng et al. *Zhongguo zhiqing shi dian* (A dictionary of China's educated youth). Chengdu: Sichuan People's Press, 1995.

Lu Ping. *Chi dao de qianhui* (Late regrets: In and Out of Prison). Shanghai: Zhishi Chubanshe, 1990.

Mao Zedong, The Writings of, 1949-1976. Michael Y. M. Kau and John K. Leung, eds. Armonk, New York: M. E. Sharpe, Inc., 1986.

McMillen, Donald H. *Chinese Communist Power and Policy in Xinjiang, 1949-1977*. Boulder: Westview, 1979.

MDDZ. Mian dui da di de zhenchan (Facing the great earthquake). Xining: Qinghai People's Publishing House, 1990.

Moseley, George. *A Sino-Soviet Cultural Frontier: The Ili Kazakh Autonomous Chou*. Cambridge, Mass: Harvard University Press, 1966.

Nong Ba Shi kenqu shihezi shi zhi (Historical records of the [Bingtuan] Eighth Agricultural Division's reclamation district and Shihezi City). Urumqi: Xinjiang People's Publishing House, 1994.

Nong Yi Shi zhi (Historical records of the [bingtuan] First Agricultural Division). Urumqi: Xinjiang People's Publishing House, 1994.

Nuclear Tibet: Nuclear Weapons and Nuclear Waste on the Tibetan Plateau. Washington: International Campaign for Tibet, 1993.

Opening to Reform? An Analysis of China's Revised Criminal Procedure Law. New York Lawyers Committee for Human Rights, 1996.

Pasqualini, Jean (Bao Ruowang). *Prisonnier de Mao*. Geneva: Éditions Famot, reprinted 1977). Trans: *Prisoner of Mao*. New York: Coward McCann, 1973.

Peng Yinhan, *Dalu jizhongying*. (Concentration camps on mainland [China]). Taipei: Shibao wenhua chubanshiye.

Pu Ning, *Red in Tooth and Claw*: Twenty-six Years in Communist Chinese Prisons. New York: Grove Press, 1994.

Qinghai sheng nongye yu nongcun jingji zonglan (Overview of agriculture and farming village economy of Qinghai Province). Xining: Qinghai People's Publishing House, 1995.

Qinghai Sheng shehui jingji tongji. . . . nianjian (Qinghai. . . . statistical yearbook). Various editions used.

Qinghai Tongji Nianjian (Qinghai Statistical Yearbook). Beijing, China Statistical Publishing House. Various editions from 1988 to 1996. The 1994 edition was primarily used.

Rocca, Jean-Louis, *L'empire et son milieu: la criminalité en Chine populaire*. Paris: Plon, 1991.

Saunders, Kate. *Eighteen Layers of Hell: Stories from the Chinese Gulag*. London: Cassell, 1996.

Shao Mingzheng. *Zhongguo laogai faxue lilun yanjiu zongshu* (Research on the legal theory of China's labor reform). Beijing: Zhongguo Zhengfa Daxue Chubanshe, 1992.

Sun Xiaoli, *Laodong gaizao xinglun* (On labor reform punishment). Beijing: China Security University Press, 1992.

— , *Zhongguo laodong gaizao zhidu de lilun yu shijian: lishi yu xianshi* (History and reality of the theory and practice of labor reform in China). Beijing: Politics and Law University Press, 1994.

Torture in China. London: Amnesty International, 1992.

Troyer, Ronald J., John P. Clark, and Dean G. Rojek, eds. *Social Control in the People's Republic of China*. New York: Praeger, 1989.

Unger, Roberto R. *The White Book on Forced Labor and Concentration Camps in the People's Republic of China,* Vol 2. Paris: Centre International d'Édition et de Documentation, 1958.

Waley-Cohen, Joanna. *Exile in Mid-Qing China: Banishment to Xinjiang, 1758-1820*. New Haven: Yale University Press, 1991.

Wang Zhongfang, ed. *Zhongguo shehui zhi'an zonghe zhili de lilun yu shijian* (The comprehensive administration of social controls in China: theory and practice). Beijing: Masses Press, 1989.

Wang Fei, ed. *Renquan jilu: Shanghai jianyu* (Human rights record: A Shanghai prison). Shanghai: Renmin chubanshe, 1992.

Whyte, Martin King. *Small Groups and Political Rituals in China.* University of California Press: Berkeley, 1974. (Chapter 9: "Corrective Labor Camp Inmates and Political Rituals.")

Wu, Harry, *Bitter Winds*. New York: John Wiley, 1994.

— , *Laogai — The Chinese Gulag*. Boulder: Westview, 1992.

— , *Troublemaker: One Man's Crusade Against China's Cruelty*. New York: Random House, 1996.

Xin Zhongguo sifa jieshi daquan (Explaining the laws of New China), Beijing: Zhongguo Jiancha Chubanshe, 1992.

XBN. Xinjiang Shengchan Jianshe Bingtuan nianjian (Yearbook of the Xinjiang production and construction bingtuan). Urumqi: Xinjiang University Press. The 1994 edition was primarily used.

XBTN. Xinjiang Shengchan Jianshe Bingtuan tongji nianjian (Statistical Yearbook of the Xinjiang Production and Construction Bingtuan). Beijing: China Statistics Press. The 1995 edition was primarily used.

Xue Meixing, ed. *Zhongguo jianyu shi* (A history of Chinese prisons). Beijing: Masses Press, 1986.

Yang Chun. *Siwang taifeng* (Deadly typhoon). Beijing: United Publishing House, 1993.

Yang Diansheng. *Laodong gaizao faxue* (The study of labor reform law). Beijing: Beijing University Press, 1991.

Yang Shiguang and Shen Hengyan, eds. *Xingman shifang renyuan huigui shehui wenti zhuanlun* (On the return to society of prisoners who have completed their sentences). Beijing: Social Sciences Press, 1995.

Yu Debin, et al., *Laogai faxue lilun* (Labor reform legal theory). Beijing: Security University Press, 1991.

Zhao Mingzheng and Zhou Mingdong, eds. *Laogai faxue gailun cankao ziliao* (Reference materials on labor reform law), Beijing: China Politics and Law University Press, 1994.

Zhongguo jiancha nianjian (China inspection yearbook). Beijing: China Inspection Press (annual).

Zhongguo laogai da cidian (Great dictionary of China's laogai studies).

Beijing: Scientific Documents Publishing House, 1993.

Zhongguo nongcun tongji nianjian (Rural statistical yearbook of China) 1994. Beijing, China Statistical Publishing House, 1994.

Zhonghua Renmin Gongheguo falü guifanxing jieshi jicheng (A collection of standard interpretations of the laws of the People's Republic of China). Jilin: Jilin People's Publishing House, 1990.

Zhongguo Renmin Gongheguo sheng, zizhiqu, zhixia shi dang zheng ji guan zuzhi jigou gaiyao (General outline of the organization of provincial-level party and government organs in the PRC). Beijing: China Personnel Press, 1989.

Zhou Mingdong, Xu Zhangrun, and Zhu Ye, eds., *Laodong gaizao faxue gailun cankao ziliao* (Reference materials on the general legal theory of labor reform). Beijing: Central Television Publishing House, 1987.

Zhu Decheng, ed. *Hubei jindai jianyu* (Hubei's prisons in recent times). N.p.: Hubei Labor Reform Work Bureau, 1987.

Index

Boldface indicates major discussion of the subject, or (after p. 225) text of the document. Italics indicates mention in a chart, table, diagram or map. A letter after a number indicates footnote on the indicated page. A § indicates a section or article number, usually in the text of a law. "Endnote" refers to the note section on pp. 264-297. The following are non-obvious but useful general categories:

> Cadres and guards
> Conditions in prisons
> Economy
> Foreigners
> Health conditions
> History
> Miscarriages of justice
> Reforming of prisoners

James D. Seymour is a research scholar at Columbia University.

Richard Anderson is an independent scholar specializing in Northwest China.